LARGE
PRINT

BIO
ANDREWS
(JULIE)

Andrews, Julie

Home work

10/17/2019

hachette
BOOKS

LARGE
PRINT

JULIE ANDREWS

Home Work

A Memoir
OF
My Hollywood Years

WITH EMMA WALTON HAMILTON

hachette
BOOKS

LARGE PRINT EDITION

Hachette Books
Hachette Book Group
1290 Avenue of the Americas
New York, NY 10104
hachettebookgroup.com
twitter.com/hachettebooks
Instagram.com/HachetteBooks

First Edition: October 2019

Hachette Books is a division of Hachette Book Group, Inc.
The Hachette Books name and logo are trademarks of Hachette Book Group, Inc.

The publisher is not responsible for websites (or their content) that are not owned by the publisher.

The Hachette Speakers Bureau provides a wide range of authors for speaking events. To find out more, go to www.hachettespeakersbureau.com or call (866) 376-6591.

Print book interior design by Tom Louie.

Library of Congress Control Number: 2019947243

ISBNs: 978-0-316-34925-3 (hardcover),
978-0-306-84598-7 (large print), 978-0-316-34923-9 (ebook)

Printed in the United States of America

LSC-C

10 9 8 7 6 5 4 3 2 1

For my grandchildren, with love.

I know that I am—all that I am.
And all that I am
is full and ripe.

All that I am is standing still,
waiting and watching
and bursting with life.

Holding the straining seams of my skin,
my passion and wit
and my sanity in.

Waiting for someone
to soothe and to say
"I understand. You're home."

—JULIE ANDREWS, 1978

Home Work

INTRODUCTION

IN MY FIRST MEMOIR, entitled *Home*, I wrote about my youth, growing up during World War II, and my experiences performing in vaudeville from ages ten to eighteen and on Broadway in my early twenties. I wanted to share what it was like in those days; living through the Blitz, touring endlessly around England, singing in the old music halls, trying desperately to learn my craft and feel at home, in spite of my transience. Only when I became moderately successful on Broadway did I dare to trust that I'd never have to go back to the bleak existence of those early days.

In this new memoir, I describe my years working in Hollywood, beginning with the filming of *Mary Poppins*. For those who did not read my first book, or who might like a reminder of what led to this next chapter in my life, I offer the following recap:

I WAS BORN in Walton-on-Thames, a small suburban village in the county of Surrey, just eighteen miles southwest of London. My mother's father was a coal miner, and her mother was a chambermaid. My mother, Barbara Morris, was just eighteen when her parents died within a year of each other. Her aspirations to become a classical pianist were cut short by the fact that she was now the primary caregiver to her thirteen-year-old sister, Joan. It wasn't long before the girls met my father, Ted Wells, an impoverished teacher. He fell madly in love with my red-haired, vivacious mother, and offered stability for both sisters, despite his economic status. When my parents married, they moved with my aunt to a small cottage, which they called "Threesome." My mother gave piano lessons, and my aunt taught dance, to augment my father's wages.

My father was the family's rock. My brother, John, was born two years after me, and Dad showed us the wonders of nature—trees, seasons, wildlife. Dad adored rivers and lakes, and often took us rowing on the Thames. He wasn't physically demonstrative, but there was never any doubt as to his love for and dedication to us.

In the summer of 1939, when I was not quite four years old, my mother was playing at a series of concerts in a coastal town. She provided piano accompaniment to a Canadian tenor by the name of Ted Andrews. They began to tour together, and just before the start of World War II, my mother left my father and moved with Ted Andrews to London. Shortly thereafter, she sent for me to come and live with them, while Johnny remained with our dad.

The time in London was a radical awakening for me. The city was filthy with soot and gray with fog, and I was unsettled by this new man in my mother's life. He was large, loud, and volatile, and as ill at ease with me as I was with him. My basement room in our apartment was hot and sterile, with bars on the windows. At night, rats ran across the exposed pipes. Air-raid sirens wailed often, and we were required to employ blackout curtains and keep all lights off after dark. Bombing raids became a regular occurrence, and we were frequently forced to retreat to the Underground subway stations for shelter.

After my mother moved away, my aunt Joan married her boyfriend, Bill Wilby. Because of the war effort, my dad had been assigned to work in a converted factory, making parts for Spitfire aircraft—and there he met a young widow named Winifred. By this time, Mum was pregnant with my half brother, Donald, and not long thereafter, she married Ted Andrews and Dad married Win.

Mum and Ted decided that my name should be changed from Julia Wells to Julie Andrews, and that I should call my new stepfather "Pop," presumably to make us feel more like a family.

In the spring of 1943, Mum, Pop, Donald, and I moved out of London to a suburban part of Kent. Pop began giving me singing lessons—perhaps in an attempt to bond with his new stepdaughter, perhaps to give me something to do, since my school had shut down briefly due to the escalation of the war. I disliked these lessons intensely. I was shy and embarrassed, but Mum and Pop were surprised to discover that I had a strong soprano voice, quite unique for my age.

Our new home in Kent had an air-raid shelter in the garden, and as the war continued, we often spent nights out there. By mid-1944, the Germans were sending "doodlebugs" to England. These were pilotless flying bombs that came across the English Channel, cut out over their target, and plummeted to earth. I could tell the difference between the sound of these doodlebugs approaching and our own fighter planes. The air-raid sirens became so constant that they prevented families from accomplishing the most basic of tasks—making dinner, doing the laundry. My mother came up with the idea that I should sit on top of the air-raid shelter with a pair of opera glasses and a whistle. Whenever I heard a doodlebug approaching, I would blow the whistle, giving my mother (and, as it turned out, many other neighborhood home-makers) time to finish a chore before running to take shelter. I was on duty in all weathers. One rainy day, I rebelled, and stayed in the house. After the bomb dropped, several neighbors came to the door, demanding, "Why the hell didn't she blow her whistle?"

My dad, Win, and Johnny moved to Chessington, about an hour away from us. I visited when I could, which was not often. Returning home from those visits was always emotionally painful.

By age nine and a half, my singing voice had improved so much that I began taking lessons with Pop's voice teacher, Madame Lilian Stiles-Allen. "Madame," an esteemed dramatic soprano, was short and stout, with a kindly nature. She was a phenomenal teacher, with whom I studied for many years. She provided me with a solid technical foundation that carried me through the decades that followed.

Soon after the war ended in 1945, I began to travel with Mum and Pop as they toured in vaudeville. I was struck by the contrast between the glamorous appearance of life in the theater and the rather shabby reality of it backstage. Just before my tenth birthday, Mum and Pop invited me to join them onstage during one of their performances. I stood on a beer crate in order to reach the microphone, and sang a duet with Pop, while Mum accompanied us at the piano. Little by little, I began to join their act more often.

Back at school, I struggled to find my place socially—ever aware of my bandy legs, buckteeth, and lazy eye, along with my ineptitude at sports. On Saturday mornings, whenever possible, I escaped into programs for children at the local cinema— it was my first introduction to the "magic" of Hollywood.

One day, just before Christmas of 1946, I was collected early from school. My mother told me that we were to perform for the troops that night at the Stage Door Canteen in London. When Mum, Pop, and I arrived at the venue, I learned that Queen Elizabeth, wife of King George VI, would be in attendance. After my parents performed the bulk of their act, I was introduced, and sang my duet with Pop and then a solo aria. At age eleven, I was the only child in the program. Her Majesty came backstage to greet the performers. When she approached me, I curtsied, and she said, "You sang beautifully tonight." I was amazed that she took the time to compliment me. At school the next day, I found myself the center of attention.

Mum, Pop, and I began touring more extensively around the country. My dad and Win had welcomed a baby girl—my half sister, Celia, nicknamed "Shad"—into the family, and the following spring my mother gave birth to my youngest half brother, Christopher.

My mother had long wanted to return to her hometown of Walton-on-Thames, and she and Pop found and purchased—with a sizeable mortgage and a down payment that took almost every penny they had—a house called "The Old Meuse." It was a major step up for us. Originally it had been the servants' quarters to a mansion next door; Mum discovered that her mother had been a below-stairs maid there in her teens, and had actually lived in our house at that time.

"It was meant that we should be here," my mother said.

The best thing about the Old Meuse was the large garden. It had lilac trees, an arbor with climbing roses, a vegetable plot, and a small orchard. There was a shabby grass tennis court, and beyond that a tiny copse of fir trees.

Of course, there was a snag; we couldn't afford to maintain it. In the early months, my mother's uncle, Harry, took care of the garden for us. When he was sober, he was jolly and kind, and there was no better gardener on earth. Harry planted vegetables, pruned, and mowed; but he drank like a fish and never came often enough. I agonized when the weeds came back and the grass grew shaggy.

My aunt Joan came to live at the house with her husband, Uncle Bill. Pop erected a tiny prefab cottage in the garden for them, and converted our three-car garage into a studio for my aunt's dancing school. Students were forever coming up and down our driveway and music echoed across the courtyard all day long. It seemed wonderful to me, for there were Auntie's classes to attend and companionship whenever I needed it—which was often, since the main house was frequently empty.

Just prior to moving into the Meuse, I had the good fortune to be cast in a musical revue in London called *Starlight Roof.* It was a glamorous evening of songs, dance, and comedy. My part involved singing one aria—a fiendishly difficult coloratura piece, "The Polonaise" from *Mignon,* that finished with a high F above top C. My debut was surprisingly successful, and I was dubbed a "prodigy with pigtails." Because we were playing two performances every night but Sunday, I had to drop out of school. A tutor was hired for me, with whom I worked four hours a day.

Mum couldn't travel back and forth to London with me every night, so sometimes Uncle Bill or Aunt Joan chaperoned me. Between shows, I would do my homework, have a bite to eat, or if I was lucky, watch an hour of cartoons at a nearby cinema.

Starlight Roof ran for just over a year, and within weeks of its conclusion, I was cast in a holiday "pantomime," *Humpty Dumpty,* playing the egg himself. English pantomimes are not in fact mimed shows; they are seasonal family-audience fare written around familiar fairy tales, with a good measure of popular music and comedy thrown in. I was barely old enough to do so, but for this show, I journeyed back and forth to London on the train by myself.

One evening, a group of rowdy boys sat in the front row during the performance. On my way home, they happened to be on the same train as I was, still giggling and being silly. They introduced themselves, and when it was discovered that we were all from Walton-on-Thames, they asked where I lived. I cagily replied, "Oh—the other side of the railroad tracks."

The following morning there was a knock at the door of the Old Meuse. It was two of the boys, who had apparently looked up all the Andrews families on the "other side of the tracks" and were hoping for an autograph. They were brothers, by the name of Tony and Richard Walton (unrelated to the name of our town). I subsequently received a charming letter from the eldest, Tony, and we embarked on an easy and pleasant friendship. He was at boarding school, but we visited when he was on vacation. I met his family, whom I adored, and whose elegant home was a stark contrast to my own.

Mum, Pop, and I spent the summer of 1949 performing in Blackpool, a resort town in Northern England. I began to notice how much my stepfather was drinking. He drank so much that during performances his words were slurred, or he forgot them. He and my mother began to have loud fights, which frequently became physical. One night, after an especially bad round, my mother tearfully begged me to telephone my aunt and ask her to come immediately. Auntie remained with us for the rest of the summer.

Pop's alcoholism escalated quickly. He would go on all-night benders, after which he would stagger up our driveway, vomit, and pass out. He tried several times to get sober, but always relapsed. Eventually, the music hall booking agents stopped hiring him. Mum and Pop began to sleep in separate rooms, and she started drinking as well. I became the primary caregiver for my half brothers, now three and seven—babysitting, fixing their meals, putting them to bed.

The more Pop drank, the more abusive he became. My brother Donald received his first caning when he was just six, due to a poor school report. This soon became a regular occurrence. Eventually, Donald was enrolled in boarding school, albeit in Walton-on-Thames, not far from our house. Soon afterward, Chris was sent there as well. He was four years old, and utterly miserable. The justification was that our parents were away so often, performing.

My dad and Win moved to Ockley, a charming country village on the Surrey/Sussex border. Dad created a thriving garden, with all manner of vegetables and flowers. Our trips through the English countryside when he would come to collect me were breathtaking, and he took great pleasure in showing me the fields of bluebells and daffodils in the spring, or listening to the sound of nightingales together in the evenings. As always, it was hard to return home from those visits.

Mum and I continued to tour around the country, now performing without my stepfather. He and Mum were in over their heads on the mortgage for the house, so it was imperative that I keep working, even though I was only fourteen. We traveled the country by train, and during those long journeys I buried myself in books. Mum, on the other hand, simply stared out the window for hours on end as we rattled through the countryside. One day, after she and Pop had been fighting dreadfully, she had a kind of nervous breakdown on the train to Aberdeen, Scotland. She wept the entire way, worrying about finances, the house, the two boys. I did everything I could to comfort her, promising that I would help make it right and would keep working, no matter what. I had no idea what I actually earned, since Mum and Pop had always given me a small allowance of £1 per week and used the rest of my earnings for household expenses. Nevertheless, I resolved to assume responsibility for the entire family as best I could.

Sometime that fall, I attended a party with Mum at the home of a friend of hers in a neighboring town. They asked me to sing, which I reluctantly did. I remember feeling distinctly uncomfortable when the owner of the house sat beside me afterward, and asked a number of questions. Mum became very drunk—so much so that I had to drive us home, despite the fact that there was a serious London fog and I was not yet old enough to have a license. During the journey, Mum confessed to me that the man at the party was in fact my biological father; the result of a brief affair.

My immediate reaction was that it didn't matter, that I would always consider my father to be the man who raised me. The following day, I tentatively asked Mum if what she had told me was true. She said it was. I never thought to ask whether the man I had always known as Dad was aware of the fact, and we never spoke of it again. In later years, after Mum and Dad had passed away, I finally discussed it with Aunt Joan. She confirmed Mum's story, and told me that Dad had indeed known the truth, and had decided to raise me and love me as his own nonetheless. The selflessness of that act knocked me sideways.

When I turned fifteen, my mother decided that a tutor was no longer necessary for me. I worried about missing further schooling, but my mother stated that I would get ample education from life. Because I was so busy working to help support the family, I didn't argue.

I was cast in another Christmas pantomime,

Little Red Riding Hood, in Nottingham, about three hours north of Walton. Mum and Auntie helped me settle in at a hotel, but then returned home. They were unable to visit much, and I was dreadfully homesick. Most nights after the performance, I ate dinner by myself in the empty hotel dining room.

Mum's and my engagements were booked by a theatrical agent named Charles Tucker, who had been my parents' manager for several years, and who became my manager when I made my debut in *Starlight Roof.* "Uncle Charlie" sent me to a good dentist, and berated my mother if he saw that I had holes in my socks or that they weren't clean. He was a great help to me and to my family in those early years.

Whenever I was working or traveling, my constant longing was to be back home at the Meuse. When I was seventeen, it was explained to me that there would be tax benefits if I purchased Mum's share of the house, which Charlie Tucker facilitated. Not long afterward, I bought out Pop's share as well. It was now solely my responsibility to keep up the payments and ensure that we all had a roof over our heads.

Tony Walton and I continued our friendship. He graduated from school and headed to Canada to fulfill his National Service duties in the air force, during which time we exchanged letters. I was very fond of him, and was aware that he felt the same way about me, but I wrestled with the desire to experience more of life before committing to a serious relationship.

I continued to tour in musical revues, playing one week each in thirty towns across the UK over the summer and autumn of 1953. Vaudeville was in its dying days at this time; most of the theaters were filthy, and in a terrible state of disrepair. The paint on the ceilings and walls was cracked, stages were splintered, and everything was dusty, sticky, and stale. I tried to create a cheery space in every dressing room I occupied, laying out a cloth to cover stains on the makeup table, buying a posy of flowers, putting up a family photo.

My days were a blur of vocal exercises, perform-ing two shows a night, traveling, and moving in and out of digs. The audiences were often drunk and unruly, their cigarette smoke spiraling down through the spotlights onto the stage. I began to have serious doubts about my prospects for the future. At seventeen, I was traveling endlessly, sing-ing the same songs night after night. I had barely any education, and no other craft to fall back on. I was supporting the family financially, but I felt as if I was going around in circles. It never occurred to me that the performance and coping skills I was gaining would become invaluable to me in the years that followed.

As luck would have it, I was cast in the title role of *Cinderella* at the London Palladium. This prestigious and historic theater was nothing like the tacky vaudeville houses I'd been playing in. The show was glamorous, the costumes fresh, and the production values dazzling, complete with four white ponies pulling the gilded coach.

At the same time, another show was playing in London: *The Boy Friend.* I hadn't seen it because of my own performance schedule, but it was very successful. To my surprise, I received an offer to play the lead role of Polly Browne in *The Boy Friend* on Broadway. The prospect of being away from my family for a year or more was agonizing, and given the situation at home—Pop's drunkenness, and my mother's and brothers' attendant misery— I very nearly turned the job down. My dad paid me a visit, and in his loving manner, he persuaded me to accept the offer.

"Chick," he said, "it'll be the best experience of your life. America will open up your head. You should not miss this opportunity."

A farewell party was planned for me at our house.

Pop became horribly drunk and ended up smashing a ceiling lamp with his cane, then went on a colossal rampage. He shattered all the windows in Auntie and Bill's house, then punched Bill in the face. The police were summoned, and my dad came to collect me, Mum, and my brothers. He took us back to Ockley for the weekend. Pop was held by the police for forty-eight hours, and Mum obtained a restraining order that prohibited him from coming near the house for several weeks, which allowed me to return and resume packing for my departure. After begging Mum to file for a divorce, I boarded the plane to America, depressed and consumed with worry. My mood was quite a contrast to the ebullience of my fellow *Boy Friend* company members, five of whom were on the same flight.

New York was noisy and hot, and I was miserably homesick. Our hotel was in Times Square, and my room was a tiny single that looked out over an airshaft. Worse still, I had no idea how to research a role or "break down" a script for a traditional musical. There were tensions between our American producers, Cy Feuer and Ernie Martin, and our director and writer, Vida Hope and Sandy Wilson. Eventually, Cy dismissed them and took over the directorial chores himself, which made for a sharper and livelier production. Yet I continued to feel at sea, and my uneven performance was resulting in an equally uneven audience response.

After our final preview, Cy took me out to the fire-escape steps in the alley beside the theater. He advised me to abandon every bit of camp or shtick, and to play Polly as truthfully as I could. I felt as if I was being given a lifeline. The show opened on the eve of my nineteenth birthday. After a rousing ovation, the audience danced the Charleston down the aisles as they exited the theater. *The Boy Friend* was a smash hit.

Although I was no stranger to hard work, I was unprepared for the amount of pressure and the sheer slog of performing on Broadway. I phoned home every week, despite the sizeable cost in those days, and looked forward to every mail delivery, in case there was a letter from Mum, Dad, or Tony. Alas, Mum and Pop were back together again, and the troubles at home had resumed. I sent half my modest salary home each week, which often left me scrambling to pay for groceries.

Performing the same role, day after day, week after week for a full year, taught me so much about the nuances of musical theater and how to conserve my energy during a long run. By the end of my contract, I was looking forward to going home.

Any problems that awaited me were overshadowed by the anticipated joy of seeing my family again.

Just before I left New York, I received an invitation to meet with Alan Jay Lerner and Frederick (Fritz) Loewe, regarding the role of Eliza Doolittle in their new musical, *My Fair Lady.* After several auditions, I was offered the part, and a two-year contract. Despite the fact that it would mean a mere three months at home before returning to New York, it was too great an opportunity to miss.

I spent Christmas and the New Year with the family, during which time I worked with Madame Stiles-Allen on the songs from *My Fair Lady.* I also spent a good deal of time with Tony Walton. Having completed his military service, he was now studying at the Slade School of Fine Art in London and working part-time at Wimbledon Theatre, with an eye toward a career in theatrical production and design. Our relationship took another step forward, and we agreed that he would join me in New York as soon as he could.

I returned to America in early January. The situation at home had not improved, and I was once again deeply anxious about leaving my family for such an extended time. I spent the better part of the flight back to the States weeping copiously.

My Fair Lady was directed by the legendary

19

director and writer Moss Hart. Moss was one of the most significant mentors in my life. It quickly became apparent in rehearsals, as it had been with *The Boy Friend*, that I was struggling with my role. Though I adapted easily to the songs, I was utterly out of my depth as an actor. I couldn't master the Cockney accent, and searched desperately for any clue that would help me play this complicated character. Rex Harrison, who played Henry Higgins, seemed completely at home in his role, and was imperious and impatient with me.

Eventually, Moss set aside a weekend to work with me one-on-one. He literally shaped Eliza Doolittle for me. For forty-eight painful hours, he bullied, cajoled, scolded, and encouraged. I returned to rehearsals with the company more grounded in the role, and Rex was somewhat mollified.

Our out-of-town opening in New Haven nearly ground to a halt as the result of a whiteout snowstorm, monstrous technical problems, and a major panic attack on Rex's part. Not being a singer, he was having trouble finding his way with the orchestra, and he threatened not to go on for the first preview. During the ensuing weeks, Moss and Alan continued to refine the show, and by mid-March, when we opened on Broadway, we were in much better shape.

The show received a phenomenal reception, and thus began another great learning period of my life; two years of nose-to-the-grindstone discipline in order to sustain my energy, my voice, and my commitment to delivering a consistent performance every night.

Tony joined me in New York City in April, and from then on, we were inseparable. He began looking for a job, and eventually took one designing caricatures for *Playbill* and other magazines. He sat for the United Scenic Artists union exam, passed it, and got a job designing sets and costumes for a production of Noël Coward's *Conversation Piece*.

During my second year in *My Fair Lady*, I was invited to play the title role in a live television production of Rodgers and Hammerstein's *Cinderella*. Live TV was a new and daunting experience, made all the more so by my discovering that the audience was projected to be in the millions. The ninety-minute special aired on March 31, 1957, and set a record for television viewership with more than 100 million people watching.

My final performance in *My Fair Lady* on Broadway was on February 1, 1958, but I had contracted to continue playing the role of Eliza for another eighteen months in the London production, where the show was a smash hit once again.

Not long after the London opening, Tony and I married. We shared a small flat in Eaton Square, where he commandeered the second bedroom as a workroom, since he was now designing a production of a new musical called *Valmouth*. Our honeymoon was a working vacation in Los Angeles, where I appeared on *The Jack Benny Program*. Immediately afterward we returned to England, where I resumed my role in *My Fair Lady*.

The stress of eight performances a week for such a sustained period of time began to take its toll. I suffered from frequent throat infections, came down with the flu, and at one point threw my back out. Tony's father, a prominent orthopedic surgeon, diagnosed the problem as congenital scoliosis. I was eventually released from my contract two months early, and felt as if I had emerged from a long, dark tunnel into the sunlight.

I had my tonsils removed and Tony and I took a much-needed vacation, but my family continued to be a worry. Mum was now spending a lot of time at the local pub, and Pop was struggling through a succession of odd jobs. Auntie and Uncle Bill had separated, and Donald was away in the merchant marines. Chris, now thirteen and living at home full-time, was a lost and lonely boy. I found a good new boarding school for him, and though I knew he would be homesick, I hoped he would at least be safe and in a more stimulating environment.

Alan and Moss offered me the role of Queen Guenevere in a new Broadway musical they were preparing called *Camelot*. It was an adaptation of the Arthurian legend in *The Once and Future King,* by T. H. White. Tony and I traveled back to New York and took up residence in an apartment on the Upper East Side.

The cast for *Camelot* included Richard Burton as King Arthur, Robert Goulet as Lancelot, and Roddy McDowall as Mordred. It was an ambitious production, stunning to look at, but fraught with problems. While we were in out-of-town tryouts in Toronto, Alan was hospitalized with a perforated ulcer. Moss held the fort in his absence, but on the day that Alan was discharged from the hospital, Moss suffered a heart attack. We soldiered on without a director for several weeks, and our opening in New York was postponed. Eventually, we limped to Broadway and did the best we could, despite the fact that Moss was still unable to be with us. The reviews were lukewarm.

On opening night, Alan made a promise to us that once Moss was well, they would return to the show and improve it, despite the fact that it was by now up and running. We had good enough advance sales to hold us until then. Three months later, he, Fritz, and Moss honored that promise. Alan did some rewriting, Fritz wrote me a new song, and Moss cut forty-five minutes. Though the show never completely fulfilled its potential, it was greatly improved, and ticket sales soared. Unbearably, Moss suffered another heart attack and passed away in December of 1961. It devastated us all.

Early in the New Year, I was introduced to a brilliant young actress and comedienne by the name of Carol Burnett. She was appearing in *Once Upon a Mattress* on Broadway, and we hit it off immediately. Before we knew it, Carol and I had signed on to do a televised concert together. I took a week off from *Camelot,* and we filmed *Julie and Carol at Carnegie Hall* on March 5, 1962. Two and a half weeks later, I received the joyous news that I was pregnant. Aside from Tony, Carol was the first person I told.

During the remaining weeks in my *Camelot* contract, Walt Disney came to see the show. He visited backstage after the performance, and told Tony and me about a combination live-action/animated musical film that he was planning, based on the *Mary Poppins* books by P. L. Travers. He then asked if I would consider playing the title role. I was overwhelmed by the offer, but told him I was newly pregnant—thinking it would negate any possibility of my taking the job. To my astonishment, he replied, "That's OK. We'll wait."

I was even more surprised when Walt turned to Tony and asked, "And what do you do, young man?" When Tony replied that he designed sets and costumes for the theater, Walt asked to see his portfolio, and subsequently offered Tony the job of designing the principal sets and all the costumes for *Mary Poppins.*

Our daughter, Emma, was born in London on November 27, 1962. Three months later, Tony, Emma, her nanny, and I boarded a plane for Hollywood, and thus began a brand-new chapter in our lives.

I FEEL THAT my professional life has consisted of four major stepping stones. The first encompassed my London debut in *Starlight Roof* at the age of twelve, and the subsequent years in vaudeville. The second was the good fortune that took me to Broadway; and the third, my film work in Hollywood. The fourth encompasses my eventual return to Broadway, publishing and directing projects, more films, and other creative pursuits that are still underway. Each has required me to learn a new craft, to place my trust in the hands of people that I did not know, and to do my homework.

The Hollywood years, the growth that followed, and most of all, the learning about myself during that time, is the substance of this book.

1

IT HAD BEEN eight years since I first made the leap across the Atlantic from England to Broadway. At that time, I was nineteen, totally on my own, and desperately worried about leaving my dysfunctional family behind and the huge unknown that awaited me. I didn't know where I would be living or how to balance a checkbook, let alone function in an overwhelming metropolis like New York City.

Now, here I was, with three shows—*The Boy Friend, My Fair Lady,* and *Camelot*—and several thousand performances on Broadway and in London behind me, beginning yet another journey into a new unknown: Hollywood.

This time, thankfully, I was not alone. My husband, Tony, was with me. We were embarking on this new adventure together, along with our baby daughter, Emma. We were green as grass, had no knowledge of the film industry, and could not possibly envision what lay ahead—but we were industrious, open-minded, and we had each other. We were also blessed to have the great Walt Disney to guide us.

WHEN WE ARRIVED in Los Angeles, our flight was met by an exuberant gentleman named Tom Jones (no relation to the singer). Tom was the head of publicity for the Walt Disney Studios, and he soon became a friend.

We rode in a limousine to a cottage that had been rented for us on Sarah Street in Toluca Lake—a two-level Tudor, with plenty of space and a pool in the back with a pretty surround. The place had been charmingly furnished in English style, most of it pulled from the Studios' furniture and prop storage. Everything had been chosen with enormous care, and every thought given to the creature comforts of "the British family" coming to stay.

Tony and I spent a few days getting over jet lag and settling in. Emma was only three months old, and we had brought her nanny, Wendy, with us to help care for her during the five days a week that we would be working. On weekends, she could take time off and we would have Emma to ourselves. I was still breast-feeding my baby, and I hoped to do so for as long as possible. I had a fair way to go to get myself back into pre-pregnancy shape, so I was grateful that there would be a period of dance rehearsals before filming began.

A few days after our arrival, I went with Tony to the Walt Disney Studios, located in Burbank. Tony and I had visited there once before, and we were again struck by the sunny ease of the place; the shady trees and beautifully manicured lawns upon which people relaxed or played table tennis during their lunch hour. Neatly arranged bungalow offices, several large soundstages, construction sheds, and a main theater were dominated by a much larger three-story structure known as the Animation Building. Walt's suite of offices was on the top floor, and below were airy workspaces where the artists and animators created their magic.

We had lunch with Walt and his coproducer/ screenwriter Bill Walsh in the commissary, long recognized as the best in Hollywood for its great food and friendly atmosphere. Walt's persona was that of a kindly uncle—twinkly-eyed, chivalrous, and genuinely proud of all he had created. His international empire encompassed film, television, and even a theme park, yet he was modest and gracious. Our new friend Tom Jones once said to me that you didn't last very long at the company if you were mean-spirited or bad-tempered.

I was provided with a car and driver for the

first two or three weeks, but eventually the Studios loaned me a vehicle of my own when it was assumed that I knew my way around. I was nervous about driving on the freeways and received guidelines: "Stick to the right lane, and get off at Buena Vista." "Stay in the slowest lane; you don't need to cross lanes at all." "Go dead straight until you come to your exit," etc. Being English, I'd never driven on a freeway, or on the right-hand side of the road, and it definitely took some getting used to.

My first weeks at the Walt Disney Studios were consumed with meetings, and wardrobe and wig fittings. I was struck by the differences between preparing for a film role and preparing for a stage performance. For a play or musical, the first few days are spent in script readings and laying out the staging of the scenes. Measurements are taken and you see costume sketches, but fittings generally don't happen until well into the rehearsal process. A film, however, is usually shot out of sequence, and in very small increments. Blocking for any scene isn't addressed until the day of the shoot. It felt odd to be fitting costume elements and wigs for a role I had yet to portray, but to some degree, seeing those costumes helped me begin to formulate Mary's character.

Walt had purchased the rights to the book,

but not to Mary Shepard's illustrations, so Tony's costumes had to be completely original, yet still evoke the spirit of the characters that P. L. Travers had created. The time period of the film had been changed from the 1930s to 1910, as Walt felt that late Edwardian England would provide richer visual opportunities, and Tony agreed.

I was awed by my husband's attention to detail: his choice of materials, colors, and accessories, like Mary's loosely hand-knitted scarf, or her iconic hat with the sprightly daisy on top. While supervising my fittings, Tony pointed out hidden touches like the primrose or coral linings of Mary's jackets, or her brightly colored petticoats.

"I fancy that Mary has a secret inner life," he explained, "and when you kick up your heels, you'll catch a glimpse of who she is beneath her prim exterior."

Tony also paid close attention to the wigs, making sure the color was right, and that Mary's hair was softer and prettier for the scenes when she was out and about with Bert. This was all hugely insightful for me as I tried to wrap my head around Mary's character. What was her background? How did she move, walk, talk? Never having made a film before, and having no specific acting training to fall back on, I was relying on instinct.

I decided to try giving Mary a particular walk. I felt that she would never stroll leisurely, so I practiced on the soundstage, walking as fast as I could, placing one foot immediately after the other to give the impression of hardly touching the ground— the end result being that the children would find it difficult to keep up with her. I also developed a kind of turned-out stance, like a balletic first position, to punctuate the impression of Mary's character when flying. I recalled certain members of flying ballet troupes from my vaudeville days who had simply let their feet dangle, and I always thought it detracted from the effect. In fact, most of Mary Shepard's original illustrations show Mary flying with somewhat droopy feet, although when she was on the ground, she was trimly turned out. I suddenly remembered that when I portrayed Eliza Doolittle in *My Fair Lady* on Broadway, I unconsciously toed-in, giving the flower girl a slightly pigeon-toed lack of grace in her clumsy boots, then I straightened my feet when she acquired confidence and poise as a "lady." It made me smile to think I was doing the exact opposite for Mary Poppins.

In addition to all the costumes, Tony designed the set for Cherry Tree Lane, which featured the exteriors of the Banks' house, Admiral Boom's, and several other townhouses. There were realistic cobblestones, blossoming trees, functional drains to carry away the rain on the pavement, and of course the façades of all the homes. Streetlamps and windows glowed; brass doorknobs and letter boxes shone. Tony also designed all the interiors in the film. It was hard to believe this was his first film venture, and his work proved that Walt's instinct about his talent had been absolutely correct.

DANCE REHEARSALS SOON began on the back lot at the Studios. The film was being choreographed by the talented young husband-and-wife team of Marc Breaux and Dee Dee Wood. Marc was tall and lithe, and devastatingly good-looking. Dee Dee was strong and spirited, with a great sense of humor. Though they had worked on Broadway, this was their first film, and I learned that Dick Van Dyke had recommended them to Walt, having worked with the couple on television.

A huge tarpaulin had been rigged as a canopy for shade in the open air, and by the time I joined the rehearsals, the group of strapping young male dancers had already learned their choreography for the chimney sweep sequence, "Step in Time." As Marc and Dee Dee put them through their paces and showed me how I would be integrated into the number, my jaw dropped.

The two of them were much influenced by the famous choreographer Michael Kidd, who was known for his vigorous, athletic style. There were somersaults, leaps, and other acrobatics using broomsticks and props. It was blazing hot under the heavy tarp, which, despite shading us, trapped the San Fernando Valley heat and smog. The male dancers stripped down to T-shirts and shorts, and none of them seemed even slightly winded. Being used to a more mild and dewy climate, and having just delivered a baby three months earlier, I thought, "Will I ever come up with the necessary strength or energy to match them?"

Eventually, I recused myself and went into a cool studio each morning to limber up—pliés at a ballet barre, stretches and so forth, which suited my scoliotic back and helped prevent injury. I finally began to get in shape again.

It was during these dance rehearsals that I first met Dick Van Dyke. He was already well established as a consummate comedian; he had starred in *Bye Bye Birdie* on Broadway and in the film, and had completed the first two seasons of his famous sitcom, *The Dick Van Dyke Show.* We hit it off from day one. He was dazzlingly inventive, always in a sunny mood, and he often made me roar with laughter at his antics. For instance, when we began work on the "Jolly Holiday" sequence, the first step we learned was the iconic walk, arm-in-arm, our legs kicking up ahead of us as we traveled. I performed Mary Poppins's demure, ladylike version of the step—but Dick flung his long legs up so high that I burst out laughing. To this day, he can still execute that step.

Dick's performance seemed effortless to me, although he did struggle with Bert's Cockney accent. He asked for help with it, so J. Pat O'Malley, an Irish actor who voiced several of the animated characters in the film, tried to coach him. It was a funny paradox: an Irishman teaching an American how to speak Cockney. I did my best to help as well, occasionally demonstrating the odd Cockney rhyming slang or a lyric from an old vaudeville song, like "I'm 'enery the Eighth, I Am" or "Any Old Iron." I don't know if it helped, but it was Dick's turn to laugh.

Dick also secretly played Mr. Dawes Sr., president of the bank, with the help of brilliant makeup disguising him as an old man. It was something he had actually begged Disney to let him do. Walt rather cheekily made Dick do a screen test for the part, and word flew around the Studios that he had been hilarious, totally persuasive and completely unrecognizable. Dick wanted the extra part so badly that he offered to play it for free, but Walt was nothing if not wily. He took Dick up on that offer, and also persuaded him to make a $4,000 donation to the California Institute of the Arts, which Walt had recently cofounded.

In addition to the dance rehearsals, we had to prerecord the songs before we could actually begin shooting the musical numbers. The delightful score for *Poppins* had been written by Robert B. and Richard M. Sherman, two brothers referred to as "the boys." They had been working for Walt for quite some time, being the first in-house song-writers he had hired under contract to the Studios. They'd written for such films as *The Absent-Minded Professor* and for Disney's television shows and his theme park, Disneyland.

Robert, the elder brother, was primarily responsible for the lyrics. He was tall, heavy-set, and walked with a cane, having been injured in World War II. Despite his gift for words and kindly manner, he often seemed quiet and somewhat removed. Richard was shorter and thinner, and was ebullience personified. He had boundless energy, always demonstrating at the piano with great enthusiasm.

My singing teacher, Madame Stiles-Allen, flew

over from England to visit her son and to work with me privately on my songs. Because I had been studying with her since I was nine years old, there was now a shorthand between us. I recognized immediately what she was asking of me in reference to a particular passage, or where my thoughts should be directed. So many times, she emphasized not reaching *up* to a high note, but rather following it down a long road, while being sure to articulate the consonants and keep the vowels true. It was all about unifying the levels in my voice, across an even plane—much like a string of matched pearls, each note placed exactly where the previous one had been. She taught me the importance of diction and breath control. Hers was a flawless technique; one that strengthened vocal cords, protected a voice from damage, and provided skills and muscle memory that stood me in good stead in the years that followed. She also counseled me about professionalism, saying, "The amateur works until he can get it right. The professional works until he cannot go wrong."

Irwin Kostal was the musical arranger and conductor for *Mary Poppins*. He and I had made two albums together when I was on Broadway. He had also conducted and arranged the *Julie and Carol at Carnegie Hall* television special that I'd done with

Carol Burnett the prior year, so working with him was easy. He was a consummate musician, and his familiar presence was reassuring.

I discovered that prerecording for a film was a very different experience from recording a Broadway cast album. The latter is normally done *after* the show has opened, by which time the cast knows exactly what is happening at that moment onstage and how to sing the song accordingly. In film, however, the songs are typically recorded in advance of shooting the scene, so I seldom knew what would be happening in terms of action, and therefore what was required vocally. For instance, if I am singing in a scene with a lot of action, such as the chimney sweep dance, a certain vocal energy or breathlessness is required to match that action, as compared to a lullaby sung by a bedside. Yet when prerecording, all the specifics of the action are still relatively unknown and must be guessed at. Fortunately, Marc and Dee Dee were at these sessions, as was our screenwriter and coproducer Bill Walsh, for whom I had great respect. I could turn to them for guidance if I was unsure about a particular moment, but to a great extent I was operating on instinct.

"Feed the Birds" was a perfect example, in that I was not even on camera for the song, and had no idea how the Bird Woman would be filmed or what she would be doing during the scene. After recording the song, I kept feeling that I hadn't quite done it justice. Tony, who had been at the recording session with me, felt the same way. "I don't think you sang it softly enough," he said. "I think you need to try it again." I asked permission to re-record it, and a month later, when we were recording other songs, I gave it another shot. I was much happier with my second version.

FILMING FINALLY COMMENCED with the "Jolly Holiday" sequence. Our director, Robert Stevenson, was English, and though he was courteous and kind, initially I found him to be a little distant. I soon realized he was somewhat shy, and hugely preoccupied with the monumental task ahead of him—juggling live-action scenes, animated sequences, and a host of special effects, many of which were being attempted for the first time. Bob had worked in the industry for more than thirty years, and had directed many films for the Walt Disney Studios, including *Old Yeller* and *The Absent-Minded Professor*. He was patient with my lack of experience, guiding me gently through what I needed to learn—simple things, like the difference between a close-up and a waist-shot, the nature of an establishing shot, the need for a reverse angle, and so on.

My first filmed scene simply required that I strike a pose, hands on my umbrella, while Bert said, "You look very pretty today, Mary Poppins!" I then had to walk past him and say, "Do you really think so?" I was extremely nervous and fretted over how to say that one simple line. I had no idea what my voice would sound like or how to appear natural on film. Onstage, you have to project your voice to be heard by the last row of the audience, and your entire figure is in full view all the time. I was acutely aware of the camera's presence, and surprised by the number of shots required to make up one small scene. Shooting a few lines was like working on a jigsaw puzzle. Not knowing which pieces of film the director would finally select in the editing process made it difficult to know when to spend my energy or save it.

Robert Stevenson didn't have time to help me much with my acting, so I worked on my scenes by reading lines in the evenings with Tony. In the end, I simply said the words and hoped for the best. If I happen to catch the film these days, I'm struck by the seeming lack of self-consciousness on my part; a freedom and ease that came from total ignorance and flying by the seat of my pants (no pun intended!).

All of the "Jolly Holiday" scenes were filmed in front of a giant yellow screen, and the animated drawings were added later. This technique, known as sodium vapor process, was very new at the time. The high-powered lights were excruciatingly bright and hot, making our eyes squint, and lending a slightly burned quality to our faces—as if we were in direct sunlight, with intense spotlights added. The wigs and costume layers made it even hotter.

I've always hated wearing wigs, and the Poppins wigs drove me nuts. My hair was long at that time, and I began to cut it shorter and shorter, the better to endure the wig every day. I also wore false eyelashes; in those days, we used strips, rather than individual lashes. Although the strips could last for a few days, they had to be meticulously cleaned after each use. My makeup man, Bob Schiffer, was well known in the business for being one of the best, but once he inadvertently used a tube of glue that had become rancid, and I got a blistering eye infection. I was unable to work for a day because my eyes were so swollen, and the company was forced to shuffle the schedule and film something else instead.

Because all animation for the film was added

long after the live action had been finished, we had little to guide us in terms of what to react to and how we should behave. For the tea party under the willows with the penguin waiters, a cardboard penguin was placed on the table in front of me. Once I'd established the sightline, the penguin was taken away, and when cameras rolled, I had to pretend it was still there. The problem was that my eyes automatically adjusted to the farthest point of vision, so it was very hard to maintain that close focus on a now-imaginary penguin. It added yet another layer to everything I was trying to concentrate on.

The turtle in the pond was actually an iron anvil, such as a cobbler might use for making a shoe. It just fit the size of my foot. I stepped on it and balanced, and they later drew the turtle and the water around it.

For the carousel sequence, the poles on the horses were attached to tracks in the soundstage ceiling. It took forever to shoot that section, because the horses had to disconnect from one track and then travel along another, much like a train changing rails. We waited hours for the equipment to be readied, then once we got on the horses, we shot each scene many times until the technical crew was content that they had what they needed.

The long waits enabled Dick and I to become better acquainted with the Banks children, played by Karen Dotrice and Matthew Garber. Karen, who played Jane, was only seven years old, but was calm and sweet, and had perfect manners. Her father, Roy Dotrice, was a well-known English actor, so Karen had been schooled in performance etiquette. Matthew, who played her brother, Michael, was the exact opposite. He had a mop of red hair, a ton of freckles, and a cheeky sparkle in his eyes. He was also very unruly at times. Bob Stevenson was endlessly patient with him, and though Matthew cost us a bit of time, you couldn't help but love him. Everything about him was authentic—his grimaces, his eyes squeezing shut in the bright light, his distractibility, his boundless enthusiasm as he thundered around the set, occasionally tearing off to explore something that had nothing to do with the scene. Sadly, he died at the age of twenty-one, after having contracted hepatitis while traveling in India. It was a tragic blow to all of us who knew him.

THE DAILY SCHEDULE was unrelenting. I was up at dawn every morning, rolling out of bed for a quick stretch on the bedroom floor, followed by a snuggle with Emma before I left for the Studios, then a full day of filming, punctuated by visits from Emma and Wendy so that I could nurse my sweet daughter and spend time with her.

Every working morning, while walking from makeup and hair to the soundstage, I would practice a series of breathing and facial exercises to help me wake up and look alive. Every evening, and on the weekends, I was a full-time mum. I seldom wanted to leave the house on my days off, so Tony and I would play with Emma in the garden, read to her from picture books, and take her for strolls in her pram or dips in the swimming pool. When Emma napped, I napped. People often ask me if I sang to her, and I did—though it was never songs associated with my work. Rather, I would sing little ditties that applied to the bond between us, such as "You Are My Sunshine" and "I See the Moon, the Moon Sees Me."

By now, Emma's personality was emerging, and to Tony's and my delight, so was her sense of humor. One day, I was in the kitchen preparing her lunch. She was sitting in her high chair, and I happened to sneeze rather loudly.

"Oh! God bless me!" I exclaimed, holding my chest and leaning dramatically against the counter. Emma began to giggle, so I hammed it up and did it again, at which point she laughed so hard, she listed sideways in her chair.

Every Sunday, I called my family—Mum, Dad, and sometimes even Auntie Joan. Those calls could take up a whole morning, and were hugely expensive, but it was important to me to stay in touch. We exchanged letters as well, and knowing it was difficult for them to visualize what I was doing, I focused more on whatever news they had shared rather than my own experiences. Mum and Pop were still together, and Mum's letters were generally circumspect, obviously trying not to worry me. These communications were never very satisfying. Dad's letters tended to be more sustaining, in that he wrote in evocative detail of the English countryside, the seasonal colors, and all the elements of home that he knew I loved.

FILMING OF THE interior scenes began with Mary Poppins's interview of (rather than *with*) Mr. Banks, played by the wonderful David Tomlinson. One of several British actors in the film, he had a comically expressive face, with what I call "upside-down eyes," in that his eyebrows slanted upward, while his eyes slanted downward. He himself thought he resembled "a disappointed spaniel." He'd had an illustrious stage and film career, and his portrayal of Mr. Banks captured exactly the right mixture of disdain and dismay needed for the role. He conjured a kind of glassy-eyed, blank stare that suggested he didn't fully comprehend what was going on. I often found it hard to keep a straight face when working with him.

Mrs. Banks was portrayed by Glynis Johns, another Brit. She was pretty, and despite seeming sweetly dotty at times, she was a fine and versatile character actress. Like me, she had been a child performer, and by this time in her career she was well established. In fact, the Sherman Brothers wrote "Sister Suffragette" especially for her, in the hopes that giving her a solo song would entice her to accept the role.

The opening long shot of Mary flying down from the clouds and arriving at the Banks' front doorstep was actually done by my stand-in, Larri Thomas. She was a wonderful dancer and accomplished stuntwoman, and we did look somewhat alike. I discovered that being a stand-in requires incredible patience and skill. Whenever there is a new scene to set up and to light, a stand-in saves the actor's energy by taking his or her place, usually wearing an equivalent costume or similar color palette that helps the director of photography do the lighting job. It's backbreaking work, because you are mostly on your feet for great lengths of time, standing very still. Larri became a good friend, and later was my stand-in on *The Sound of Music*.

Every flying sequence was conjured at least six different ways so as to distract the audience from how it was achieved. I had read the *Mary Poppins* books and script, so I knew I would be flying in the film. What I hadn't bargained on was how many different tricks it would take to pull it off on-screen. Sometimes I was suspended on wires; other times I sat on a seesaw or atop a ladder, depending on the camera angle. In the tea party scene with Uncle Albert—played so adorably by the legendary comedian Ed Wynn—we shot some takes with the set completely turned on its side. When the film was ultimately righted to match everything else, no wires were apparent.

Many of my costumes needed duplicates in a larger size to accommodate the harness I wore when flying. This was a thick elastic body stocking, which started at my knees and ended above my waist. The flying wires passed through holes in the costume and were attached to steel panels on either hip. I literally did a lot of "hanging around" between takes, and when I was suspended, the steel panels pressed on my hip bones, which became very bruised. Sheepskin was added, which helped, although it was barely enough, since I couldn't look too bulky.

My most dangerous flying sequences were saved

for the end of our filming schedule, presumably in case of an accident. In one of my last takes, I'd been hanging in the rafters for quite a while, waiting for the tech team to be ready. Suddenly I felt my supporting wires drop by about a foot. I became extremely nervous, and called down to the stage manager below:

"Could you let me down very gently, please? I felt the wire give a little. It doesn't feel safe."

I could hear the word being passed along the full length of the studio, to where the man who controlled my wires and counterweights was standing.

"Let her down easy, Joe!"

"When she comes down, take it *realllly* gently . . ."

At which point, I fell to the stage like a ton of bricks.

There was an awful silence, then Joe's disembodied voice from afar called, "Is she down yet?"

I have to admit, I let fly a stream of colorful expletives. Fortunately, I wasn't harmed because the balanced counterweights did their job and broke my fall, but I landed hard and was quite shaken.

It is amazing to me that, even now, one doesn't see the technical difficulties in *Mary Poppins* that were ever-present while shooting. In those days, there were no computers to assist with the special effects. Every single scene had to be storyboarded, and these hand-drawn renderings created the visual road map for the film. Bob Stevenson worked hard to make sure that each shot faithfully followed those designs, and that no one could spot the brilliant technical work behind the Disney "magic." So often, the film called for something that had never been achieved before in terms of special effects. It was up to Walt's brilliant technical crew to figure out how to make it happen.

In the scene where I sang "A Spoonful of Sugar," I worked with a mechanical robin, which was one of the Walt Disney Studios' first Audio-Animatronics. It was attached to a ring on my hand, and the wires that manipulated the bird went up under my sleeve to my shoulder, then down the back of my dress to an operator, who was crouching on the floor beside me. The wires were painted with black shoe polish to minimize any bounce from the lights, but I also participated in the camouflage, hiding them with my thumb, or by stroking the robin's chest with my other hand. Bob Stevenson had originally hired a professional bird whistler to voice the robin, but it didn't sound right. I've been a good whistler all my life, so I ended up trying it myself and it somehow worked better. Filming this scene was all about the robin, who received a good deal more attention and direction than I did.

As for the carpetbag, and my pulling all those impossibly sized items out of it—the standing lamp, mirror, etc.—there was a hole in the table and in the bottom of the bag. All the items were actually under the table, so that I could just reach through and grab them. After the scene was shot, the rectangular space under the table was spliced out and replaced with a separate piece of film featuring Michael crouching down to see where everything was coming from.

For the tidying-of-the-nursery sequence, in which it appears that clothing is folding itself and, along with the toys, jumping into open drawers and cupboards which then shut themselves—the Disney magicians simply filmed everything in reverse. Drawers were pushed open from the back and folded clothing expelled *out* of them . . . and the footage was later run backwards.

One of my favorite scenes to film was "Supercalifragilisticexpialidocious." The song so resembled the patter songs I'd heard in my vaudeville days, and I instantly embraced it. Marc and Dee Dee came up with fancy footwork to match the tongue-twisting lyrics, incorporating elbows, knees, toe-taps, and bounces in response to the tambourine slaps of the animated Pearly band—all of it performed at breakneck speed. We were in the middle of filming the sequence when my Tony suddenly suggested that Mary might show off a bit by saying the long word backwards. I ad-libbed the dialogue, and it worked. I also had great fun voicing one of the Pearlies myself, drawing on my old Cockney skills from *My Fair Lady* to sing the "Um-diddle-iddle-iddle, um-diddle-ays."

The "Step in Time" musical sequence was the most arduous to shoot. Having rehearsed it for six weeks on the back lot, we now filmed sections of it day after day for a full week, the dancers racing up and down the angled roofs, dancing on chimney tops, jumping in *and* out of them, suspended on wires, some of it quite dangerous. Again, the music was played at breakneck speed, and once Mary Poppins was "invited" into the dance, I galloped and spun my way around the soundstage, trying breathlessly to keep up with the dynamic energy of the chimney sweeps.

A series of trick shots had been prepared for me during the sequence, ending with my being strapped to a pole on a lazy Susan and whipped around like a spinning top. I tried to focus on one spot, as per my ballet training, but still ended up feeling extremely queasy.

One unexpected bonus of this number came from the makeup department. The chimney soot needed for the rooftop sequence was actually a kind of mineral-rich clay compound known as fuller's earth. It was often used in Hollywood films to create effects involving dirt and dust. For years, I had been plagued by a wart on my thumb, which I had attempted to treat in a number of different ways. It had become large enough for me to want to hide it by any means possible; mostly by clasping my hands, one thumb over the other. After several days of shooting "Step in Time," I noticed that the wart was shrinking. As the days passed it became smaller and smaller, until finally, to my delight, it vanished altogether, leaving my thumb smooth and unblemished. It has never returned. I can only attribute it to some magical ingredient in the fuller's earth.

The great skyscapes and vistas of London surrounding the rooftops were added later, by a process called glass shots, or mattes. These were designed by the brilliant artist Peter Ellenshaw—a lovely, unassuming Englishman. He had done the matte work for *Spartacus, Treasure Island, 20,000 Leagues Under the Sea,* and many other important movies. Peter and his team of fellow artists created these matte shots by painting on glass, leaving a blank or clear space in which the live-action film could then be inserted. The glass and film were put together and re-filmed as a composite. So, for the great shots of St. Paul's in "Feed the Birds," for instance, the Bird Woman sat on a limited set with nothing much around her. The matte painting of St. Paul's was added later, and was supplemented with special effects like animated pigeons and mist. Apparently, there was only one camera in existence at the time that could combine the matte shot and live film, and of course it was conceived, owned, and operated by Disney.

Another aspect of filming that I had to learn about was continuity work. I didn't know that all films have a script supervisor whose job it is to make note of every detail in any scene, so that all the shots—wide angles, close-ups, etc.—match in terms of gestures, arrangement of costumes, objects, and so forth. We didn't have instant replay in those days, so that continuity person was the eyes and ears of the entire film.

Our supervisor would say, "No, Julie, you picked your handkerchief up on the *third* beat," or "You sipped from that glass *before* you spoke," or some such reminder.

Initially I was irritated by all the interruptions, because it felt as though I were being picked on. Eventually, I came to appreciate the value of continuity work, and began to pay closer attention to those details myself.

TONY AND I had promised P. L. Travers that we would keep in touch with her during the process of filming *Poppins*. I was aware that there had been tensions between her and Walt Disney. She had originally tried to control everything, wanting to cut out songs and even the animation. Walt finally gave her a firm understanding of her boundaries, and she returned to England. My letters were an attempt to mollify her and improve the situation to whatever extent I could. In a way, I understood where she was coming from. After all, Mary was her creation, and she'd protected her for so many years. I tried to keep whatever I wrote positive and focused on what I thought she'd like to hear, such as how well the film was coming along and how talented the cast and crew were.

Walt visited the set from time to time, and when he did, everyone was thrilled to see him. He was always very encouraging and full of bonhomie— I never heard him critique what he saw. He was clearly very excited about this new project. I got the feeling that he would have liked to visit more often, but he wanted to be tactful and not appear concerned or be intrusive. There was always a special aura when he was on the set; that charismatic sparkle that he conjured so well.

One day, he and I did some publicity shots together. A tea table was placed on the set, dressed with good china and all the trappings of an English tea. Even though we had to pay attention to our photographer, I think Walt enjoyed sitting down and chatting as much as I did. Although I don't recall what we discussed, I do remember thinking how pleasant it was to spend time with him.

Occasionally, Tony and I were invited for a weekend at the Golden Oak Ranch, in Santa Clarita. The ranch was owned by the Disney family, and used for location filming when needed. There was a lovely lake, an abundance of American oak trees, and the whole place was extremely rustic. Although Walt was never there when we were, it was always a welcome respite for us—despite the live peacocks that sometimes let loose piercing screams during the night, causing us to bolt upright in bed, ears ringing and brains reeling.

Tony and I tried to socialize when we could, but it was mostly accomplished by inviting friends to dinner at our house, including members of our film company, such as David Tomlinson, Irwin Kostal, and Marc and Dee Dee, and friends like Carol Burnett and Roddy McDowall. Dick Van Dyke and I were never able to socialize, alas. He had a large family, and a television show to get back to, but we remain fond of each other to this day.

In addition to his work on *Mary Poppins*, Tony was designing two operas—Benjamin Britten's *The Rape of Lucretia* for the Edinburgh Festival, and Prokofiev's *The Love for Three Oranges* for the Coliseum Theatre in London. These required that he make several trips back and forth to the UK during production for *Mary Poppins*, and at the end of June, roughly halfway through our shooting schedule, he returned to London full-time. His work for the film was complete, and all his sets and costumes were up and functioning. He was also preparing the transfer of *A Funny Thing Happened on the Way to the Forum* from Broadway to London, and was serving as coproducer of that as well as designer. Needless to say, it was not easy being apart for such a long period of time, especially since Emma was growing and exhibiting new and delightful personality traits almost daily. We did our best to write letters and make long-distance phone calls whenever possible.

Principal photography for *Mary Poppins* finished shooting in August, yet there was still a ton of postproduction work to be done, including all my "looping" on the film. I discovered that sound defects often disturb a scene—an airplane flying overhead, wind blowing across a microphone if we were outdoors, a camera being bumped, a body mic rubbing against clothing or being brushed by a hand, and so forth. The smallest flaw necessitates re-recording that piece of dialogue in a sound booth. Sometimes, it's actually possible to improve a performance, with better emphasis on a word here or more nuance there. Between looping and all the animation and special effects that still had to be added, it was several months before I saw any part of the film assembled, and another year of editing, color-correcting, and sound balancing before *Mary Poppins* was finally completed.

In retrospect, I could not have asked for a better introduction to film, in that it taught me so much in such a short period of time. The special effects and animation challenges alone were a steep learning curve, the likes of which I would never experience again. I had as yet no idea how to assess my performance, or how the film might be received, but I did know that the hard work had not precluded my enjoyment of the process. From the kindness and generosity of Walt Disney himself, to the camaraderie on set, the pleasure of performing the songs, and of course, the creative collaboration with my husband, it had all been an unforgettable experience.

One day, during my last weeks in Los Angeles, I happened to be driving across the valley toward the Hollywood Bowl. I passed the Warner Bros. Studio, where the film of *My Fair Lady* had just commenced shooting, with Audrey Hepburn playing the role of Eliza Doolittle opposite Rex Harrison and Stanley Holloway, both of whom had been in the stage production with me on Broadway. Though I totally understood why Audrey had been chosen for the role (I'd never made a movie, and was a relative unknown compared to her world-wide fame), I felt sad that I would never have the chance to put my version of Eliza on film. In those days, archival tapes of an original stage production were still a thing of the future.

As I was driving by the great Warner gates, an impish feeling came over me. I rolled down my window and yelled, "Thank you *very* much, Mr. Warner!" I was being facetious, but at the same time genuine; so aware of how extremely lucky I was that Jack Warner's choice of casting for Eliza had rendered me available for *Mary Poppins*.

2

A T SOME POINT during the *Poppins* shooting
schedule, Walt Disney very generously screened
some of the film-in-progress for two gentlemen who
would become responsible for casting me in my
next two films: producer Martin Ransohoff and film
director Robert Wise. I was told that it was highly
unusual for Walt to allow *anyone* to see footage from
a film in progress, and I considered it the utmost
courtesy that he did that for me.

Ransohoff was producing a film in partnership
with MGM called *The Americanization of Emily*,
and Bob Wise was embarking on plans to direct a
film adaptation of *The Sound of Music*, to be shot
the following year. I understood that Bob was considering me for the role of Maria von Trapp, but in
the meantime, to my surprise, Ransohoff offered
me the title role of Emily, which was to commence
shooting in England almost immediately. Needless
to say, the prospect of making my next film at
home was very appealing.

The film had been loosely adapted by the great screenwriter Paddy Chayefsky from a novel by William Bradford Huie. The story is centered on Lieutenant Commander Charlie Madison, an American "dog robber"—a general's aide who procures anything needed to keep his boss happy, from booze to cigarettes to pretty ladies—and Emily, an English girl with strong values who falls in love with him. The film takes place in World War II London in the weeks leading up to D-Day.

Marty Ransohoff was a stocky fellow with a wispy comb-over. His reputation for using objectionable language and the casting couch preceded him, but I experienced none of that. He teased me good-naturedly, and I found him to be rather lovable. I learned that originally the film was to have been directed by William Wyler. Mr. Wyler wanted to make some changes to Paddy's script. Ransohoff refused, and replaced him with Arthur Hiller—a newer, younger face in Hollywood. It was unusual for a producer to support a screenwriter over a director of such esteem.

I felt that I was a rather odd choice for Emily. Certainly, I didn't feel sophisticated or experienced enough to show all the nuances I sensed in Paddy's marvelous screenplay. This was only my second venture into filmmaking, and I still had so much to learn. While I was very nervous, I simply couldn't turn the role down. I recognized that it would be a wonderful contrast to *Mary Poppins,* and perhaps help me to not be typecast if *Poppins* were successful and if I were later cast as another nanny in *The Sound of Music.* So I told my agent to accept Marty's offer.

EMMA AND I flew back to London to join Tony at the end of August. Our little flat in Eaton Square seemed to have shrunk. Emma's arrival had forced Tony to surrender the second bedroom, which had been his studio, to Emma and Wendy, so he had begun working in the living room. Now, his design projects having tripled, his work was spread all over the apartment. Costume sketches, ground plans, elevations, and renderings were stashed behind curtains and under our bed, leaning up against chairs and spilling over his giant drafting table. Realizing we desperately needed more space, I spent the next few weeks looking at houses and larger apartments.

We found an estate agent who showed me various places around London. Nothing was size- and price-right. Everything was either too tight, too dark, without a view, or too expensive. Finally, our agent said, "I know this isn't as central as you'd like, but there's a wonderful house on Wimbledon

Common that's been divided into apartments." Wimbledon is about seven miles southwest from the center of London, and half an hour's drive from Walton-on-Thames, where Tony's and my families still lived. The apartment had been tastefully converted, and more than suited our needs. We bought it at the end of September, and began making plans to move in.

A Funny Thing Happened on the Way to the Forum opened on October 3, 1963, at the Strand Theatre (now the Novello Theatre). In those days, as often as possible, I would search for an opening-night outfit that in some way complemented Tony's designs for the play. Just before I left Hollywood, I bought a velvet suit with an orange, red, and purple pattern that directly corresponded to the riotous colors in Tony's sets and costumes for *Forum*. I was pretty smug about having found something so appropriate, and Tony was tickled by my choice.

Forum was as big a success in London as it had been on Broadway, and it remains one of my favorite musicals. Tony's designs once again received accolades, and more job offers began to flow in for him, both in New York and in London.

NOT LONG AFTER I had arrived back in London, Marty Ransohoff said, "I want to show you a guy

who I think would be perfect for the lead in *Emily*."
He arranged a screening of a comedy starring Doris
Day. The leading man was attractive and a fine
actor; there was no doubt that he'd be spectacular
in the role of Commander Charlie Madison. His
name was James Garner, and I was delighted when
he agreed to play the part.

Arthur Hiller had been a prolific television director on stellar series such as *Ford Playhouse 90*, *Perry
Mason*, *Gunsmoke*, *The Barbara Stanwyck Show*,
and *Alfred Hitchcock Presents*, to mention but a few.
He was Canadian, small in stature, with a black
mane of hair and a gentle voice, which reflected his
nature. He was also very smart, with a good sense
of humor. He was relatively new to feature films,
and he'd lobbied hard to get this job. Arthur made
a bold, creative decision to shoot the movie in
black-and-white, as he felt it best suited the subject
matter and the period.

Just prior to our first day of shooting, I received a charming and thoughtful letter from Walt
Disney:

I thought you might be consoled to know a
little something about Arthur . . . His first
movie, as you may know, was our *Miracle of
the White Stallions*. I think you will like him.

He's an understanding guy . . . not the shouting type, by any means. As a matter of fact, the only thing I can think of that isn't in his favor is that he doesn't have the experience and background of Willie Wyler.

As to James Garner, well, he's an up and coming young actor, and has done very well for himself over here.

I think you may find that this is going to turn out alright in the long run.

I was very touched that Walt had taken the time to reach out to me. Clearly, he'd sensed my anxiety about making the right choice in terms of a film that would follow *Mary Poppins*. I was still so naïve about the ways of Hollywood, and his fatherly kindness meant the world to me.

AFTER OUR INITIAL read-through at MGM's studio at Elstree, we filmed some exteriors, and I shot two small scenes. Once again, I felt I understood from the script what was required of the character, yet I lacked the acting skills to put it into practice. In those days, it never occurred to me to find an acting class or coach. I foolishly thought it a sign of weakness to do so, and that I was supposed to draw from an innate talent and instinct. It's a horrible feeling to know that you understand a role, but don't know how to get there. As with my first days on *Poppins*, I simply opened my mouth and said the words as best I could. Happily, Paddy's brilliant dialogue did a lot of the heavy lifting for me.

Ten days into filming, Marty Ransohoff suddenly announced that he intended to pull the entire production and take it back to Hollywood to shoot there, where he could better manage costs and union regulations.

This came as a big shock to me, because I had been looking forward to the pleasure of being home for a stretch. Having been away in Hollywood for so long, I was keen to be with Tony again, and to spend time with my family. Though the situation in Walton with my parents had calmed down, I was anxious to keep an eye on Mum, and also Auntie Joan, who was by now divorced from her husband. Donald had recently joined the British South African Police Force in Rhodesia, and Johnny had earned his pilot's wings earlier that year, while Chris was still at school. Tony and I were also in the middle of moving into our new apartment—but suddenly I was being called back to Hollywood. Since I had started shooting already, there was nothing I could do about it. Tony was understanding, as his next projects were taking him back to New York. Nevertheless, it was not easy for either of us.

Tony, Emma, Wendy, and I packed up once again, and before we knew it, we were getting our bearings in a small, Spanish-style rental house on Bowmont Drive, off Coldwater Canyon, in Beverly Hills. Poor Tony spent the next few weeks flying back and forth between L.A. and New York, where his latest show, Jean Anouilh's *The Rehearsal*, opened. He was also coproducing the transfer of the musical *She Loves Me* from Broadway to London.

One day, as I was driving to the MGM studio at an ungodly early hour, I was pulled over by a policeman. He told me that I'd just driven through a stop sign. I had been completely unaware of it. When he asked to see my license, I rummaged in my glove compartment and pulled it out with a flourish. "It's an English license," I said cheerfully. "But I understand I'm allowed to use it here temporarily."

He looked at it, then looked at me. "Ma'am, are you aware that this license expired five years ago?"

"WHAT?!" My jaw dropped. "What can I say, Officer? I had no idea. I am *so* sorry." I thought back to the hours I'd spent driving back and forth to the Walt Disney Studios for months on end, never realizing my license was invalid. I was appalled.

He must have sensed that my words were genuine, because he said, "Listen. Will you promise to apply for a license by the end of the day?" I swore on my honor that I would . . . and I did.

ON FRIDAY, NOVEMBER 22, we were filming a party scene at MGM when we received the devastating news that President Kennedy had been shot in Dallas. All work ground to a halt, and a pall descended over the entire studio. Tony was away, and I was alone with my feelings of sadness and confusion. I remained glued to the television, trying to make sense of it all.

Four days after the assassination, we resumed filming. Over the next few weeks, our company formed a special bond; not only because of the shared grief, but also because our script dealt with the folly of man. Most of the men in the company had done military service, including Paddy Chayefsky, Arthur Hiller, Melvyn Douglas (who had served in two wars), James Garner, and James Coburn. They all knew the truth of what they spoke, and they threw themselves into Paddy's substantive characters with relish.

The role of Charlie Madison seemed tailor-made for James Garner. He was so perfectly chiseled and square-jawed—so leading-man handsome, with his dark hair, flashing eyes, and devilish smile—and the thoughtful nuances in his performance were eye-opening to me. I learned a lot from simply observing the natural ease he brought to the role.

James Coburn, who played Lieutenant Commander "Bus" Cummings, was fairly new to the film scene. He was an instinctive actor, and quite unique with the stiff walk and rigidity of stance that he adopted for the role, along with his toothy grin and earnest manner. Arthur Hiller commented that his was the most dangerous character in the film. Bus was an Annapolis man, and his total dedication to duty and honor is such that he becomes fanatical. Jimmy Coburn's larger-than-life approach to Bus's extremism was seriously funny, and unsettling at the same time.

When Melvyn Douglas was on the set, the entire company was reverential. Even if we weren't in the scene, we flocked to the set, riveted by his every move. One only has to remember *Captains Courageous*, *Ninotchka* with Garbo, or *Hud* with Paul Newman to know how accomplished he was. He went about his work with such quiet authenticity, it was breathtaking. Despite his fame, he was a team player, and never pulled rank.

The English comedienne Joyce Grenfell played my mother in the film. I had worked with her once or twice in my teens. She was a headliner in radio and the music-hall variety shows of the early 1950s. Her forte was playing oddball roles with a vacant, eager-to-please air, which made her hugely popular with the British public. Offstage, she was professional and gracious, and we got on like a house on fire.

Paddy Chayefsky visited the set from time to time. Stocky and somewhat unkempt, as though he'd slept in his suit, he had tousled hair and a faraway gaze that belied his brilliance for observation. The cast would gather around him, hoping for pearls of wisdom. I didn't get to know Paddy well, but his easy presence made me feel totally accepted.

One of the more memorable scenes I shot early in the film was the first love scene between Charlie and Emily. This was certainly outside my experience of *Mary Poppins*. I had never played a love scene before, and I had no idea how to approach it. How "authentic" was a kiss supposed to be, for instance? Should I fake it, or do it for real?

The scene takes place in Charlie's bedroom. Our first kiss was very respectful.

"Oh! So that's the way it's done!" I thought.

However, the script called for some seriously steamy passion, which took most of the afternoon to shoot. Sometimes I was on top of Jim, other times he was on top of me. The camera crept ever closer. We were rolling one way or the other, talking, tearing at each other's clothing, but mostly, we were just kissing, and kissing—and kissing.

I began to think, "It's getting a bit hot in here . . . ," followed by: "I can handle this. I'm a professional."

Hours later, after multiple takes, Arthur called a wrap. When I got up off the bed, my legs literally buckled beneath me. I suspect the scene got to Jimmy, too. As we headed back to our respective dressing rooms, I tried to appear nonchalant. Walking beside me, Jimmy suddenly gave me a big hug and one last kiss on the head, as if to say, "That was fun."

The goodbye scene in which Emily and Charlie stand in the pouring rain, battling their emotions and each other, was a challenge of a different sort. It's a heartrending scene. You know that these two are crazy for each other, but suddenly everything tilts and the conflict in their values and ideals rises to the surface. We shot the scene at night on the tarmac at the Santa Monica Airport. Huge rain machines were brought in, and the downpour was driving and incessant. I learned that in order for rain to register on camera, it has to be twice as heavy as it might be in real life. Despite wearing plastic linings under our raincoats, we became soaked to the skin. Having a monumental fight about morality in war, and showing the pain of loving someone with opposing values, becomes even more challenging when water is dripping off your nose and trickling down your neck.

Shooting for *Emily* ended the day after Christmas. Tony joined me in L.A. on Christmas Eve, and we saw a very rough cut of the film on January 2. Being a dramatic black-and-white war film, it was quite a contrast to the vibrant color and musicality of *Mary Poppins*. It was difficult for me to assess my performance, although I enjoyed reliving the experience of working with such a fine group of people. Today, it is one of my favorite films, and I know that James Garner felt the same way.

TONY, EMMA, WENDY, and I headed home to London to resume the task of readying the long-awaited flat in Wimbledon. We also needed to find a replacement for Wendy, since she was getting married. I knew that once again it would be a fleeting visit. Robert Wise had offered me the role of Maria von Trapp in *The Sound of Music,* and we were to begin shooting in L.A. at the end of February.

While we were home, Tony and I received devastating news: T. H. White had died. Tim had remained a beloved friend since the days of

Camelot, and Tony and I had visited him at his home on the Channel Island of Alderney many times. He had inspired us to buy our own little cottage there, and he'd stayed with us on numerous occasions in London and New York.

We traveled to Alderney for Tim's memorial service, but our time there was short and bittersweet. As I headed to the States to begin rehearsals for *The Sound of Music,* I wondered how I could continue to balance a home life in England with the professional opportunities that were increasingly pulling me back to Hollywood.

3

Tony and I had seen *The Sound of Music* on Broadway, and I'm ashamed to admit that at the time we weren't wildly impressed. We loved the music, but the show seemed rather saccharine to us—so much so that Carol Burnett and I did a spoof of it called "The Pratt Family Singers" in our 1962 television special. Who could have predicted then, as we gleefully indulged in satire, that I would be invited to help bring this now-classic musical to the screen?

Bob Wise, who was directing the film version, and Saul Chaplin, his producer, explained to me that they intended to take a less sentimental and more substantive approach to the material. This helped allay some of my anxieties, but all my life I have struggled with making decisions—which I blame on being a true Libra—and I still had lingering doubts about accepting the job. It would be my second nanny role, almost on the heels of the first. I worried that I might need to affect an Austrian accent, and also it was going to be a long haul, with a lot of time away from home. However, Bob Wise and his team were reassuring and persistent. My British manager, Charlie Tucker, had introduced me to a respected Hollywood agent named Arthur Park, in hopes that he could assume some of the responsibilities that Charlie couldn't handle long-distance. Arthur very much encouraged me to accept the job, and I'll be forever grateful for the nudge over the fence that he and Bob gave this nervous and insecure young woman.

Tony and I had managed to hold on to the same rented house in L.A. that we had used during *Emily*. Kay, Emma's delightful new nanny, traveled from London with us, and Emma took to her immediately. Tony helped us to settle in, but a week later he had to return to London, where he was now working on a stage production of *Caligula* and preparing for the opening of *She Loves Me*. As we always did when we were apart, we spoke on the phone a lot, but it never seemed enough.

I had expected 20th Century Fox to be bustling with activity, but it seemed eerily quiet. The studio had just produced *Cleopatra,* starring Richard Burton, Elizabeth Taylor, and Rex Harrison, at enormous cost, and as a result Fox was virtually bankrupt. When we arrived, very little else was happening there, but I enjoyed the feeling of having the place to ourselves.

Marc Breaux and Dee Dee Wood were choreographing *The Sound of Music,* and Irwin Kostal was our music director. Having so loved our collaboration on *Mary Poppins,* I was delighted that we were all working together again.

For the better part of March, we rehearsed and prerecorded most of the musical numbers for the film. Bob, Saul, and our phenomenal production designer, Boris Leven, had already been to Salzburg for a "recce" to scout shooting locations. They had brought photographs and dimensions back to Marc and Dee Dee, so they could begin working on the movements for each song. Elements of those locations, such as steps or the rim of a fountain, were marked out with colored tape on our studio floor.

The seven "von Trapp" children had already been rehearsing for a week when I arrived. They greeted me enthusiastically, and I hoped that I could live up to their expectations. They were learning the choreography, working with a dialogue coach to affect a "mid-Atlantic" accent, absorbing the songs and harmonies, and keeping up with their schoolwork. My heart warmed to each one for different reasons.

Gentle Charmian Carr (playing the eldest child, Liesl) was trying to navigate being both the teenager she'd been cast as and the young adult she really was. Shy and handsome Nicholas Hammond (Friedrich) grew six inches during the shooting schedule, necessitating some creative framing when others were in a shot with him. Freckle-faced Heather Menzies (Louisa) had an endearing gravitas about her; she was circumspect and shy. Huggable Duane Chase (Kurt) was all boyish exuberance and dimpled charm. Beautiful Angela Cartwright (Brigitta) was the most seasoned actress of the group, with a natural ease and authenticity on camera. Sweet Debbie Turner (Marta) kept losing her teeth, but bravely soldiered on with prosthetics that gave her an adorable lisp. Cuddly Kym Karath (Gretl), the baby of the bunch, was a pint-sized force of nature in her energy and confidence.

We learned the choreography, running around singing our heads off and marching up and down the supposed steps. We were taken out to the back lot to practice our bike-riding skills, and to time our pedaling to the tempo of "Do-Re-Mi," pushing forward and pulling back rhythmically on certain music cues.

There was so much going on those first weeks—costume fittings, hair and makeup tests, rehearsing and recording the musical numbers—not to mention getting to know the rest of the cast and crew.

Dorothy Jeakins, one of the finest costume designers in Hollywood, had designed such films as *Friendly Persuasion*, *South Pacific*, and *The Music Man*. Her costumes for *The Sound of Music* were exquisite in their materials, texture, and authenticity. As I had done with *Mary Poppins*, I found myself absorbing the character from the outside *in*, sensing the nuances of Maria's personality from the images that confronted me in the mirror when I put on the nun's habit, or the rough, shabby dress that even "the poor didn't want."

Dorothy said to me, "I think once Maria gets married, she becomes more of a woman." Therefore, the soft, girlish dresses in the early part of the film gave way to more mature outfits, such as beautifully tailored suits, all of which helped me understand the evolution of Maria's character.

Then there was the issue of my hair. Having cut it short during *Mary Poppins* to accommodate the wigs, I had kept it that way ever since. I had added a few highlights to enliven my mousey brown, but on camera the back of my head was still too dark. Bob decided that I should have more highlights, which was fine with me. Unfortunately, there was a mistake in the color processing, and I ended up with a bright orange mop. My hair had to be cut even shorter, and what was left of it was dyed pure blonde. As luck would have it, this gave me a more Austrian look. Initially it was a shock to be so yellow-blonde, but I got used to it. Having it so short was actually more convenient, especially whenever I needed touch-ups on location. That close cut was also more authentic in terms of playing a nun, since most novitiates kept their hair short under the wimple.

Prerecording the songs for the film was one of the most enjoyable parts of the entire project. The music was recorded in a vast studio at 20th Century Fox. To walk in through the heavy door and see and hear seventy musicians tuning their instruments, practicing a phrase, leafing through a score, is enough to make your stomach somersault with nerves— but it's also a thrill. For me, there are few pleasures greater than singing with a large orchestra.

For the first run-through of every song, I stood next to Irwin Kostal, to hear the layout of the orchestration. For the recording itself, I went inside a small, soundproof glass booth. I had a view of the orchestra, and Irwin on his podium, and I could hear the musicians through my headphones. I prayed that I could come up to their level of brilliance.

Because we'd already learned the choreography for our musical numbers together, the children and I were able to imagine what it might really be like when we actually shot the scenes—when we would be skipping, marching, and so on. But singing the solo title song that opens the film was a different thing altogether. I had no idea—and I'm not sure Bob, Marc, or Dee Dee did either—which field or which mountainous area we'd be filming in, and what movements would be required. In fact, the sweeping turn that I make at the beginning of the song was an idea Bob only came up with once we were on location, so in recording the song I had to rely on my imagination and instinct. Irwin's orchestrations were gorgeous, and as the score climbed to my opening phrase, I intuitively sensed—and the music indicated—the grandeur of the landscape around me. I knew that the moment had to be thrilling. I simply shut my eyes and let the music be my guide.

Oscar Hammerstein's lyric for "The Sound of Music" tells us so much about Maria herself; her love of nature, her loneliness, the things that make her heart sing. To convey all of this through my vocal interpretation before we'd even shot a single scene felt like an impossibility. I hung on to the words and the images they conjured for me as best

I could—though I will confess that "a lark who is learning to pray" is an image that has always eluded me. My solution there was to push through that line and topple into the next phrase and associated image as quickly as possible. I hoped that what I had laid down on the track would suffice when the time came to shoot the scene, several months later.

PRINCIPAL PHOTOGRAPHY FINALLY commenced at the end of March, with the scenes in Maria's bedroom and the song "My Favorite Things." I was very nervous. I'd never worked with Robert Wise before, but I knew that his impressive résumé included *Somebody Up There Likes Me* and *West Side Story*. I had also never worked with seven children before, but I imagined they might be even more nervous than I was. I spent as much time as I could telling them stories, making faces at them behind the camera when Bob needed a good close-up, and generally trying to put them at ease. The adorable grin I elicited from Duane Chase in "Favorite Things" was reward enough. Even though *Mary Poppins* hadn't been released yet, the children had heard about it. They kept asking me to say "supercalifragilisticexpialidocious" for them, which I did—and then to their delight, I said it backwards.

Ernest Lehman, our screenwriter, had written the screenplays for such films as *West Side Story* and *North by Northwest*. He disliked when characters in musicals burst into song without warning, and he wanted to avoid having to write clichéd dialogue to facilitate a segue to the music. So he suggested that I simply speak the first phrase of "My Favorite Things" as a continuation of dialogue, then once the orchestra established itself, ease into singing. I was very pleased, because it felt more real to me when the song grew organically out of the story.

I have always enjoyed singing "My Favorite Things." It has such a strong and spare chord structure, and its lilting melody is irresistible. "I'm in Love with a Wonderful Guy" has the same compelling drive. I feel Richard Rodgers stands alongside the Strausses and Henry Mancini as one of the great "waltz kings," and Oscar Hammerstein's brilliant lyrics render these songs unforgettable.

Incidentally, there's something I want to set straight. Rumors abound that I was the author of a tasteless send-up of "My Favorite Things," which I supposedly sang at an AARP benefit at Radio City Music Hall. I'd like to state for the record that I never had anything to do with it. I didn't write it, I didn't sing it, and I have no idea where it came from. I have never sung at Radio City—and more importantly, why would I denigrate such a beautiful song, which I was so honored to sing?

The "Favorite Things" scene concludes with the arrival of Captain von Trapp, played by Christopher Plummer. Our paths had crossed only once or twice during my time on Broadway, but I knew Chris to be an esteemed classical actor, which I found intimidating. My background was in vaudeville, the complete opposite of "legit" theater, which Chris had done *so* much of. I thought, "How can I match up?" He had initially struck me as a surprisingly dark choice for the Captain, and I'd heard that he almost hadn't accepted the role. On that first day of filming, I realized he'd been brilliantly cast. He just *was* Captain von Trapp.

The first piece of direction I recall receiving from Bob Wise was when I was kneeling at the bedside praying, while Liesl creeps into my room through the window. Bob demonstrated the image he had in mind for Maria in that moment: hands clasped, elbows on the bed, head bowed. It sounds like such a simple thing, but the posture felt instantly right, and it cemented my trust in our director.

Bob was gentle, patient, and considerate. Whenever Emma came to the set, he would lift her onto his knee while I was doing a scene and let her watch with him from behind the camera. He also allowed me the freedom to improvise occasionally, and only reined me in if he felt I had gone too far.

At the end of the "Lonely Goatherd" sequence, for instance, there's a shot of me staggering around the corner of the little puppet theater, exhausted. I initially hammed it up to such an extent that Bob burst out laughing. I said to him, "But Bob, I think she *would* be that exhausted! Why wouldn't she show it?" He replied, "It's wonderfully funny, Julie, but it's too much . . . Bring it down."

For that number, we all had to learn how to operate the marionettes; no easy task. I'd prerecorded some of the extra voices, including a goat, which was great fun. However, the one thing I *couldn't* do was yodel. In the original Broadway production, Mary Martin yodeled brilliantly. Although I practiced and tried my best to make the required "break" in my voice, I don't think I fooled anyone. Having spent so many years working with Madame Stiles-Allen on trying to erase any vocal "gear-changing," it was hard for me to put a glottal shift back in. In the years since, I've heard a great deal of authentic yodeling in Switzerland and Austria, and I'm always impressed by the skill it requires.

Bob taught me a great deal about how to perform on camera. He said to me, "Julie, when the camera is in a tight close-up, and you're looking at someone, try not to move your eyes back and forth from one side to another. Onstage you'd never notice, but on the big screen it's very distracting." I learned to either focus on the space between the eyebrows of my fellow actor, or simply look at the eye closest to the camera. Bob also encouraged me to blink less. Neither of my previous directors had mentioned these things, and I now realize it was probably because *Poppins* and *Emily* were filmed in 35 mm, whereas *The Sound of Music* was shot in 70 mm Todd-AO—a much wider format, making every facial tic more apparent.

THE WEEKEND BEFORE I traveled to Austria to commence location shooting, Tony and I managed to meet up in New York City for just two nights. It was precious little time together, but we were happy to have even that. His sweet, familiar presence always made me feel safe again. Tony was taking production meetings for the upcoming musical of Clifford Odets's *Golden Boy*, starring Sammy Davis Jr., for which he would be designing sets, costumes, and projections. The show was to have a long tryout period in Philadelphia, Boston, and Detroit, before opening on Broadway. I was immensely proud that Tony's career was taking off in such meteoric fashion, but I don't think either of us yet grasped how long we would have to be away from each other, or how these extended separations might take a toll on our marriage. We'd known each other for almost seventeen years and had often been apart for work-related projects. At this point in our relationship, it seemed natural to allow for each other's professional commitments. We couldn't always expect to work together as we had done with *Mary Poppins*. I hoped Tony would be able to visit me in Austria.

Emma, Kay, and I traveled from New York to Salzburg on April 21. I had never visited Austria before, and it was exciting to see the historic city where Mozart was born, and its beautiful surrounding mountains. The film company had housed the cast and crew in several different hotels. I was in the rather staid Hotel Österreichischer Hof—the name itself was daunting—now called the Sacher. Chris Plummer was in the ritzier and more popular Hôtel Le Bristol. I think the studio felt that the Österreichischer Hof would be quieter and more comfortable for Emma, Kay, and me.

The day after I arrived in Austria, we shot the massive wedding scene inside the Basilica St. Michael by the lake of Mondsee. It had taken our cinematographer, Ted McCord, and his crew several days to light the exquisite church. The scene was made all the more challenging by the number of locals who'd been brought in to act as spectators, dressed in the ir traditional Austrian finery. It took quite a bit of crowd control.

Maria's wedding dress, designed by Dorothy Jeakins, was one of the most beautiful costumes I have ever worn, before or since. As I walked down the center aisle, clutching my bouquet and matching my steps to the soaring musical playback, it was thrilling to glimpse the camera through the magnificent archways, dollying sideways along a separate aisle to keep me in frame. I could see Chris waiting by the altar at the top of the steps, and as I climbed to join him and reached out to take his hand, I was reminded of my aunt Joan's lessons in graceful arm extensions and "finishing the line."

We moved from the church to the Felsenreitschule, or Rock Riding School, which is the amphitheater where the Salzburg Festival is held each year. The arena is carved out of stone, and the long nights that we shot there were perishingly cold. My heart went out to the more than one thousand extras, who had to simply sit in the audience and couldn't retreat to a warm trailer. In a bizarre twist, someone had assumed that the song we were all to sing, "Edelweiss," would be known by Austrians. In fact, having been written by Rodgers and Hammerstein, the song was new to the locals, and the assistant director had to take up valuable time teaching it to them and rehearsing them between takes.

"Edelweiss" is the last song Oscar Hammerstein ever wrote, and it is my favorite song in the film, despite the fact that I only sing it with the von Trapp ensemble. I have, however, sung it many times in the years since. To me, it's an anthem that speaks to one's homeland, no matter where that may be, and it moves me deeply. I spent so much of my early life trying to unify my need for home with my commitment to work. These days, I've come to realize that home is a feeling as much as it is a place; it is as much about loving what I do as being where I am.

SOMEONE HAD EVIDENTLY forgotten to mention to our production crew that Salzburg has Europe's seventh-highest annual rainfall. Since we had shot most of our interiors at the Fox studios in L.A., most of our locations in Austria were outdoors. The rains began in our first days there, and from then on, our budget and our schedule were totally governed by the weather. The crew had found cover sets to grab a few additional interior shots if needed . . . but those were quickly used up. At that point, we had no choice but to go to one of our exterior locations, which were sometimes miles away, and wait—and wait—for the weather to clear.

For the alpine scenes, our equipment trucks were parked at the foot of whatever mountain we were filming on. There were no roads, just fields and rutted tracks, so the camera equipment had to be carried up on an ox-drawn cart, and the rest of us had to walk. It was always cold in the Alps, and walking up wasn't easy. On one particularly chilly day, the wind was blowing hard and there was a lot of mud. Bob said to me, "Sit on the ox cart, Julie, with the cameras. We'll give you a lift." I climbed into the cart, and off we plodded. I happened to be wearing a fur coat (it was the 1960s, after all!), and the humor in the contrast between my attire and the mode of transport wasn't lost on any of us.

Once we reached our designated location, tracks were laid, and cameras were set up, then temporarily covered with tarps. We actors would settle somewhere, under a tent, or in a barn if there was one, to wait out the weather. When nature called, we went into the woods—not easy for us women!

The fields where we filmed were owned by various

Austrian farmers, who had been paid for our use of their land. One of them had been specifically asked not to cut the lush grass, but we arrived to discover that it had been reduced to stubble. Perhaps it was the language barrier. We had to find another field, another location, wasting precious time.

A different farmer was apparently a little over-stimulated by having "Hollywood" come to visit. He accosted me with a lascivious leer and let fly a stream of obscenities. He was speaking in German, yet there was no doubting his intent. The local members of our crew were outraged, and he was henceforth kept far away from me.

Sometimes a kindly farmer would provide us all with homemade schnapps when we wrapped at the end of the day. It tasted like nectar after the damp, blustery working conditions.

Many days went by when we only got a single shot—two if we were lucky. To pass the time, I'd run lines with the kids or practice my guitar. I'd been taking guitar lessons, learning basic fingering and simple chords so that I'd appear to know what I was doing. (Sadly, I didn't stick with it, though I wish I had. I guess it just wasn't my instrument.)

Saul, Marc, Dee Dee, and I would occasionally indulge in singalongs. We called ourselves "the Vocalzones," after the throat pastilles I always carry.

Whenever the meal wagon showed up, it felt like a momentous event.

Ted McCord would regularly produce his view-finder and peer up at the sky. "Everyone stand by! In about five minutes, we *may* get a glimpse of sun!" When the moment came, we'd throw off our blankets and dash out, only to do about two seconds' worth of filming, if we were lucky, before the weather closed in again. We had to be in a constant state of readiness in terms of makeup, hair, and costumes.

To meet Ted, you would never have guessed he was a cinematographer. He was always pressured, often irritable, and not at all social. However, he had an extraordinary eye, and his lighting was magnificent. He was "old school," and fretted about shooting me after 5 p.m., worrying that there'd be unflattering shadows under my eyes. (If only he'd been around later in my life, when I had to shoot television close-ups at two-thirty in the morning!)

I'll never forget the day he proudly showed me his lighting scheme for the scene where Maria leaves the abbey for the von Trapp villa. Standing in shadow in the dark courtyard of the abbey, she says, "When the Lord closes a door, some-where he opens a window." She then pushes open the gate and comes out into bright sunlight, mirroring the physical and emotional transition she is making in her life. Once Ted pointed that out to me, I was able to internalize it in my approach to the scene.

I DIDN'T SEE much of Chris Plummer beyond the workday, as he spent most of his spare time at the Bristol. Word spread that he was becoming renowned for his late-night performances at the piano in the hotel bar. In his youth, he had trained to be a concert pianist, and he was very good indeed. He apparently spent his evenings at the bar getting quite smashed and playing Rachmaninoff or Tchaikovsky until the wee hours. That said, Chris was the glue that held us all together; the one who always kept us from going too deep into the saccharine side of the story. He was so disciplined in his acting, so knowledgeable, that he was appropriately imposing as the Captain. Yet he was very gentle, and constructive, too. He'd make suggestions as to how we might play a certain scene. For instance, when we worked on the argument between the Captain and Maria after the children have been boating, he said, "Don't be afraid to *really* let me have it!" He'd even come up with a good ad-lib in the heat of the moment.

That boating scene was particularly challenging

to shoot. It called for the children and me to stand up in a small, shallow boat, and then for it to tip us all overboard. Just before we shot the first take, the assistant director waded rather urgently through the water toward me. As I leaned over the edge to hear him, he whispered, "The little one can't swim . . ."

"WHAT?!"

"Yes," he said. "We'd be most grateful if you could get to her as quickly as possible once you're in the water."

Kym Karath was only seven years old, and she was being very brave. I was supposed to go over the front of the boat to land right beside her. The first take went perfectly, but Bob felt he needed another shot. Unfortunately, in the second take, the boat rocked so violently that I went over the back as Kym went over the front. I have never swum so fast in my life. I could see the poor child flailing away and going under at least twice. Crew members dove into the water to help save her, and mercifully we got there in time. Little Kym threw up all the water she had swallowed, and we bundled her in blankets and made a big fuss over her.

The von Trapp family villa in the film was a composite of three different locations—none of them the actual villa, which was dark and gloomy, and not particularly photogenic. The front façade of the film's villa was one location, and the back garden, terrace, and lake another. As mentioned earlier, most of the interiors were shot in the studio in Los Angeles.

The real von Trapps had only twenty-four hours to evacuate their home when they escaped Austria, and the film fictionalizes their journey. In reality, they didn't go over the mountains to Switzerland, as our script suggests. There was a railway line at the bottom of their garden on which the train to Italy came through. The family packed small rucksacks and crept out at five in the morning to board that train, and never went back. It's hard for me to imagine abandoning your home and everything in it, but their lives depended on it.

That sad villa was subsequently acquired by Heinrich Himmler, and when Hitler came to visit, there was always a train steaming at the ready in case the Führer had to make a quick getaway. Himmler made Jewish prisoners build a high wall around the property, and once that was completed, he lined them up and had them shot. If he suspected a member of his staff had overheard something they shouldn't, he'd send that unfortunate person down to the courtyard to fetch something, and then shoot them himself from his upstairs office window.

I never visited the real von Trapp villa while filming *The Sound of Music,* but fifty years later, when Diane Sawyer and I were in Salzburg for the anniversary of the film, we went there and we both got chills. Despite the fact that the villa is now a museum devoted to the von Trapp family and there is no mention of the German occupation, you can literally feel the evil that once permeated those walls.

I HAD BEEN so busy working that I had very little time to do any sightseeing or socializing. When I learned that my good friend from London, Svetlana Beriosova, would be dancing with the Royal Ballet at the Munich Opera House, I arranged for a bus to take thirty of us on our one free day to see her perform. The ballet was superb, and afterward we were given a backstage tour of the opera house. It was great to see my old friend, even so briefly, and I think she was equally happy to see me.

The only other event I attended was a beautiful chamber music concert. It was at the invitation of Peggy Wood, who played the Mother Abbess; Eleanor Parker, who played the Baroness; and Portia Nelson, who was Sister Berthe. The ladies had done quite a bit of sightseeing together in their spare time, and realizing that I hadn't, they insisted that I come with them.

The concert was held in the Salzburg town hall. A small ballroom had been set with chairs, music stands, a white piano, and a yellow-gold harpsichord. Chandeliers hung from the ceiling, and two tall candelabras flickered on either side of the orchestra.

"Rather schmaltzy," I thought. I was cold, and felt I'd be glad when the concert was over and I could go home to a much-needed night's rest.

The musicians entered, and from the moment they began to play, something magical happened. That evening, when I returned to my hotel, I wrote:

The acoustics in the room were incredible. The musicians were young and dedicated. To be so near them, to see their serious faces, hear them breathe, see them frown and communicate with each other was riveting. But mostly, to hear such purity, to drown in glorious sound, to feel it wash over and through me—Haydn, Purcell, Mozart of course—was to be spiritually uplifted.

The image I have now was that everything was golden. The instruments, the parquet floors, the gilt chairs—all glowed in the candlelight. The experience was utterly sensual. I had always believed composers like Purcell and Mozart to be rather formal and precise, but they're *not*. To hear and see the music played in its authentic setting was to feel the composers' passion and emotion in a way I never had before.

I stumble around Hollywood, thinking I might just be contributing something worthwhile, flattering myself that I'm "growing," gaining strength in my work, beginning to feel it pulling together . . . when all along the group that played tonight have been making a perfect contribution to a world that, until tonight, I knew nothing about. In contrast, my work seems slap-dash and haphazard.

Something happened within me tonight. I gained perspective on an elusive thread that I couldn't quite catch, but almost did—and I just want to record it on paper, so that one day I might read it again and remember how *alive* I felt.

Despite how busy I was, I felt lonely for much of the time in Salzburg. Because of his own work commitments, Tony was unable to visit me, and long-distance phone calls were few and far between, given our competing schedules and time differ-ences. My resources weren't substantial enough to allow for visits from my family, although my great friend the photographer Zoë Dominic came from London to take publicity shots at one point, and I was unbelievably grateful to see her.

I took Emma with me everywhere I could. She and Kay came to the flat locations in Salzburg, but I couldn't bring my seventeen-month-old daughter to the more challenging alpine locations. On those days, Kay would keep her occupied, visiting the Mirabell Gardens, going on sightseeing excursions, or taking pony rides.

However, when Emma wasn't around, I was often blue. It was reminiscent of the melancholy I had felt in my teens, when I was touring in vaudeville and had no family members accompanying me. I knew I would have to return to L.A. to finish the film. Would I then wish to return to London, and the empty apartment awaiting me in Wimbledon? Would work continue to pull Tony and me apart? It certainly seemed that it might—Tony's work was more and more centered in New York, and mine, now, was based in L.A. How could Wimbledon be a home base if we were so seldom in residence and so often away from each other?

One day, I was having a particularly difficult

time. I shared a company car with Richard Haydn, who played the impresario Max, from our location back to Salzburg. He must have recognized that I was struggling emotionally, for he proceeded to make me laugh the entire way home. I didn't really wish to engage—I just wanted to look out the window and process my thoughts. However, that dear man persisted until I finally laughed so hard that I temporarily came out of my funk.

DURING PREPRODUCTION, Bob Wise, Saul Chaplin, and Ernie Lehman had decided that we needed a new song to capture Maria's journey from the abbey to the Captain's house—something that conveyed her anticipation, excitement, and anxiety. Saul was a consummate musician, and in addition to being our producer, he was the unofficial music supervisor for the film, which encompassed every aspect of the film's sound. (It was, after all, *The Sound of Music*.) Saul asked Richard Rodgers to write something appropriate for this moment in the film, but Richard delivered a song that was surprisingly solemn and slow.

Saul tried his best to have Richard rework it, but the result wasn't satisfying. So, with Richard's permission, Saul cobbled bits and pieces of music from the score that had not been used thus far, and added in some music of his own, along with new lyrics. Richard reluctantly gave his blessing, stating that he liked the original better, but that Saul's was "OK to use." Saul never told me until many years later that he was largely responsible for "I Have Confidence," because he was afraid of what my reaction would be. His fears, alas, were well founded.

When I first heard the song, I was genuinely puzzled by some of the lyrics, which were hard to make sense of. Because I have always relied on lyrics to anchor me in a song, it was hard for me to sing. I decided that the only way to get around those lyrics was to have Maria be so nervous about her upcoming job that she works herself into a state and becomes a bit dotty. I talked with Marc and Dee Dee about it, and they mercifully agreed. So, as the song progressed, I started flinging myself about, skipping and swinging and tripping over my suitcase to make it seem as if I was babbling with nerves.

The "I Have Confidence" sequence was further complicated by the ever-present Salzburg rain. As I had learned during *The Americanization of Emily*, it takes a great deal of rain to register on camera, and I doubt anyone viewing *The Sound of Music* noticed that when I was peering through the gate of the villa, it was actually raining. It wasn't strong enough to prevent our shooting the scene, but it did make for another soggy day's work.

During the making of the film, Saul fell in love with our continuity lady, Betty Levin, and she later became his wife. Poor Betty really had her hands full with this picture. One of the biggest challenges for her was the "Do-Re-Mi" montage, which was shot in multiple sections and filmed in nine different locations. We were all over Salzburg—on the mountains and in the town, riding in a horse and buggy, cycling along a river path. We ran over the Mozart Bridge, around the fountain, and down the covered allée in the Mirabell Gardens. The montage showcases Salzburg as a principal character in the film, and establishes its importance to the von Trapp family. It also shows a passage of time in which the children fall in love with Maria and revel in their newfound freedom. Betty nearly went crazy noting every child's specific movements, where they were in relation to me and to each other, and what each of us was doing at any given moment.

The orchestration for the montage builds as the children become more accomplished musically, culminating at the steps of the Mirabell Palace. Saul conceived of the last eight steps as representing the notes of the musical scale, and Marc and Dee Dee choreographed a devilishly complicated series of movements for the children. As I climb a straight line to the topmost step, the children on either side of me jump up and then back down to match the intervals between the notes in the solfège. By the end, we are in full-throated crescendo. This prompted me to ask if I could cap the scale with an octave leap to get us to the last note. Despite its complications, the sequence was tremendous fun to do, and it gave the entire company a real sense of achievement. So many people contributed their considerable talent to those scenes, not the least of whom was our editor, Bill Reynolds, who cut the whole nine-minute number together so skillfully as to appear seamless.

TOWARD THE END of my work in Salzburg, I heard that the next film scheduled to be shot there would be *The Great Race*, directed by Blake Edwards and starring Tony Curtis and Jack Lemmon. When the new company came in, a lot of our local crew would be re-employed. I had received word from my agent that there had been an inquiry as to whether I might play the role of the suffragette journalist who drives the race car for her newspaper. I was aware of Blake's work on the *Pink Panther* films and *Breakfast at Tiffany's*, and I admired it tremendously. I dearly hoped the production could wait for me. Unfortunately, with all our delays and more shooting still to do in Los Angeles, I wouldn't be finished in time for their start date. Instead, the role went to the lovely Natalie Wood.

Ironically, most of our film's magical opening sequence was the last thing we filmed in Austria. Bob had envisioned an aerial shot to be filmed from a helicopter that would discover me—a speck in the vast alpine landscape—walking toward the camera. He selected a beautiful stretch of country-side high in the mountains, flanked by woods on two sides. Our huge playback speakers were camouflaged among the trees, as was our crew, so that no one else was in view.

I was placed at one end of the meadow. A heli-copter hovered behind the trees at the other end, waiting for me to begin my walk toward it. Initially, I couldn't hear my cue since the crew's voices were muffled by the trees. Even the playback, turned up as loud as possible, was almost inaudible over the "clackety-clack" of the helicopter. Finally, Marc Breaux was given a bullhorn, through which he yelled, "GO, JULIE!"

I began my walk, and as I did, the helicopter rose up and over its cover. It came at me sideways, looking rather like a giant crab. A brave camera-man named Paul Beeson was hanging out of it, strapped precariously to the side where a door would have been, his feet resting on the runners beneath the craft. Strapped to him was the heavy camera equipment. As the helicopter drew closer, I spun around with my arms open as if about to sing. All I had to do was walk, twirl, and take a breath. This required several takes, to be sure that both the helicopter and I hit our marks correctly, the camera was in focus, there was no helicopter shadow, and that everything timed out. Once the take was complete, the helicopter soared up and around me and returned to its original position. At that point I'd run back to the end of the field to start all over again, until Bob was satisfied that he had the perfect take.

The problem was that as I completed that spin and the helicopter lifted, the downdraft from the jet engine was so powerful, it dashed me to the ground. I'd haul myself up, spitting mud and grass and brushing it off my dress, and trek back to my starting position. Each time the helicopter encircled me, I was flattened again.

I became more and more irritated—couldn't they see what was happening? I tried to indicate for them to make a *wider* circle around me. I could see the cameraman, the pilot, and our second unit director on board, but all I got was a thumbs-up and a signal to do it again. Finally, the shot was deemed acceptable, and I was grateful to return to my hotel and take a long, hot bath.

By this time, largely due to the weather, we were three weeks behind schedule, seriously over budget, and the studio had summoned the rest of the cast back to L.A. We tried to capture the next small section of the song for several days, but the relentless rain thwarted our attempts yet again. Day after day, we waited for a break in the clouds, everyone cold, damp, and longing to go home.

There was still quite a bit left to shoot, as each small segment of the song was its own little scene. The brook, for example, was actually man-made, dug out by our crew, lined with plastic and filled with water, boulders, and ferns. Our host farmer lost patience with us, claiming that the film crew's presence was disrupting his cows' milk production. Overnight, he took a pitchfork to the plastic lining and punctured it enough times that all the water drained away. Bob was devastated—the 20th Century Fox bigwigs were hounding him to wrap things up, but they had no idea of the obstacles that he was wrestling with.

Finally, Bob promised the studio that if he didn't

get the last shot he was waiting for, he'd wrap the company nonetheless and come home the following day. By some miracle, that afternoon the clouds parted for a brief half hour, the sun came out, and we got our shot. Bob later said that those constant lowering cumuli set against the magnificent Alps gave the film the drama and authenticity it needed—something we couldn't have achieved any other way.

WE RETURNED TO Los Angeles and resumed filming at the studio two days later. We were now shooting the interior scenes in the villa; Boris Leven's production design crew had built the set for it while we were in Austria. Boris was known for designing *Giant* and *West Side Story,* among many other notable films. Being the wife of a production designer, I had already admired Boris's work before we left for Europe: the vast courtyard of the abbey, the incredibly realistic cloisters with the tombs that conceal the von Trapp family before their escape. But the interior of the villa was even more spectacular. It was a vast set that included the main hall, the staircase, the great mirrored ballroom, the living room, the dining room, and the outside courtyard. Boris's attention to detail was extraordinary, and it was a thrill to arrive home and discover what he had created in our absence.

Of all the scenes we shot in the film, there are three that will always stand out in my memory. The first is just after Maria and the Captain have had a blazing row by the lake and he has fired her. The Captain walks into his house and hears his children singing the song they have prepared for his fiancée, the Baroness. Maria is about to walk up the stairs, but she stops to listen for a moment. The Captain spots her and comes out to speak with her.

"You brought music back into this house. I had forgotten," he says, and then, "I want you to stay; I . . . *ask* you to stay."

Looking down at Chris from the stairs, I found his performance deeply moving. I spontaneously clapped my hands together with joy—I didn't know what else to do—and dashed up the stairs. It's the sort of moment that Bob let me run with, and I believe it worked so well because Chris had genuinely moved me.

Another moment was dancing the *Laendler* with Chris in the courtyard outside the great ballroom during the party. Although it remains unspoken, it is the moment where the Captain and Maria recognize their love for each other. Everything about the scene worked beautifully; Richard Rodgers's music,

Marc and Dee Dee's choreography, Boris's setting, Ted's lighting, and above all, Bob's sublime camerawork, culminating in that very intimate close-up between the two would-be lovers.

The third was when Maria is wandering sadly by the lake at dusk. The Captain has just told the Baroness that he is unable to marry her, and he now joins Maria outside.

"Nothing was the *same* when you were away, and it'll be all *wrong* again after you leave!" he says to Maria. Chris played it like a sweet, sulky little boy, and as I watched him, I thought, "You are simply adorable!" How he knew to find that surprising aspect of the grown man's character still delights me.

The scene concludes in the gazebo with the song "Something Good," which coincided with my last day of shooting on the film, August 13, 1964.

Ted McCord had hung huge klieg lights above the octagonal gazebo to create shafts of moonlight. Because these arc lamps were tilted so sharply, the carbon rods inside—which rubbed together to create the light—began to protest, groaning and making loud raspberry-like sounds at the most intimate moments in the scene.

After several interrupted takes, Chris and I began to get the giggles—me especially, partly from the idiotic noises and partly from the sheer exhaustion of the preceding five months. Chris and I were nose-to-nose, and I could see in his eyes that he, too, was struggling to hold it together. That only made things worse.

Shot after shot, we'd get to a certain point, a lamp would groan or emit a seemingly blistering comment on our performance, and we'd collapse with laughter. Bob would say "Cut!" and we'd have to start all over again. Eventually, Bob called an extended lunch break, thinking it would give us time to compose ourselves. I was a basket case, panicked that I would never be able to get hold of myself. I took a long walk around the lot. Two hours later, we tried the scene once more. The carbons heated up, protesting anew, and Chris and I lost it again, leaning against the scenery, too weak with laughter to even stand up straight.

In desperation, Bob came up with a brilliant idea. "We'll shoot it in the dark!" he said. He asked us to walk to the door, out of the moonlight, and stand in silhouette, so that our mirth would be hidden. Of course, the moment there were no lights on us, the pressure was off—and with much relief, we easily finished the scene. Ironically, that adjustment made the end of the gazebo sequence even more touching.

It was the end of my filming for *The Sound of Music*. I had a considerable amount of looping to do, which meant I would still go to the studio every day for the next few weeks, but my on-camera work was complete.

When I look back at this time, I realize that my senses were suffused with all that I'd seen and experienced in Austria. Those vast mountains are forever seared in my memory; the smell of the fresh air; the showers and the downpours on the fields and flowers. Above all, the *music*, still—and always—lives in my bones and in my soul.

At this point, I had made three films, yet not one had been released. I had no idea how successful they might be, or what lay in store—but I did know what a gift I had been given. The privilege of having played those three roles would have been enough to satisfy me for a lifetime.

4

Tony joined me in Los Angeles at the end of July, and though I'd so looked forward to being reunited as a family, our time together was once again all too brief. We attended a screening of *The Americanization of Emily*. Johnny Mandel's score had not yet been added and there was still much editing work to be done, but the film held together well. Watching myself on-screen, I saw places where my lack of experience showed through; I wished I hadn't rushed some scenes, or that my voice could have been less shrill in others. I had learned a bit more about my craft from working on *The Sound of Music*, so the gaffes were more obvious to me now—but in the end, it wasn't so bad that I wanted to run away and hide.

Four days later Tony headed for Boston, where *Golden Boy* was to open next. The production was fraught with problems—Sammy Davis Jr. was demanding, the playwright had passed away, and the original director had been replaced. The civil rights themes and biracial relationship depicted in the show were prompting hate mail. Tony was trying to keep his contribution intact, while navigating all the larger-than-life personalities and problems. We were both so busy with our respective professional commitments that we were like two ships passing in the night.

A few days after Tony departed, I received a surprising invitation. Cole Porter asked me to come to dinner at his home. I had never met him, but admired him enormously, and was delighted to accept.

I was ushered into a small study where the great man himself was lying on a sofa. I knew he was very frail; he'd lost a limb years ago as the result of a riding accident, and was now in the final stages of kidney failure. He was dressed in a sort of white pajama suit with a mandarin collar, and had a light blanket covering him from the waist down. Everything seemed white, including his extremely pale skin, the only exception being his piercing eyes.

Dinner was served on television tables. Cole was propped up on the sofa, and I sat opposite him in a comfortable chair. He asked me question after question; where was I born, how did I begin my career, and so forth. I tried to comprehend why he had chosen to invite me. I guess at that time

I was the new girl in town. Since I was the only guest there, I did my best to keep up my end of the conversation and to amuse him. It was a shock when, just two months later, I read that he had passed away.

MARY POPPINS FINALLY premiered on August 27, 1964, at Grauman's Chinese Theatre in Hollywood. The Walt Disney Studios pulled out all the stops; it was a glorious, old-fashioned kind of premiere. All the classic Disney characters were there, welcoming people as they pulled up in their limousines. There were crowds in the bleachers, screaming with delight, and huge searchlights raked the sky. On the large parking lot adjacent to Grauman's, a tent had been erected for the after-show party. It was glamorous, grand, and gaudy all at the same time.

Tony and I arrived in a company limousine provided by Disney, with my dad, who had come to visit for two weeks. This was Dad's first trip to California, and we were beyond thrilled to share the experience with him, and to give him such a splendid glimpse of Hollywood glamour. He had made the journey all by himself; my stepmother, Win, had stayed home with their daughter, Shad. Dad rented a white tuxedo jacket, which I picked up for him early in the day. As he had done at my wedding, and on several visits to *My Fair Lady* in New York and London, he acted the part of my squire and protector, in a quiet but proud way. Charlie Tucker, my long-time agent and manager, had also flown over from England. Surprisingly, P. L. Travers came as well. Given the tensions that had existed between them, Walt showed great restraint that evening, and was polite and decent to her. She never said a word to me about her opinion of the film. She did send a note to Walt, in which she called it a "splendid spectacle," and complimented my "understated" performance. High praise!

Unfortunately, my mother could not attend. I had invited her and hoped that she would come, but she said that her arthritis was giving her tremendous pain and she'd prefer not to travel. I had a feeling that she was worried about not measuring up in some way. I would have given anything to have had her with me—I had a daughter's desire to share my good fortune with both my parents and to make them proud. I'm sure Mum was, but I always sensed that she hid some embarrassment about how she conducted her life, relative to what she thought I had become. It made me sad.

Tony, Dad, and I walked along the red carpet toward Walt and his wife, Lillian, flashbulbs popping everywhere around us. Dorothy Jeakins had designed an Empire-style, cream-colored silk jersey gown for me. On top I wore a little mink stole that I had rented for the evening. Tony wore a tux, which was a rare occurrence for him. Tom Jones had warned me that I would need to pause for interviews before entering the theater. Even so, I was unprepared for the pressure and scrutiny; the feeling of being pulled, poked, and shouted at by the phalanx of TV and radio reporters. There were so many people to attend to that after we arrived, I barely saw my dad or Tony for the rest of the evening.

At the party in the tent afterward, Tom continued to steer me around, a gentle hand at my elbow, introducing me to guests and more members of the press. I never sat down, and I don't recall eating a morsel. Feeling overwhelmed, I couldn't wait to go home, to be somewhere quiet where I could process what was happening.

Happily, the audience seemed to love the film. I was so dazed by everything that was transpiring that I couldn't watch it with any perspective. I do know that it received a raucous ovation, and the reviews were extremely positive.

The following morning, I had to be at 20th Century Fox by 9:30 a.m. for looping on *The Sound of Music.* That same day, Tony flew to Detroit, where *Golden Boy,* still beset with problems, was now playing.

Two days later, my dad and I flew to New York, where *Mary Poppins* had just opened. I did four days of back-to-back interviews in the city, during which time Tony briefly joined us. There wasn't a second to spare, except in the evenings, when we managed to treat Dad to a couple of Broadway shows. After emotional goodbyes, Tony went back to the dramas in Detroit, and my dad flew home to London. I returned to L.A., and to my Emma, whom I always hated to leave behind.

The weeks that ensued became an assault of epic proportions that I could never have foreseen. I did more publicity than I have ever done in my life, before or since. After an onslaught of *Poppins*-related activities in L.A., I embarked upon my first promotional tour, traveling to San Francisco with the Disney press team for the premiere of *Poppins* there; then on to Chicago, Detroit, New York again, Philadelphia, Washington, DC, and Boston.

I am well aware how irritating it is when people who have been graced by good fortune complain about its rigors. However, this was the first time I had encountered such widespread attention, expectation, and accountability. I was a small-town English girl, naïve, undereducated, and considerably younger than my years, suddenly confronted by a scrutiny that I had no context or experience with which to manage.

The press bombarded me with questions that called for me to be introspective, to examine things about myself and my work that up to this point I had never considered, let alone formed an opinion about. I floundered about, trying to appear sophisticated, while feeling as though I were playing dress-up in my mother's clothes.

It never would have occurred to me to say no to any of the things that the studio asked of me. I felt that I owed them every interview—one paid one's dues, so to speak, and I honored every obligation and went wherever they asked me to go.

During this whirlwind, I saw a rough cut of *The Sound of Music,* which was the first time I'd seen any of the footage assembled. I marveled at its beauty, its energy, its joyousness. It seemed even larger than *Mary Poppins,* and I felt it was going to be a stunning film. It put in perspective the amount of work we had accomplished over the past months—no wonder I was exhausted!

I returned to New York for Tony's birthday, which coincided with the low-key opening of *The Americanization of Emily.* In contrast to the pomp and ceremony of the *Poppins* premiere, *Emily* simply opened at a regular cinema, with no fuss. Since it was a relatively quiet drama, the studios didn't feel a fancy premiere was warranted. Nevertheless, it received fine reviews, and the film has subsequently become something of a cult favorite.

TENSIONS HAD BEEN escalating with my British manager, Charlie Tucker. I had taken the liberty of sharing with my Hollywood agent, Arthur Park, my concerns about the contract renewal I had signed with Charlie some eight years before while I was performing on Broadway. Charlie had represented me since my earliest days in vaudeville, and he had managed my career and my money. He never told me how much I made, or where the money was going; he simply sent my living expenses, and I submitted receipts to him. It seemed disrespectful to question his judgment or management style. I knew that a percentage of my income went to my mother and other family members, but over the years, my concerns had grown. Charlie would lightly mention a company here, or an account there, and he always assured me that there was nothing to worry about. I was conflicted; although grateful for how much Charlie had done for me, I was no longer a teenager. I was almost thirty years old, yet he still seemed to perceive me as a child.

Prior to meeting Arthur, I had asked a lawyer in England to look into the contract situation, but Charlie had swiftly dispensed of him. When Arthur read the contract, he was aghast. He claimed it was far too restrictive, and that Charlie was taking too high a percentage of my income. Once Arthur began to ask questions, Charlie became hurt and defensive. The process of trying to resolve the issues began. It took months, but at least it was under way.

Arthur Park introduced me to a business manager whom he felt would be helpful to me in my financial matters. Guy Gadbois was one of the finest men I've ever known. He shared an office with the actor James Stewart. They were great friends, and I was thrilled to run into Jimmy whenever I popped in. Arthur and Guy represented a breed of businessmen that was new to me. They were circumspect, caring, and decent. I felt I had stepped up in the world, and I also felt more safe.

On the other hand, I was becoming aware that the ongoing separations from Tony were affecting our marriage. We had spent more time apart than together in the previous year, yet because we'd called and written often, until that summer I hadn't been fully aware of the extent of my loneliness. It was becoming ever more clear that for professional reasons, Los Angeles was where I needed to be based. Yet Tony's passion was the theater, which was centered in New York and London—and he was now much in demand. This made being based in Los Angeles difficult for him. It was also unthinkable in those days for a husband to compromise his career in support of his wife's. On top of all that, the attention being directed at me was becoming increasingly seductive. One or two men were showing more than a passing interest in me, which I found confusing but flattering. It was an enormously challenging period for both Tony and me to navigate.

Around this time, our dear friend Mike Nichols, whom Tony and I had known since our early days on Broadway, came to my house for dinner with a few other friends. I noticed how focused and clearheaded he seemed to be. His composure seemed such a stark contrast to my own emotional turbulence. Mike mentioned that he was in psychoanalysis, and I asked him a lot of questions about it. I envied him the clarity that he seemed to have. Mike sensed why I was asking, and he very generously gave me a better understanding of the process.

Soon after that, my friend Masud Khan, Svetlana Beriosova's husband, came to L.A. on business.

"Sudi" was a brilliant London psychoanalyst. He invited me to accompany him to a dinner with the head of psychiatry at UCLA.

It was a fascinating evening. I was seated next to another eminent psychoanalyst, Dr. Ralph Greenson, who was charming and a wonderful conversationalist. The more we talked, the more I felt he might be someone who could help me.

A day or two later, I took what felt like the biggest leap of courage I had ever taken. Without informing Tony, I phoned Dr. Greenson's office and made an appointment to see him. I wept copiously during that visit and felt exceedingly embarrassed. I conveyed that my marriage was in trouble, but that I truly wanted to save it. His reply surprised me: "Well, that's very admirable. Usually people come in here seeking the support to end their marriages."

Greenson was incredibly kind, but his calendar was totally full. He recommended a colleague and, steeling myself once again, I made an appointment with the new doctor.

During my entire first week of psychoanalysis, I wept through every session. I could barely get a word out as I attempted to share my life story. The doctor waited patiently and said very little. At the end of the week, I managed to stammer, "I suppose the first thing I should figure out is why I'm crying all the time." He nodded, and summed it up for me.

"I believe I know why. I think it's the cavalry."

"I don't understand," I said.

"I suspect you've been holding on to a lot of painful feelings for a very long time . . ." I promptly burst into tears again. "It's a little like a western," he went on. "The enemy has attacked, the wagons have drawn into a circle, all seems lost. Suddenly the cavalry comes over the hill. The relief is so huge that it's safe to let go, to cry."

I began to understand that the stress of trying to keep my family together all those years—supporting them at such a young age; my mother's depression; my stepfather's alcoholism; striving to hold on to the house that meant so much to us all—combined with the pressures of the war and touring all over England year after year, followed by the steep learning curve and rigorous demands of Broadway, a marriage and a child, and now Hollywood . . . all of this had generated powerful emotions inside of me, which I had buried in order to survive. Indeed, I barely knew what I was feeling at all. I did recognize how fortunate I was to have been given the gift of my voice, and because of that, so many extraordinary opportunities. But now, having arrived at what would seem to be a safer haven in my professional life, my marriage was in trouble.

I began to see the good doctor regularly—five days a week at first. I was so hungry for any information to help me better understand myself. I couldn't be sure that psychoanalysis would do the trick, but I kept at it . . . and my God, am I glad I did. Little by little, I began to unload the emotional baggage I'd been carrying, disposing of old fears and finding new coping mechanisms. I had a long way to go, but it was a start.

One day, the doctor asked me what I wanted most out of life.

"Oh . . . to be loved, I suppose, and to be healthy. To do something well . . ." I struggled to articulate what I actually did want.

"Don't you want to be happy?"

"That sounds like a rather selfish thing to say," I replied. "I want, I want. There are so many people who have so much less than I have."

He surprised me by smacking his thigh with an open palm. "Good God, woman! Do you think you were put into this world to be *un*happy?"

"Oh—er, well . . ."

"Don't you think it is your God-given right to seek happiness, no matter what, providing you don't hurt anyone along the way?"

Ridiculous as it may sound, I'd been so focused on keeping everyone else happy that I hadn't really thought of it in that way.

Another day, I was brainstorming alternative careers that might appeal to me. I mused about being a pianist, a painter, a botanist, even a newscaster.

"You could do those things," the doctor replied. "And if you were willing to wait twenty years or so, it's possible you would become very good at them. But you already do one thing very well. It would seem a shame to waste that gift and take away the pleasure it gives to others."

"But I've always had to work so hard at it," I stammered. "I don't know if I really *love* singing . . ."

There was a pause, and then, very quietly, he said, "Maybe you love it too much?"

His words hung in the air for a moment. Then the dam burst, and I exploded into tears once again. He was right, of course. I realized then that singing had become such a part of me, was so profoundly ingrained in my soul, that if the wonder and the joy of it were ever taken away, I might not survive.

ALL THIS WORK on myself and my best intentions notwithstanding, the problems in my marriage persisted. I knew it was largely my fault. I wanted so much to make it better, to be the loving and adoring wife that Tony deserved. I felt such a deep connection to him—a bond that remains unchanged to this day—but I couldn't give up the opportunities that were now being offered to me in Hollywood, nor could I expect him to give up his work in London and New York. My life was opening on so many levels, and I simply had to keep exploring whatever lay on the path ahead of me, rather than turn my back on it and shut it all down. Although we did our best to keep up appearances for the time being, for Emma's sake as much as anything, I think we both knew that we were heading for a separation.

IN EARLY JANUARY of 1965, Lyndon B. Johnson was inaugurated as president of the United States. He had been sworn in as president immediately following Kennedy's assassination in 1963, and had gone on to win the subsequent election in November of '64. There was a preinaugural gala at the National Guard Armory in Washington, DC. It was a monumental occasion, with many Hollywood luminaries paying tribute in an evening that included Mike Nichols and Elaine May; Carol Channing; Woody Allen; Marlon Brando; Alfred Hitchcock; Harry Belafonte; Barbra Streisand;

Bobby Darin; Ann-Margret; Margot Fonteyn and Rudolf Nureyev; Peter, Paul and Mary; Sophia Loren; Gregory Peck; Johnny Carson; Carol Burnett; and me.

Carol and I were asked to re-create a fifteen-minute medley from *Julie and Carol at Carnegie Hall*. We had two days of rehearsals. It rained heavily, which Carol was thrilled about because she had a long-held superstition that rain was a lucky omen.

Mike Nichols was not due in town until the evening before the gala. We were all staying at the same hotel, and Mike said that if it wasn't too late when he arrived, he'd come and say hello. Carol joined me in my suite, and we waited and waited. We changed into our pajamas and dressing gowns, thinking that if Mike didn't come, we'd return to our respective rooms and turn in for the night. At the very last second, the phone rang.

"Am I too late?" Mike asked breathlessly. "I just got in. The train was delayed because of the foul weather."

"No, no," we said. "We're in our jammies, but come on up."

"I'll be right there," he said.

We decided to meet him at the elevator. We padded down the hall, feeling rather foolish in our dressing gowns and slippers. In front of the bank of elevators there was a sofa. Carol and I sat on it together and waited.

One of us suggested doing something to make Mike laugh when he saw us. I don't remember whose idea it was—Carol says it was mine, and I say it was hers—but we thought it might be fun if Mike found us kissing.

At this point, one of the elevators went "ping!" so I whipped Carol across my lap, making it look as if I had her in a full embrace. The doors opened . . . and the elevator was packed with Secret Service men. Nobody got out, nobody got in. As the doors closed, they collectively leaned toward the center so they could get a better view. Carol and I simply cracked up.

Suddenly another elevator went "ping!"; I quickly dipped Carol over my knee again. The doors opened and a lone woman stepped out, glanced at us both, and then hurried on down the hall. By now, we were both weeping with laughter. Carol slid off my knee and crawled behind the sofa to hide.

"What are you *doing*?" I asked.

She couldn't even reply, she was laughing so hard. With a touch of panic, I noticed that the lady who had just passed us had turned around and was now coming back. Leaning over the sofa, she inquired, "Excuse me, are you Carol Burnett?"

In a strangled voice, Carol said, "Yes!" Then raising a hand above the sofa to point at me, she added, "And this is my friend, Mary Poppins!"

That set us off again. The lady beat a hasty retreat, no doubt thinking we were sloshed. The elevator went "ping!" for a third time. I dragged Carol out, saying, "It's *gotta* be Mike this time! Come on!"

We plunged into our embrace once again, and Mike stepped out of the elevator. Without pausing or even breaking a smile, he casually said, "Oh, hi, girls," and continued down the corridor. *Touché!*

TO MY AMAZEMENT and delight, I was nominated for a Golden Globe Award for my role in *Mary Poppins*. The event was held at the Ambassador Hotel in Los Angeles. I sat at the Disney table with our screenwriter/producer Bill Walsh, his wife, Nolie, and Roddy McDowall, among others. There was some talk at our table about the fact that if I'd been cast in the film *My Fair Lady*, I wouldn't have been free to accept the role in *Mary Poppins*.

I jokingly said to Bill, "Well, if I win, I should probably thank Jack Warner, shouldn't I?"

"Oh, Julie, do it!" he said.

"I wouldn't dare!" I gasped.

"Julie, I promise you, everyone will love it."

To my astonishment, when my category came up, I was announced as the winner. I wasn't sure what I would say, even as I went up on stage to accept the award. After thanking Walt and the Foreign Press for the honor, I took an enormous gamble:

"Finally, my thanks to a man who made a wonderful movie and who made all this possible in the first place . . . Mr. Jack Warner."

There was a pause of about five seconds— during which I contemplated the possible end of my career—followed by an explosion of laughter. Happily, Jack Warner had the good grace to laugh as hard as everyone else.

LATER THAT MONTH, I began rehearsing a television special with Gene Kelly. He was one of my idols, and while I was awed by the honor of working with him, I worried that I wouldn't be up to the task of dancing with him. Thankfully, he choreographed our pieces himself, making what we did together appear effortless. We rehearsed for a week, whereupon I flew to New York, delivered Emma to Tony for a brief visit, and attended the premiere of *The Sound of Music* there.

As with the *Poppins* premiere, it was almost impossible for me to watch the film with any degree of perspective. I was learning that this kind of evening is all about working the event, which is jam-packed with people and press, all of whom want contact, a sound bite, a personal connection. It is a moment in time when you are responsible for representing the hundreds of people that have contributed to making the film possible. I was aware that I was being watched—before, during, and after the screening—so I was focused on carrying myself in the way that was expected. I did have an ear attuned to the audience's response to the film . . . I sensed that they were gripped by the story, and of course, by the beautiful music.

After the screening, during the crush in the lobby, I suddenly saw Bette Davis approaching me. I had never met her before, though I was a huge fan. As we shook hands, she said, "YOU, my dear, are going to be a *very big star.*" I had always imagined she might be crisp and aloof, but her warmth and generosity bowled me over.

The next morning, I flew back to Los Angeles, where rehearsals for the special with Gene Kelly resumed, followed by a week of taping. In my "spare" time, I continued my daily sessions with my analyst, and attended the L.A. premiere of *The Sound of Music.*

Reviews for the film were mixed. The *New York*

Times assaulted the musical for being too sentimental. The Hollywood papers credited the technical aspects—the design, the locations, the score. Some recognized the pitfalls we had faced, and things we had fought to overcome. Most acknowledged the challenges it took to bring the musical to the screen, raved about Bob Wise's work, and were kind to me and the rest of the cast. A few, however, were scathing across the board. Thankfully, the public embraced the film and this many years later, it seems they still do.

5

MY AGENT, ARTHUR PARK, sent me a script based on James Michener's book *Hawaii*. It had been written by Dalton Trumbo, screenwriter for *Roman Holiday*, *Exodus*, and *Spartacus*, among others.

The film was being produced by the Mirisch Corporation, and the director was George Roy Hill. The brilliant Swedish actor Max von Sydow, who had recently played the role of Jesus in George Stevens's *The Greatest Story Ever Told*, was to play the lead role of missionary Reverend Abner Hale. I was being asked to play his wife, Jerusha Bromley. I was very taken with the screenplay—though, as always, I worried that I wouldn't be up to the job. This was a sweeping drama, and there were no songs to help anchor me in the role. That said, the film was to be shot in the Hawaiian Islands, which was very appealing, as was the fact that my friend Dorothy Jeakins was designing the costumes. After some deliberation, I accepted the offer.

Rehearsals began at Goldwyn Studios on April 5, 1965—the same day as the 37th Annual Academy Awards. I had been nominated for my role in *Mary Poppins*, and happily, Tony had also been nominated for his inspired costume designs in the film.

The other nominees in my category were Sophia Loren for *Marriage Italian Style*, Debbie Reynolds for *The Unsinkable Molly Brown*, Kim Stanley for *Seance on a Wet Afternoon,* and Anne Bancroft for *The Pumpkin Eater*. I fully believed that Anne would win, because of her extraordinary performance. Both Tony and I felt fortunate just to be nominated.

Dorothy Jeakins created an exquisite primrose-yellow chiffon dress for me for the evening. The edges were hemmed with satin piping, and Dorothy said, "I think it will flutter like a moth behind you as you walk." She chose a crystal necklace to go with it, the only other accessory being a pair of long white gloves.

I sat beside Tony in the Santa Monica Civic Auditorium. Sidney Poitier was presenting the Best Actress award, and I was stunned when he called my name.

I went up on stage and stammered into the microphone, "I know you Americans are famous for your hospitality, but this is really ridiculous!" I was escorted backstage to the press room, where a crowd of journalists and photographers were gathered, and it was quite a while before I could return to my seat.

Rex Harrison had been nominated for Best Actor for his performance as Henry Higgins in *My Fair Lady*. He won the award, which was presented to him by Audrey Hepburn. She herself had not been nominated, which I felt was a shame. I suspect Rex was walking on eggshells that evening, although he said something generous about honoring his "*two* fair ladies."

Sadly, Tony did not receive an Oscar that night—though he would go on to win one, along with many other awards, in subsequent years. The Oscar for Best Costume Design that evening went to Cecil Beaton for *My Fair Lady*.

At the end of the ceremony, all the winners and presenters were asked to pose for photographs together. I stood next to Audrey, who looked absolutely gorgeous. She quietly said to me, "Julie, you really should have done *My Fair Lady* . . . but I didn't have the guts to turn it down." I told her that I completely understood, and in the years that followed, we became good friends.

As we departed for the Governors Ball, Anne

Bancroft came up to me, and in another example of class and generosity, she congratulated me on receiving the award.

"Oh, Miss Bancroft," I stammered. "I was so convinced it was going to be you! It *should* have been you."

I'm embarrassed to say that, despite being thrilled to receive it, I kept the Oscar in my attic for a while, rather than displaying it anywhere. I also didn't mention it to my analyst for over a week. I honestly felt that I didn't deserve it, and that perhaps it had been given to me as a kind gesture because I hadn't been cast in *My Fair Lady*. These days, I proudly display it in my office.

REHEARSALS FOR *HAWAII* continued the following day. Though Michener's epic novel encompassed the entire history of the islands, Dalton Trumbo's script only dealt with the first third of the book: the arrival of the Christian missionaries and their impact on the Hawaiian people. George Roy Hill wanted to tell the story from the Hawaiians' point of view; to convey what it meant for them to be so overwhelmed by Western culture and its attendant ills.

Filming commenced in mid-April in Sturbridge, Massachusetts. The previous weeks had been busy with costume fittings. There were screen tests for makeup and hair, and all the while I was trying to figure out who Jerusha was, and how to play her. She was the daughter of a minister, from an upper-class household, and very pious and stoic—all of which felt far from my own experience.

We flew into New York on Easter Sunday, and I shared a car with Max von Sydow from New York to Sturbridge. I sat beside this tall, reserved, Swedish gentleman as we were driven through the night to our hotel, and found it bizarre that this total stranger and I were about to play husband and wife. We talked politely for a while, but I was very tired and longing to sleep. I wished that I knew him well enough to fall asleep on his shoulder.

We began location shooting the following day at a place called Old Sturbridge Village; a "living history museum" that replicates a rural New England town of the 1830s. The first scene we shot was Abner's proposal to Jerusha. I knew I was acting rather busily, because George kept saying, "Julie, I want you to be as still as you possibly can. Don't blink if you can help it, don't move your hands, or head. Jerusha must be utterly serene."

I simply couldn't do it for him. I have a fairly ebullient nature, and I felt constricted, stiff, and without any technique that could help me find what he wanted. During the following week I became depressed because George kept stopping the takes, riding me hard, conveying how essential it was that Jerusha's gentle nature contrast with Abner's Puritan gaucheness. I was embarrassed to find it so difficult to do what George was asking of me, but ultimately that early drilling did help me find Jerusha's character.

Because we were filming just after Easter, Sturbridge was teeming with visitors. Our dressing rooms on location were Winnebago trailers, with facilities for hair and makeup. Not long after shooting began, I was dressed and ready for a scene, and waiting in my trailer to be called to the set, when the tourists apparently sussed out which trailer was mine. I suddenly heard people scratching on the walls, tapping on the door, talking and calling to me.

The Sound of Music having opened four weeks prior, and with my having just won the Oscar for *Poppins*, people were hoping for a glimpse of me. Eventually, the crowd thrust so close that the trailer began rocking and shaking. Alas, there was no phone to summon help. I pulled down the blinds and sat inside that tiny space, feeling trapped, while on the other side of the walls people were jammed against each other like sardines.

When I was finally summoned to work, the production team forged a narrow pathway through the crowd for me. As I walked past, people reached out to touch me, pinching, poking, plucking at the fabric of my dress. I had been shyly keeping my head down, yet the more I withdrew, the more it seemed they wanted my attention.

I don't know what made me do it, but I suddenly lifted my head and made eye contact, smiling and saying hello as I passed. The crowd fell back, almost as one, and I was able to move on. It was an interesting lesson; making that simple connection was all it took.

Emma had been staying with Tony in New York for the few days that I was in Massachusetts. He was about to head overseas again to begin work on the film version of *A Funny Thing Happened on the Way to the Forum*. We had finally made the sad decision to officially separate, but we hadn't announced it yet, as we still had much to sort out. There was no need to rush into a divorce, and we didn't want the press getting wind of the separation until we were ready. When Tony brought Emma back to me, we were tender with each other, although it was miserably painful for us both. Emma, her nanny Kay, and I returned to Los Angeles the following day.

Shooting for *Hawaii* resumed at Goldwyn Studios,

where the interior of our sailing ship had been rigged on hydraulic rockers so we could enact the effects of the great storm at sea. In those early weeks, George continued to be tough on me. I knew it was in order to get a better performance out of me, but I also sensed that he enjoyed seeing whether I could stand up to the pressure. Eventually, maybe because he saw I had a certain kind of resilience—and I recognized that he was such a good director—we became mutually respectful. In fact, in the months that followed, we became firm friends.

KAY, EMMA, AND I traveled to Honolulu in early June of 1965. The view from the plane as we touched down was breathtaking; beautiful aquamarine sea with rolling breakers, lush green mountains, and a brilliant blue sky. Hawaii was still young in its statehood, and there was very little Westernization as yet. It looked as close to paradise as anything I'd ever seen.

We were the last off the plane, since the press was waiting. I was painfully aware of how creased my dress was, and of a run in one of my stockings. As we came down the airplane steps, I felt the gentle trade winds and smelled the incredible perfume of the islands. But so many flowered leis were placed around my neck that I felt smothered, as if by a warm blanket, and quickly became a sweaty mess. Perspiration ran down my back and off the end of my nose. Photographs and questions were being fired from all sides. Dottie Jeakins had come to greet us, and she mercifully ushered us into a waiting car, which whisked us off to the house where we would be staying. It was a pleasant beach house, with lots of bamboo and straw mats; light and airy, with a magnificent view of a narrow beach and, beyond that, a beautiful lagoon.

Location filming began with two days at sea, on board the old Danish trader that had been converted into our double-masted brigantine, the *Thetis*. In the days that followed, I became windblown and sun-ravaged. My feet and legs ached from balancing against the mountainous swells—the ship rolled and bobbed like a cork—but the experience was amazing. The ship's real-life captain had ten young sailors working under him; beautiful, bronzed, tousle-headed boys of varying nationalities, fascinating to watch as they scrambled over the rigging, pulling ropes and hauling canvas.

I had been warned that the "head" (the toilet) on the *Thetis* was worse than the black hole of Calcutta. It was belowdecks, all generator fumes and other smells, pitch-dark, and everything damp with seawater. Eventually I had to brave it. I took a small flashlight, stumbled and slipped and hung on, becoming a contortionist in my efforts to hike up my nineteenth-century dress, all the while holding the flashlight between my teeth. Finally, I emerged, triumphant, and was greeted with cheers. Apparently, I was the first member of the crew to have survived the head without becoming seasick.

Our filming shifted to the historic Hawaiian village that had been built for us on the other side of the main island: an entire community of grass huts on a stunning white beach, an hour and a half away from where I was staying. Dozens of mostly naked extras, children included, roamed around, along with the occasional dog or pig. It felt like stepping into the past.

Filming with so many extras was challenging, however, as were the problems of water reflection, wind, and frequent rain showers that interrupted our shooting daily. George was concentrating on the Polynesian cast members, most of whom had never acted before. We inched along, averaging about two takes a day.

Richard Harris was playing Captain Rafer Hoxworth, the sailor whom Jerusha had originally hoped to marry. I liked Richard, but I found him difficult to work with. He was undisciplined as an actor, changing his approach or dialogue with every take, questioning everything he was asked to do. This resulted in long, huddled arguments between director and actor, while I sat around, fuming with impatience. Eventually, I got used to his improvisations, and began to figure out how to work with him, although I sensed that he found me very boring.

WORD LEAKED OUT that all was not well behind the scenes between the producers, Walter and Marvin Mirisch, and George, due to our many delays and attendant budget overages. Our shooting schedule was all over the place. I would get a call at 11 p.m. to come out to the set for a night shoot, which would then be canceled two hours later.

Meanwhile, out in the "real world," the hostilities in Vietnam had escalated. The news reports coming in daily were beyond disturbing, and the contrast between our creative work in that island paradise and the atrocities going on in Southeast Asia preyed on me.

The state of my marriage was also a continuing concern. I spent hours wondering whether to make one last effort to remain with Tony, or to formalize our separation. However, I always came up against a block that wouldn't let me break through and decide. I missed Tony's friendship, his dignity and gentleness, and wanted to hold on to that. I worried that I risked losing it by not making up my mind. My sleep was chaotic and disrupted, and I wrestled with fearful dreams, loneliness, and depression.

One evening, I saw a hive of activity on the water in front of my house. Little lights bobbed and weaved, and larger lights moved majestically along behind them. I suddenly realized I was witnessing the arrival of the first of the yachts in the Transpacific Yacht Race originating in California. I raced up to Diamond Head to find hundreds of other cars, radios blaring, and the big lighthouse lamp blazing across the water. The beautiful ketch *Ticonderoga*, or "Big Ti," was just slipping through the beam and over the finish line as I arrived, setting a new world record. The sight of its shadowy, billowing sails was so poetic, it made my heart ache. The boat felt like a direct link to Los Angeles, which I was considering more and more to be home.

I longed to resume work with my analyst, and finally managed a quick trip back to L.A. Seeing him helped to allay some of my anxieties. I also saw Arthur Park, and learned that although the situation with Charlie Tucker was almost straightened out, I would need to keep working as much as possible, since most of my savings had gone toward the severance settlement. Arthur mentioned that Paul Newman had been signed to play the lead in *Torn Curtain*, a Hitchcock film in which I had been offered a role. Knowing this made me inclined to accept.

Around this time, my business manager, Guy Gadbois, told me that there was a house in Coldwater Canyon that he felt would be a good purchase. He reasoned that I was spending too much money on rent. I loved the place, and my lifelong craving for continuity, for a true home, suddenly kicked in. This desire had been sidelined by years of work-related transience, and a constant sense of obligation to others—to my entire family in England, to Tony, to Emma, to agents and managers.

I still needed to make a final decision about our marriage and the apartment in Wimbledon, but I was in a dangerous mood. I was anxious to take some action that I could control; to establish something that was mine alone. Within a week of being back in Hawaii, and without consulting anyone else, I signed on to do the film with Hitchcock, and the house was mine.

THE TENSIONS BETWEEN George and the producers proved to be real, as at the end of July we received news that George was to be replaced. I was stunned, as was the entire company. I felt that with the chronic weather problems, the number of nontheatrical extras in the film, and the huge technical challenges, it was unlikely that any other director would be able to do better. There was a great deal of kerfuffle, and the entire Polynesian cast, led by Jocelyne LaGarde, who was playing the majestic Hawaiian queen, staged a walkout in protest. Twenty-four hours later, the situation had reversed itself. George agreed to heavy cuts, and filming resumed.

In the midst of all this, my youngest brother, Christopher, arrived for a visit. I had asked my mother to come, but she had declined. Instead, she begged me to treat Christopher to a vacation, saying that he was going through a bad patch and could use the break.

I almost didn't recognize him when I picked him up at the airport. At nineteen, he looked pale, gaunt, and lost, with a heavy beard and unkempt hair. I had begun keeping a diary on this film, and one entry reads:

It disturbs me deeply to see Chris. So many memories surface as he talks of life at home . . . layers of suburbia, and prejudice, and conditions over which he has no control. The question is, what should I do? Do I help or hinder by exposing him to my comparatively broader world? I know there's a gentle, bright soul locked away, oh so deeply . . . I wonder if he'll be strong enough to seize the opportunities that could lie ahead.

I chose to watch and wait; to decide how best to help him once he'd settled in and we had spent more time together.

THE COMPANY BEGAN shooting the big sequence involving the fire at the church. One night, I very nearly got burned to death. The cameras were rolling. George was yelling "Get in there, Julie!" so I dashed in under a flaming roof, and caught a blast of heat from the burning wall. I staggered out to witness real fire engines racing up the hill. Apparently, our church actually *had* caught fire. We all watched as the firemen stilled the blaze, leaving a charred, steaming mass of straw and debris in their wake. There were cinders and ashes in our pores, hair, noses, throats . . . even inside my bra. The next day, I had little blisters all over my cheeks.

Another hair-raising episode involved a scene in

which two pieces of burning pitch were supposed to hurtle past me from the roof (carefully aimed by a Hollywood grip), and one was to ignite the hem of my dress. This couldn't be done with a stunt double; the cameras were too close, and George wanted authenticity.

I was wearing long fireproof underwear and an asbestos underskirt. A fuse was attached to the hem of my chiffon dress to help ignite the garment. I don't think I have ever been as scared as I was that night. I kept wondering at what age women had heart attacks, and whether I might faint, or burst into tears, from the tension.

At the first tentative rehearsal, when the flaming pitch was thrown down, my skirt caught fire so fast that fire extinguishers were sprayed and blankets were thrown on me. A new skirt had to be sent for.

I became almost sleepy with fear as we waited for the next shot. I sat slumped in a chair, unable to talk to anyone. I couldn't help thinking that a dreadful accident might occur. I was terrified my flimsy sleeves would also catch fire, or that my long wig would go up in flames—and having that wretched fuse attached to my hem made me intensely claustrophobic.

The first take went well, although the burning

wall was too hot, and the breeze was blowing the flames in my direction. But everything worked, and afterward I was liberally doused with foam and smothered with blankets once again.

George, however, wasn't satisfied. "Not enough flames on the skirt!" he pronounced. So we had to do it once more. At this point, things became really dicey.

I could feel the intense heat creeping up my backside, and looking down, I could most definitely see the flames . . . but from where George was sitting, they didn't register on camera. Again and again I darted into the fire, all the while muttering, "Christ, it's hot!" and then yelling, "Goddammit, George . . . NOW?"

"No, no, not yet . . ." George replied. "Stay in the flames!"

As the heat started to scorch my waist, I finally screamed, "Put it *out*!" More foam, more blankets— and *still* he felt we hadn't got the shot.

"Dinner break!" the assistant director called. I realized I would have to sweat it out for another hour and a half while everyone had supper. I was unable to eat a thing.

By this time, I was seriously pissed off. I had a sneaking suspicion that George was getting a slight kick out of my misery. After yet another failed attempt, I yelled at him, "*You* do it! If you can do it, *I'll* do it." Given that it was in front of the whole crew, he couldn't lose face.

He headed straight for the burning wall, then broke right, making a complete circle and emerging on the other side, saying, "It *is* a bit hot in there, isn't it?"

It made everyone laugh but me. Eventually, we got the shot. After it was over, I hit a high C to ease my tension, and got a round of applause from the crew.

Several days later, we saw the dailies. The camera had picked up every detail of the flames engulfing my skirt, yet we could hear George's voice in the background insisting, "No, no, can't see a thing!" At that point, I joined in the laughter until I nearly wept.

Immediately after the fire sequence, we shot the devastating measles epidemic. From storms to fires to plagues, our film was an epic account of the never-ending disasters the missionaries encountered, and subsequently imposed upon the Hawaiian people.

AS I'D HOPED, my brother Chris did indeed blossom during his stay with me. He took to the sun, the fresh air, and the beauty of the island. He confessed that he'd been getting into drugs at home. Lovely Hawaii gave him a new perspective.

In early August, Chris and I were invited to Schofield Barracks to visit the 25th Infantry Division. The feeling was that our visit might cheer the troops before they shipped out to Vietnam.

We traveled by army helicopter to a mock-up of a typical Vietnamese village. We were accompanied by Major General Weyand, who was enormously tolerant of my being there. I felt sure that this sort of visit must be a pain, and a waste of time for him. We were given a live demonstration of how a village was captured and taken, with explosions, gunfire, and fake blood. We also watched a fake ambush enacted with bombs and machine-gun fire, which was extremely realistic and disturbing.

Afterward, I met with about a hundred and fifty young men, all of whom were due to travel to Vietnam within the next two weeks. When presented with a scroll stating that I was the first honorary member—and first woman—of the 25th Division, I was at a loss for words. Feeling emotional, I mumbled something about being deeply touched, and said that my love and thoughts would be with the men, and that I hoped they would come home safely. Major General Weyand quickly steered me away, quipping that no one would go at all if I carried on much longer. I signed soldiers' caps, and a number of the fellows gave me their badges, which I still cherish. Those young men nearly broke my heart.

I HAD A few days off, and jumped at the opportunity to go back to L.A. for a short spell. I managed to see my analyst for one brief session, and discussed Chris; whether I should help him further, and if so, how. Chris was passionate about photography, and I decided to look into photography colleges, either in London, New York, or Los Angeles. When I mentioned this to Chris on my return to Hawaii, he seemed most keen to try his wings outside of England. He decided to come to L.A. I knew this would mean extra responsibility for me, but he was doing so well, and I wanted that to continue.

While in California, I met briefly with Alfred Hitchcock regarding the upcoming film, *Torn Curtain*. As I walked into his office, the famous profile was silhouetted against the window.

"You sent for me, ma'am?" he intoned, in a voice resembling Jeeves the Butler. He was so famous that I was frightened he'd be unapproachable and that we wouldn't connect, but he turned out to be just the opposite. He was funny and lugubrious about himself, and I learned that he was a great connoisseur of wine and art. I left feeling excited to be working with him.

Back in Hawaii, we tackled one of my most difficult scenes in the film: the childbirth scene. It took two days to shoot, during which I was "bearing down," yelling, screaming, acting my head off, flat on my back. I almost passed out from hyperventilation.

Max was incredibly generous as we filmed this sequence. We seemed to share an unspoken agreement to not break the mood between takes, so while grips, technicians, soundmen, and others went about their work, we stayed together on the bed, chatting quietly and trying to sustain the personal connection the scene required.

At the end of the day, I was amazed that we'd managed to shoot such an intimate scene in front of the entire crew. I had hardly noticed they were there.

That evening, my phone rang.

"Hallo, Julie?"

"Yes?"

"This is Max von Sydow."

"Oh . . . hallo, Max!" The formality of his using his full name made me smile.

Throat clearing. "Er—how are you?"

"Fine . . ."

A pause.

"Actually, I called for two reasons—well, three. First, I wanted to say I thought you did a wonderful job today. Er—second, that I enjoy working with you. And also—I finished reading *The Once and Future King*, and I want to thank you for introducing me to T. H. White."

I was touched. It had been the most totally absorbing week I'd spent on the film thus far, and I sensed that Max felt the same way.

THERE WAS ONE other day on *Hawaii* that I will never forget. Max and I had been summoned from our trailers to the set. As we walked along the golden stretch of beach, Max mentioned that he had always wanted to do Restoration comedy. I was surprised, having only seen him in the dark, dramatic films of Ingmar Bergman.

To prove the point, he suddenly began doing wonderful antics—whisking a handkerchief out of his sleeve, bowing, cavorting. Being so tall, with elbows and knees so sharp and pointed, and dressed in his narrow black suit and stovepipe hat, he resembled a Jules Feiffer cartoon. I laughed so hard, and he seemed delighted to be amusing me.

CHRIS EVENTUALLY HEADED back to London. I hoped that when he returned to attend college in L.A., he would still be in good shape.

My birthday was approaching, and Emma was near to bursting in the days leading up to it. Kay had told her to keep my gift and cards a secret, but my two-year-old kept whispering to me, "We got you a present . . . but shhh! It's a secret!" Finger to lips, very conspiratorial and dear.

A couple of days before my actual birthday, she suddenly burst into a full rendition of "Happy Birthday to You," with dance steps thrown in for good measure.

On the big day, Emma was beside herself. She and Kay brought me breakfast in bed, along with presents, and another rendition of "Happy Birthday." Emma kept stroking my arm, saying, "It's your *birthday*, isn't it, Mummy?" And then of course she opened every gift for me. Adorable!

At one point during the making of *Hawaii*, I did a photo shoot with Philippe Halsman for *Look* magazine. Emma and I strolled along the beach, splashing about and playing with two Labrador retrievers that showed up, Philippe photographing us all the while. The photos were lovely, but I later realized, when the issue was out on the stands and I saw myself and my little girl on the cover, that I had been foolish to allow her to be so publicly exposed. From that moment on, I made a concerted effort to keep Emma away from all cameras, other than my own.

MY LAST DAY on the film was October 8. Although there were still two weeks left for Max to shoot, there was an early wrap party, and we enjoyed a festive luau.

Back in Los Angeles, my dear friend Mike Nichols asked if I would like to see a screening of his film adaptation of Edward Albee's *Who's Afraid of Virginia Woolf?* starring Richard Burton and Elizabeth Taylor. He offered to pick me up, and we planned to dine at his place afterward. I brought a delicious trifle for our dessert, knowing how much Mike loved them.

Mike had recently acquired a Rolls-Royce, and as I slid into the front seat with the trifle bowl on my lap, I marveled at the immaculate soft leather and the exquisite "new car" aroma. We set off, and suddenly Mike had to brake. I watched in horror as the trifle slithered back in its dish toward me, then reversed course and hurtled forward, out of the dish, disappearing into the Rolls air-conditioning vents. I was utterly mortified, but Mike roared with laughter, and assured me it would clean up fine. I later learned that the next time he turned on the air-conditioning, rancid custard squirted all over his passenger.

SHOOTING FOR *TORN CURTAIN* began at Universal Studios on October 18, 1965, and the following weekend, Emma and I moved into our new house on Hidden Valley Road.

The first scene that Paul Newman and I shot was the opening love scene. Both of us were supposedly nude, in bed. Although we'd met briefly during the on-camera tests, we'd barely had a chance to say two words to each other.

The scene took place aboard a ship heading to Russia. Hitchcock wanted to suggest that while it was bitterly cold outside, buried beneath several duvets and blankets, we were warm and cozy and making love. It may sound dreamy, but it was anything but. Despite only being clad in undergarments, with all the hot studio lights and with so many covers on us, both Paul and I became seriously overheated. Eventually, since we were shooting in close-up and sweat was now dripping off our faces, the covers at the bottom of the bed were lifted and a large fan was aimed at our bare feet. It didn't help much.

Paul was easy to get along with—and oh, those blue eyes! There was something endearingly collegiate about the way he dressed, always with white socks and sneakers. We didn't get to socialize much, though he did tell me about his morning ritual when working on a film: plunging his face into a bucket of ice water upon rising. He claimed it worked wonders to firm his skin and freshen him for the day ahead. I considered trying it myself, but never had the guts to do so.

HITCHCOCK WAS AS large in personality as he was in size. His main objective was to manipulate his audiences; scaring them to death one moment, then making them laugh with relief the next. He was enormously creative in his concepts, but once the script had been written and he'd chosen his shots, he seemed to feel that the actual filming was an afterthought.

Early in the schedule, Paul and I realized that neither of us was very happy with the screenplay for the film. We asked if we could take a meeting regarding a scene we thought could use some better dialogue. Hitchcock's reply was "Say anything you like," which surprised us.

Paul and I did try to improve the dialogue, and at the time, we thought our adjustments made more sense than the original. Looking at it now, I don't think we did Hitchcock any favors.

Hitch was equally detached directing his actors. One day, I was shooting a scene on an airplane, sitting by an exit door that opened to the tarmac. Hitchcock said, "Julie, in this shot, I'd like you to look left as though the door has just opened."

"What am I looking at?" I said.

"It doesn't matter," he replied.

"Well, I mean . . . are there photographers out there, or press, because in the script they seem to know I'm coming?"

"It doesn't *matter*," he repeated. "I just want you to be looking forward, and then turn your head. That's all you have to do."

It didn't give me much to work with; there was nothing behind my eyes, but that was the way he wanted it, I suppose. Considering that he had worked with so many incredible actors, it didn't seem right to complain.

That said, Hitch couldn't have been more generous to me regarding the technical aspects of filmmaking. One day, a cameraman asked him about a close-up on me, and whether he should put a certain lens on the camera. Hitchcock was aghast.

"On a *woman*? Good heavens, no! You should use a such-and-such."

I was suddenly ashamed of how little I knew about lenses, and I said so.

"Come with me," Hitchcock stated. "Every actress should have a good understanding of what the camera is doing to her." For the next twenty-five minutes, he drew lenses for me and explained their differences. I wish I'd retained more, but I do remember him saying, "You see, the lens that our cameraman wanted to use would have widened your nose in profile and made it grow. You should never use that one in a close-up."

Another day, he was preparing a two-shot of me and Paul.

"Look! I've made a Mondrian," he said.

I went over and peered through the camera. The background was indeed like a Mondrian painting—red on one side and blue on the other, with our two heads in between. Hitchcock was very pleased with himself. I was just grateful that I knew the artist he was referring to.

As was his wont, Hitch gave himself a small cameo appearance in the film. He planted himself in the lobby of the supposed Hotel d'Angleterre, with his back to the camera and a baby seated on his lap. For years, people have thought that the baby was Emma, but it was not. Emma was three at the time, and the baby in the shot is barely a year old.

I got the impression that Hitchcock loved his

actresses, even to the point of being a little posses-
sive. I was sitting in a tall director's chair one day
and someone I was due to have lunch with arrived.
Hitchcock came over to chat with me, and I looked
over his shoulder and called to my guest, "I'll be
right with you."

Hitch then moved directly into the center of
my focus, putting a hand on either side of my
chair and blocking my view. He continued to hold
my attention, talking to me and not allowing any
distraction until he chose to let me go.

Once shooting was over, I made the mistake of
saying in an interview that I was not very happy
with my performance in the film. I got a terse
letter from Hitch, saying that he hoped I would
never do that again. I realized that when a new film
is coming out, you should never reveal that you
aren't pleased with any aspect of it. I wrote back
and apologized. It was an important lesson.

6

Ⓘ N EARLY JANUARY of 1966, my mother and
stepfather finally came to Los Angeles for a visit.
They accompanied my brother Chris, who was to
be staying with me for the next few months until
he got settled in school and was ready for his own
apartment. Though Mum and I had spoken on the
phone most weekends, I hadn't seen her or Pop for
nearly two years. I was nervous about how it would
be having them in my new home, and especially
how Pop might behave—but to my surprise, he
was sober and appeared to be in a relatively good
place, though he was puffy and overweight. Mum
was rather quiet, though she seemed to take pleasure in seeing my new home, playing my piano,
and spending time with Emma. She and Pop
stayed in the guesthouse by the pool, and Chris
moved into a small bedroom off the kitchen in the
main house. It was hard to get a reading on how he
was doing. I was still shooting *Torn Curtain* and
seeing my analyst every day, and Chris started his

photography classes almost immediately, so we didn't see much of each other.

One day when I was driving to my analyst's office, I stopped at a median in the center of Sunset Boulevard to wait for traffic to clear. A Rolls-Royce going in the opposite direction pulled into the median alongside me. I looked across at the driver, didn't think much of it, and went on my way. A few days later, the same thing happened. The third time it happened, there was a slight smile from the driver of the Rolls. He rolled down his window.

"Are you going to where I just came from?" he asked. We were at the intersection of Roxbury and Sunset, and almost every psychoanalyst at the time had an office on Roxbury.

"I—think so . . ." I replied.

"Well, it's a pleasure to meet you. I'm Blake Edwards."

"Oh! Very nice to meet *you*."

"Good luck," he said, and drove off.

A couple of weeks later, Arthur Park called and said, "Blake Edwards has asked to speak with you about a role in a movie he's developing."

I remembered how much I had wanted to do *The Great Race*, and how much I had admired Blake's other films. I was curious.

There was some dithering as to where we would meet. He suggested my house, but I didn't want him to come there because having just moved in, I still had very little furniture—plus, Mum, Pop, and Chris were in residence. I suggested we meet at the Beverly Hills Hotel, just down the road.

"I'm not going to keep you more than five minutes," he insisted. "Really, it's no problem for me to come to you."

It was early evening when he showed up at my house. My family tactfully retired to the kitchen and shut the door. My living room had a couch, a grand piano, and a fireplace, but that was about it—except for the worst carpet imaginable, which I had commissioned. It was white, with a huge orange-and-red sunburst in the middle. At the time I commissioned it, I thought it would be very chic, but I hated it the instant it was in the house.

Blake sat down on the edge of the couch, and we swapped pleasantries. I found him charming, and surprisingly attractive. At forty-three years old, he was slim, fit, and elegantly dressed, with a sharply etched face and dark eyes that seemed to know something. He told me the story of the film he was thinking of writing, to be called *Darling Lili*, about a British spy during World War I, very loosely based on Mata Hari. He asked if it was a role that might appeal to me.

It was hard to say yes to something that hadn't been written yet, but I tried to be tactful. "It sounds very interesting . . . I hope you'll write it."

I asked him what he was currently working on. He said, "I've just finished a film called *What Did You Do in the War, Daddy?* Actually, I'm having a private screening of it next week for some friends. Would you care to come?"

I hesitated, feeling shy about not knowing anyone there. But then I thought it might be good for me to get out, and this man was certainly intriguing. I accepted, and he said he would pick me up on the way.

Six days later, Blake arrived at my house as promised. At the screening, I met a number of his friends, including Dick Crockett, an esteemed stuntman who often worked on Blake's films. Dick seemed very protective of Blake, and indulged in a few inside jokes with him that went over my head—perhaps he was a little threatened by my presence. But once the movie began, it was so funny that I completely forgot my discomfort and laughed so hard I practically slid off my seat.

After the screening, everybody said their good nights and Blake asked, rather shyly, if I would care for a bite to eat. I was famished, so we went to La Scala, took a booth, and talked for a while. We discovered that we were both separated from our former spouses. I learned that he had two children who lived with their mother, and that he missed them very much.

We made a plan to go out again a few nights later, but he then called and said he was in bed with the flu. I asked if I could help in any way, but he said he was fine and would be in touch as soon as he was better.

I assumed I'd been given the brush-off, but on Valentine's Day, an enormous bouquet of flowers arrived. The note said, "Happy Valentine's Day—Blake." Then he did call, and asked me out again—but by this time, I had come down with the flu.

Once I felt better, we attended an Arthur Rubinstein concert together at the Music Center, but Arthur Park accompanied us since he had provided the tickets. Two days later, the composer Leslie Bricusse invited me to a party, saying that Michael Caine was coming, among other people whom I might enjoy meeting.

"May I bring someone?" I asked.

"Er, yeah . . ." he replied, and Blake escorted me to the Bricusses'. I later learned that Bricusse was hoping to pair me up with Michael, but since I'd brought Blake, Leslie abandoned his matchmaking mission.

Shortly after that, I had to appear at an evening for the Producers Guild. Blake asked that I call him when the event was over, and I did.

"Would you like to go for a drive?" he asked.

"But I'm all dressed up . . ." I said awkwardly.

Within a few minutes he arrived at my door, and we drove down to the beach and along the Pacific Coast Highway. It was unbelievably romantic; his Rolls purring along, the radio on, and the two of us chatting easily. Blake eventually pulled onto the Malibu Bluffs and parked the car. We gazed out at the full moon hanging over the sea, and he quietly took my hand.

I thought, "If he doesn't kiss me, I am going to go crazy."

Then he did just that.

OUR RELATIONSHIP PROGRESSED fairly quickly. One Sunday afternoon, Blake called and said, "I'll pick you up and we'll decide what to do."

"I don't mind what we do," I said. "It's just pleasant being together."

"Well, actually, I do need to do some grocery shopping . . ." he replied.

"Then let's go to the market!"

He seemed rather stunned, even slightly impressed. I think the ladies he usually dated would have expected to do something more grand.

We also visited art galleries together, particularly along La Cienega Boulevard. We'd park the car and stroll along, window-shopping and comparing preferences. Once, we stopped to admire some bright, bold seascapes in a gallery window. The following day, I arrived home to find one of the larger paintings propped up against my bed.

Amazed, I called Blake and said, "That is the most generous gift I have ever received!"

I decided to give Blake a gift of my own. In an attempt to re-create a little bit of England, I had recently bought three lilac bushes for my garden. Knowing that Blake had just purchased a new home at the top of Rising Glen, off the Sunset Strip, I thought he might appreciate having one for his own place.

Blake took me to see the new house, and as we drove up to the front door, I innocently said to him, "Blake, would you like a lilac for your garden?"

He looked at me, aghast. "What?"

"I've purchased a couple of lilac trees," I said. "Would you like one?"

There was a long pause, and then he said, "Oh . . . you know, don't you?"

"Know what?"

"Don't do that to me!" he said. "Who told you?"

"Honestly, I have no idea what you're talking about!"

"Well, you're either very good at perpetuating the joke, or you really don't know. I'd better tell you."

He proceeded to relate that a couple of weeks before our first meeting, he had attended a party where my name came up. The question circulating was whether I had received the Oscar for *Mary Poppins* because of my talent in the role, or as a conciliatory prize for losing the part of Eliza in *My Fair Lady*. Everyone had ventured an opinion, except Blake. He bided his time, and spoke last.

"I know why she won," he said. All eyes turned to him. "She has lilacs for pubic hair."

Apparently, the room erupted with laughter, and somebody said, "With your luck, you'll probably meet the lady and end up marrying her!"

As he finished his story, he looked at me sheepishly. "I'm so sorry," he said.

"That's all right." I smiled. "But—how did you know?"

He got his tree, and from that day on, lilacs were a theme at every birthday and anniversary.

Blake's new home was built into the side of a steep

hill. It was pseudo-modern, with a French-style mansard roof. Long and narrow, with bedrooms at one end and a kitchen at the other, it had a sunken living room in between, featuring a magnificent view of Hollywood. On a small second floor, he had an office, which was accessible from the outside by a spiral staircase.

Blake shared the house with a huge, pink-eyed, rather dumb Harlequin Great Dane by the name of Beatle, who had some odd habits, to say the least. The dog seemed to love heights, and climbed that spiral staircase every chance he got. On my second visit, as I stepped out of my car, I had the distinct feeling that I was being watched. Not seeing anyone, I glanced up and nearly jumped out of my skin. Beatle was staring down at me from the roof, having gotten himself stuck there after one of his climbing sessions.

BLAKE THREW A small housewarming party, which I believe was as much to introduce me to his friends and family as it was to show them his new home. He was particularly keen for me to meet his uncle, Owen Crump. Blake's father, Don Crump, had deserted his wife, Lillian, when she was pregnant with Blake, and then had seemingly vanished off the face of the earth. Blake had never met his father or had any contact with him, and Owen, who was Don's brother, had been a surrogate dad to Blake all his life. I sat next to Owen at the party, and we talked at length. He was a writer/producer, with an elegant demeanor and a shock of silvery-white hair. He was easy to talk to, and I liked him instantly. He later told Blake that he very much approved of his new girlfriend.

On the other hand, Blake's mother, Lillian, was slower to warm to me. She was a diminutive lady, originally from Oklahoma. My first impression was that her small stature did nothing to conceal her determination to keep any girlfriend of Blake's firmly at arm's length. She had a deeply lined face, iron-gray hair, a voice that could cut steel, and a beady eye that missed nothing. After her husband's desertion, she had left Blake in Oklahoma with her older sister, Thyrza, and moved to California. There, she met and married Jack McEdward, a Hollywood production manager. He was the son of J. Gordon Edwards, the famous director of epic silent films, most notably *Cleopatra* starring Theda Bara in 1917. Jack was tall, Cornell-educated, conservative, and rather locked up emotionally, but he was a good man. Lillian sent for Blake when he was about three years old, whereupon he took his new stepfather's last name. Later, when registering in the Writers Guild, Blake discovered there was another McEdward on the roster, so he simplified his name to Edwards.

I began to grasp what a difficult childhood Blake had had. He was a rebel, so unmanageable in his early teens that Lillian and Jack had dispatched him to military school, from which he promptly ran away. How this troubled, angry young man had become the stylish, complicated, brilliant gentleman that I was trying not to fall in love with completely eluded me. I'd never met anyone quite like him. He was unbelievably charismatic, and seemed to have an uncanny understanding of human nature; he could assess someone at a first meeting, and his instincts were almost always spot-on. He was devastatingly funny; wicked, even. Blake took delight in tilting at authority, but was generous, humanitarian, and always championed the underdog. He loved taking creative risks, pushing buttons and boundaries. There was something dangerous about him, which was irresistible to my play-it-safe nature. Why he chose to woo me was a total puzzlement—we couldn't have been more different. I likened us to a lion and a squirrel.

I took to calling him "Blackie," partly as an endearing adaptation of "Blake," and partly because he had such a black sense of humor. When he was being wicked, his dark eyes had an anthracite flash to them. He took the nickname in stride, and told me that in fact, one or two other people also called him that. Apparently, when he arrived in Cortina d'Ampezzo, Italy, to film exterior scenes for the first *Pink Panther*, he was welcomed by a huge local committee. They had strung a banner across the street, which read "Welcome Blak Edwards." It was a source of much amusement to Blake and the crew, and "Blak" had morphed into "Blackie."

Emma took to calling him Blackie, as well. Their first meeting was not until several months into our relationship. Blake stood in front of my fireplace, legs astride, hands clasped behind his back. My three-year-old came into the room, sized him up, and then walked to the fireplace and stood beside him in an identical pose. Looking down at Emma, Blake grinned at her spirited display of equality. In retrospect, it was very much a symbolic representation of what their relationship would eventually become.

IN MARCH, BLAKE and I escaped to Ojai for a weekend away. My mother and Pop had left the day before, somewhat to my relief. My mother had flirted outrageously with Blake, showing a leg and betraying her bawdy nature. I went streaking off to my analyst to complain about this behavior. With a quiet smile, he said, "I think it's rather delightful that this lady of a certain age still has enough spirit to play the coquette."

Some mutual friends had very kindly agreed to let Blake and me borrow their farm for a couple of days. We arrived late in the afternoon, and went down to the local market to get some food.

As we were leaving, we spotted a record player. We knew there was no radio up at the farm, so on a whim, we bought it and looked to see what albums we could find. We picked one of Ravel, along with a few others.

At dinnertime, Blake declared, "I'm going to make you one of my famous hamburgers."

I had no idea what a great cook he was. He served up the biggest hamburger I had ever seen in my life, trimmed with peanut butter, crushed peanuts, cheese, tomato, mayo and mustard on a bun. It was absolutely delicious, but I only managed to get through about a quarter of it. He pretended to be very hurt, but he knew that I'd loved it.

We plugged in the record player and lay on the carpet. The first thing we played was Ravel's Piano Concerto no. 2. The perfumed Ojai air, the romantic setting, and that glorious piece of music made for a magical evening. That concerto became a beloved favorite of ours, and from then on, Blake and I developed a habit of listening to classical music together. If, after work or a dinner out, say, we heard a compelling piece on the car radio, we would remain in the darkness even after we'd pulled into the garage, and hold hands until it concluded.

SOON THEREAFTER, MY new beau asked me to come with him to Newport Beach. He wanted to show me his boat.

"You have a *boat*?" I asked.

"As a matter of fact, I have three."

"Well, lah-di-dah!" I thought.

"I'm in the process of selling two of them," he explained. "This is a small motor yacht that I've just acquired. She's called *Tempest*."

Tempest was trim and classy, and I instantly fell in love with her.

Over Easter, Blake and I escaped on the boat for a week's vacation. Emma was on holiday with Tony, so I had the luxury of time to spare. We boarded on Good Friday, intending to head south to Mexico. All was panic and bustle. I met Blake's associate producer, Ken Wales, and his wife, Kären, who were joining us for the trip, along with the boat's skipper and first mate. There were cases, crates, cartons, a typewriter, a vacuum cleaner, and endless paper bags filled with foodstuffs lying around everywhere.

By the time we pulled away from the harbor, I thought I might burst with impatience and happiness. I stood on the bridge and gazed out at the sea, inhaling the fresh air. The skipper pointed out John Wayne's boat—the *Wild Goose*—heading in the other direction, going home to Newport. We pulled into San Diego in the early evening.

That night I wrote in my diary:

A million thoughts . . . and a feeling of expectation. What will this trip reveal? Will I be mentally refreshed? Will I ever want to work again? Blake and I look a little grey in the bright light. We'll soon change that, I think.

We had decided to travel all day and night to make it to Turtle Bay in Baja California by Easter Sunday. I adored the feeling of being rocked by the sea as I slept . . . though I quickly discovered that showering while under way was something of a comedy act. We saw whales and porpoises, flying fish and seabirds, and as I so often did, I thought of my dad and how much he would have loved it.

Days and nights blended into one long round of sleep and sun and sea. We spent nights in Santa

Maria and Cabo San Lucas, dining on local abalone and fresh yellowtail caught by our crew. Blake and the others planned to sail on to Acapulco, but I had to return to L.A. at the end of the week. I had been nominated for an Academy Award for *The Sound of Music*, and had agreed to be a presenter and to accept on behalf of Bob Wise if he won for directing. Julie Christie won for Best Actress that year, which was expected, since actors don't normally receive Oscars two years in a row. Happily, our film picked up five awards, including Best Picture and Best Director.

Alas, it was a while before I saw *Tempest* again, as I was about to start work on a new project.

SOMETIME DURING THE shooting of *Torn Curtain*, George Roy Hill had come to my house to discuss another film he hoped we would do together. *Thoroughly Modern Millie* was a stylized valentine to the 1920s. Ross Hunter, who specialized in glamorous comedies and dramas, was the producer for Universal Studios.

George described a concept he'd been toying with for the look of the movie. Though it was to be shot in color, George envisioned a black-and-white palette, with one additional key color for each important scene. He also envisioned that I would engage in direct-to-camera glances from time to time that would break the fourth wall.

The more we read through the script, the more we laughed.

"It's so *silly!*" George kept saying. I had to agree. Seeing him crack up, I realized that I had never known this side of him on *Hawaii.* That had been such a huge, serious endeavor, and had made so many demands on us both. Since we were now good friends, the opportunity to work together again, especially on something lighthearted, was very appealing.

Shooting for *Millie* commenced in May of 1966. Joe Layton was our choreographer, and his assistant, Buddy Schwab, had been in the company of *The Boy Friend* with me on Broadway in 1954. The cast included Carol Channing, Mary Tyler Moore, Beatrice Lillie, John Gavin, and James Fox.

Elmer Bernstein was to score the film, and André Previn was commissioned to arrange and conduct all the songs, which were mostly standards from the 1910s and 1920s, along with a few original songs by Jimmy Van Heusen and Sammy Cahn. Having had an early exposure to twenties music in *The Boy Friend,* I delighted in the familiar flat cymbals, the soprano saxes and clarinets, and the spare, wacky sound.

Ten days after we began shooting, I received word that my stepfather, Pop, had died after a series of small strokes. My brother Chris was still living with me and attending photography school. Mum telephoned us with the news, and I told her that we would get on the first flight possible. It would have to be a mad turnaround, as the studio couldn't spare me for more than a day or two.

Fortunately, Emma was away with Kay visiting Tony in New York, so I didn't have to make arrangements for her. I made a plan for Chris and me to get on a red-eye flight to arrive in London the following morning, attend the funeral that afternoon, and return home the same evening. Strangely, our flight was canceled, and there wasn't another until the following day, by which time we would have missed the funeral. I called my mother to tell her, and she agreed that it didn't make sense to come.

To be truthful, while I was saddened, I felt a measure of relief at the thought of my mother finally being released from Pop's alcoholism and abuse. Even so, I knew Mum wished I could have been there, and I was wracked with guilt that I wasn't able to support her when she needed it most.

I BEGAN TO notice that Chris was behaving in a strange manner. I said to Blake, "I don't know what it is with him. He's evasive; he's never really present. He sleeps till all hours, and his room is an absolute mess."

Blake looked at me for a moment, then said, "Julie, he's probably on drugs."

"What? How do you know?"

"Believe me," Blake said. "I know."

Given what Chris had told me in Hawaii, it made sense, but I hadn't connected the dots. My analyst advised me to get Chris into therapy, and I promptly did, but I was beginning to have doubts as to whether I could do anything to truly help my youngest brother with his troubles.

THESE DISTURBING EVENTS notwithstanding, the work on *Millie* was a pleasant distraction. I think the entire company felt it was a joyful experience. Every nuance we found as we went along delighted us. The film allowed me to be something of a clown, which was welcome after the seriousness of *Hawaii* and *Torn Curtain*.

Mary Tyler Moore and I became fast friends. I'd originally wondered if I should play her role and she should play mine, because she was so great at comedy. But George was insistent that my sort of "chirpiness" would be the appropriate thing for Millie, whereas Mary was better suited to being the classy Long Island heiress.

Her character's name was Miss Dorothy, and some years later, seeing her in a supermarket, I yelled across the aisle, "Miss Dorothy!" She responded instantly, "Millie!" We never referred to each other as anything else.

Carol Channing was charmingly eccentric. Though she was the darling of Broadway, she'd made very few films, and she had serious problems with her vision. This contributed to her signature look of wide-eyed vulnerability. Carol confided to me that she was quite nervous about being on a film set, so I made it a point to be there for her whenever I could, and she seemed to really appreciate it.

When I heard that the great comedienne Bea Lillie was cast, I was thrilled. I don't think anyone else knew how huge a star she had been in England. Sadly, she was now suffering from early dementia, and she couldn't remember her lines. We used cue cards, and when I was off-camera in a scene with her, I fed her the lines and she repeated them back to me. Nevertheless, her comic timing remained faultless.

One day, we were filming a sequence outside a supposed Chinese fireworks factory. We were on the back lot of Universal, and there was a large crowd of extras all dressed in Chinese "pajama" suits. Suddenly, someone slammed into my shoulder, and I stumbled.

I turned around and said, "Oh, I'm *so* sorry!" thinking it had been my fault for not looking where I was going.

As I made eye contact, I realized I was speaking to Blake's friend Dick Crockett, the stuntman who had been prickly with me at the screening we'd attended. I'm pretty sure he bumped into me deliberately to see how Blake's new lady would respond. The fact that I didn't show any irritation must have won him over, because from then on, he became my protector and friend.

Toward the end of the film, I inadvertently closed a set for the second time in my life due to laughter. I was doing a scene with John Gavin, who was absurdly handsome and playing a "Dudley Do-Right" sort of character. The square of his jaw and the jut of his pipe between clenched teeth, combined with an extra-silly line reading, set me to giggling. Eventually I put my head on the desk and simply sobbed with laughter. My "vamp" makeup ran in rivulets, and it would have taken at least an hour to repair, so George called a wrap for the day. I slunk home, shamefaced but grateful.

Shooting for *Millie* wrapped at the end of August. Unfortunately, Universal Studios decided that the film was going to be a box office bonanza, and they refused to make any of the cuts George wanted. He'd envisioned a light soufflé of an entertainment, but the Universal brass wanted to keep it road-show length, and even burdened it with an intermission. I met with Lew Wasserman, the head of the studio, to advocate for George's version, but received a condescending put-down in response. George quit before the film was scored and finished. Although there is much to love about *Thoroughly Modern Millie*, I feel that it could have been an even better movie if our director's cut had been allowed.

DURING THAT SUMMER of '66, my dad and stepmother, Win, came to visit. When Blake and my father first met, they were as wary as two bucks circling each other. I think that Dad wanted to carefully assess this new man in my life.

One evening, contrary to pleasant dining protocol, we got into a discussion about capital punishment. To my total surprise, my dad said, "I believe in an eye for an eye, and a tooth for a tooth. The punishment should match the deed."

I'd never heard him express that point of view. Blake argued for incarceration and studying the criminal mind to better understand what led to aberrant behavior. The conversation became quite heated, and the evening ended on an acrimonious note. Blake thought nothing of it, but I said to him later, "I'm so sad. My dad used to be the most open-minded, generous man. He was nonjudgmental and fair to everyone. I guess there comes a time later in life when one's opinions become inflexible."

The following morning, I went for an early swim. I heard a splash, and discovered my dad in the pool beside me. We did a couple of laps together, then he rested his elbows on the tiled edge and said, "About last night, Chick . . . I'm not sure— but Blake's got a point, I think."

I loved him for that more than I can say. Later, I relayed the story to Blake. "Dad still has an open mind," I said. "It just takes him a little longer to get there these days."

From then on, Blake and my dad embarked on a friendship rooted in affection and mutual respect.

HAWAII HAD ITS premiere in New York in early October. While I was there, I saw several of the productions Tony had designed, including screenings of *A Funny Thing Happened on the Way to the Forum* and *Fahrenheit 451*. Our friendship had never wavered—after all, we'd known each other since we were twelve and thirteen years old. Despite the fact that I was dating Blake, and Tony had just started seeing a lovely lady by the name of Genevieve (Gen) LeRoy, who had a daughter just a year younger than Emma, my "ex" very generously escorted me to the premiere of *Hawaii*. The film was warmly received by the critics, and I was delighted with the way George's monumental piece of work had turned out.

On my return to L.A., I went into the hospital for foot surgery. For most of my life I had suffered from painful bunions, aggravated by wearing too-tight shoes as a child, since my parents could seldom afford new ones. The 1920s-style pumps I wore in *Thoroughly Modern Millie* had cut across my instep and caused further inflammation; I was now in chronic pain, constantly removing my shoes to rub my sore feet. It was clearly time to do something about it.

Blake insisted that I recuperate at his house, for which I was truly grateful. Emma and I moved in with him for two weeks, during which time Blake spoiled me royally with flowers, meals, and chauffeured follow-up visits to the doctor. The surgery had involved cutting bone, and the recovery was painful and slow. I couldn't wear proper shoes for weeks. My surgeon suggested that I buy a pair of sneakers, cut out the toe box, and leave the sole and laces, giving me a platform to walk on and a modicum of support, with no pressure on my scars.

When I was just able to get up on my feet, I visited my analyst. After my session, I came out of his door and began shuffling slowly to the elevator. I heard a door open behind me, and suddenly felt an arm around my shoulders. A complete stranger said to me, "Oh, come now, it can't be *that* bad . . ." He was another analyst on the same floor as mine, and he had obviously assumed that I'd just had the worst therapy session ever. I pointed to my feet, we both laughed, and he apologized profusely.

ON NEW YEAR'S EVE, Blake and I invited some friends, including André Previn and his wife, Dory, over to my house for a late supper. We had just finished drinks and hors d'oeuvres when the most exquisite sound emanated from the courtyard. I looked out the window, then said to Blake, "There's a whole group of people outside!"

"Well, open the door!" he replied, with a twinkle in his eye.

It was the Young Americans, a singing group

comprised of young men and women between the ages of fifteen and twenty-one, who were all the rage at the time. Blake had invited them to come and serenade us into the New Year.

"This is amazing!" I said. "But—I don't have food for everyone!"

"Honey, relax," he said. "Hot chocolate and dinner for all is being delivered as we speak."

The Young Americans spread out in my living room, on the steps of my open staircase, on the floor, and all along the hearth. Some had brought guitars; André played the piano; I sang, they sang, and we all shared a magical evening of music, long into the night.

7

DURING *THE SOUND OF MUSIC*, Bob Wise and Saul Chaplin had discussed with me a possible film based on the life of the famous British actress and singer Gertrude Lawrence. The darling of London and Broadway in the 1920s and '30s, "Gertie" was well known for her friendship with Noël Coward, who wrote several highly successful plays for her. Her career culminated in the role of Anna Leonowens, opposite Yul Brynner in the Rodgers and Hammerstein Broadway musical *The King and I.*

The idea of my portraying Gertie had cropped up a few times in my life, since there were so many parallels between her early years in vaudeville and mine, but I'd always hedged, feeling I couldn't do her justice. However, when Bob explained his concept for the movie, I felt a familiar tingle of excitement.

I had to be patient. Bob had *The Sand Pebbles* to do; I had *Hawaii* and then *Millie*; and of course, a script had to be written and cast, and preproduction organized. By the beginning of 1967, all was finally in place. Rehearsals for *Star!*—as the film was called—commenced in February.

When shooting began, I went through my usual period of insecurity. Was I making the right choices for the character? Were those choices believable? Although by now I had a better knowledge of filmmaking, I was still figuring out the process of creating a character from scratch each time, and in this case, one based on a real person. These early nerves continue to be a pattern for me whenever I begin a new project. After floundering around for perhaps two weeks, there comes a moment, if I'm lucky, when a feeling of being on the right path comes over me, after which I push ahead with more confidence.

Bob and Saul had cast Daniel Massey for the role of Noël Coward. Dan was Noël's godson in real life, which gave him a unique perspective.

I was thrilled that Michael Kidd was creating the choreography, but I worried about finding comfortable shoes for all the dancing I would be doing. Although two months had passed since my bunion surgery, I still had bandages on my feet, and I couldn't yet wear regular shoes.

I had a series of meetings with Bob and Saul Chaplin, who was on board once again as producer.

Saul had collected recordings of all the musical numbers in the film, many of them sung by Gertie herself. We spent an afternoon discussing ways to re-create the songs. How authentic should I be? How imitative of Gertie? That would depend on how I played her character in the dramatic scenes, of course. That afternoon, as we discussed each song and its place in the script, ideas began to take shape in my mind. I decided that since I didn't look much like Gertie, I couldn't totally re-create her, so I opted instead to try to give a suggestion of her voice and the period in which she sang.

The Fox production team provided me with a lovely dressing room/apartment on the studio lot. It was beautifully furnished, down to the last teaspoon. I'd arrive at nine o'clock each morning and do an hour's singing practice, then meet Mike Kidd and his assistant Shelah Hackett and work on the dance numbers. After a quick break for lunch, I'd dash back to the apartment, rest briefly, then meet Saul and Lennie Hayton, our conductor and arranger, to continue working on the songs.

At the end of the first day of rehearsals, I wrote in my diary:

I'm stiff!!! And *oh*, my poor, sore feet!

For weeks, it seemed I did nothing except attend music and dance rehearsals, take meetings, and have hair and makeup tests and endless costume fittings. The clothes for the film, which spanned three decades, were designed by the eminent couturier Donald Brooks, and they were simply gorgeous. My roughly one hundred outfits required at least two or three fittings each.

My makeup man from *The Sound of Music*, Bill Buell, and my hairstylist from *Hawaii*, Lorraine Roberson, were with me once again. We tested my own hair, rinsed red, but it wasn't good enough. We then decided I would wear wigs, and we struggled to find the right color for so many changes of length and fashion.

Madame Stiles-Allen came to L.A. again, and I managed to squeeze in some singing lessons with her. It also seemed essential to continue the work with my analyst, since I had only just begun to unpack the myriad issues that had brought me into analysis in the first place. On any given day, I was examining my past, the present, my dreams, my behavioral patterns, my reactions and emotional responses. At some point, my analyst recognized that what I needed most was to make up for my lack of education. Having been shortchanged in that respect, I always felt a fundamental sense of inadequacy. He set about filling in the gaps. Some sessions were devoted to history, others geology or math, and I lapped it up. He seemed to know everything about everything. It was like going to school for a master's degree, but in this case the main subject was myself.

Emma was now in nursery school, which made things somewhat easier, although I wanted to spend as much time with her as possible, as well as with Blake. I was trying to accomplish twelve things at once; to say that I was feeling pressured is an understatement.

Thankfully, I had hired a new assistant. Joan Mansfield was vivacious and seemingly inexhaustible. She organized everything from my calendar to my wardrobe, and quickly proved to be an indispensable asset to me.

BLAKE'S CHILDREN WERE due to visit for their Easter vacation, and Blake felt that it was finally time for me to meet them. They were now living in London with Blake's ex-wife, Patricia Walker, a former actress. Both children adored their dad, and missed him desperately, as he did them.

I learned that neither of them had seen *The Sound of Music*, and they were keen to do so. I asked Bob Wise if he could arrange a private screening at Fox

Studios one afternoon. Knowing that the film had an intermission, I brought a picnic tea with me.

I was nervous to meet them, and realized it must be equally daunting for the children to meet me. I wondered what they would think of this new lady in their dad's life.

Jennifer was rail-thin, with long, blonde hair and wide eyes. Having just turned ten in March, she seemed astute beyond her years. Geoffrey was seven, equally fair and sweetly vulnerable. They were both rather rambunctious during the screening, probably due to the length of the film—but the picnic scored me a few points.

During their holiday with him, the children visited Blake on the set of the film he was currently directing, *The Party.* Someone on the crew noticed Jennifer and mentioned her to Delbert Mann, a director who was looking for a young actress to play the lead in his upcoming television production of *Heidi.* Jennifer did a screen test and got the part, and we were all thrilled for her.

PRINCIPAL PHOTOGRAPHY FOR *Star!* commenced in April. We filmed many of the musical numbers first. Michael Kidd's choreography, though brilliant, was extremely physical, and my feet continued to give me hell.

The scenes of young Gertie in early vaudeville were immensely evocative of my own touring days. The extras in the theater audience were seriously convincing—leering, jeering, beer-swigging, cabbage-slinging, and noisy. I had a familiar feeling of panic as the first cabbage landed at my feet.

Before heading to New York on location, we shot one of the most challenging numbers—"Burlington Bertie from Bow."

I had seen the famous Ella Shields perform this song when I was in vaudeville, and I loved it. Michael's staging was full of stylish tricks. It took three and a half days to shoot, and Michael was demanding, making me do everything so precisely that I became bad-tempered. At one point, I buckled and had a rare tantrum.

"MICHAEL!" I exploded. "You ask too much! I simply *cannot* do it!"

He looked surprised, then crestfallen. He called a break in the shooting, and I sat on the stage, my head on my knees. After a couple of moments, Michael came over.

"Jools, I didn't mean to be cruel," he explained in a quiet voice. "I just knew that when you saw yourself on film, you wouldn't be pleased."

Canny fellow that he was, he knew exactly what

to say. We did the take again, and this time, I nailed it.

I traveled to New York with my dear chum Zoë Dominic, who had been asked to do some photography for *Star!* Emma had gone to spend two weeks with Tony, Gen, and her daughter, Bridget, in San Francisco, where he was working on the film *Petulia.* I missed my sweet Em, but I was relieved that she was going to be happily engaged.

Arriving in New York was depressing. We'd been diverted to Philadelphia due to bad weather, and the storm battered us on the drive to the Big Apple. Sense memories of the exhaustion and loneliness that I'd felt during the long haul of *My Fair Lady* washed over me.

I had one day to unpack and prepare for filming. The first scene we shot was of Gertie singing Kurt Weill's lovely ballad "My Ship" on the stage of an empty Broadway theater. The song is a reverie, a wish for fulfillment with a true love. It stirred up so many feelings and memories for me, including sadness surrounding the failure of my marriage, that I suddenly choked up. It didn't hurt the scene, but I wonder if anyone suspected how personal that moment was for me.

EVENTUALLY, AFTER MY initial resistance to being back in New York had faded, the city proved to be stimulating, and I began to enjoy myself. One evening, I indulged in a rare treat: I went to see the great Birgit Nilsson in one of my favorite operas, *Turandot*, at Lincoln Center. I got goose bumps when I heard the dramatic soprano's voice fill the auditorium without any amplification. Her technique was like that of Madame Stiles-Allen; warm yet airy, and with enough strength to reach the last row of the balcony. For many years I struggled to emulate that technique, but I could never achieve it. My voice was a thin coloratura, and lacked her gravitas. But I always continued to aim for a similar vocal placement in practice.

ONE DAY WE were shooting at the Music Box Theatre. Irving Berlin had once had an office above the auditorium, and that space had been loaned to me for a dressing room. One of Berlin's pianos was still there, along with his desk and other memorabilia.

While I was changing, the phone rang. On an impulse, I picked it up.

A voice said, "May I speak to Miss Andrews?"

Surprised, I replied, "This is she . . . ?"

"This is Irving Berlin. I just wanted to welcome

you to the Music Box, and say that I hope you're very comfortable there."

"Thank you *so* much!" I stammered, feeling starstruck. What a thrill . . . and thank goodness I answered the phone!

THROUGHOUT THE FILM, I wore a lot of fabulous jewelry on loan from Cartier. Gertrude Lawrence apparently loved jewels, and spent a fortune on them at the famous boutique. A kindly armed guard named John was always stationed near me to protect the glorious stuff, which on some days was valued at as much as $2 million. It's a daunting responsibility to have that level of investment draped around one's body. John became a sort of personal bodyguard to me, elbowing his way through crowds, getting me in and out of cars or through doors in a hurry, and generally looking out for my well-being.

Cartier held a big party for the cast, crew, and press in their salon on Fifth Avenue. They lent me some earrings and a ring for the occasion. When it came time for me to leave, the main entrance was jammed with sightseers, so John arranged for a car to pick me up at the back entrance. This happened to be in the basement, which was smelly, hot, and filled with garbage cans. As I left the building, I removed my priceless gems and handed them to John, feeling very much like Cinderella returning to her broom and ashes.

I HAD BEEN missing Blake, and to my delight, he flew in one weekend for a visit. At the time, we were filming on a barge in the Hudson River with a piece of scenery on it that made it appear we were on the Staten Island ferry. My dressing room trailer was perched incongruously in the middle of the barge. There was nothing else on board except a couple of deck chairs, the camera equipment, and the inevitable coffee wagon. Between takes, Blake and I sat together gazing at the New York skyline as we floated across the river. It felt very romantic.

We shot some scenes at Cape Cod's Dennis Playhouse, the theater once owned by Gertie's husband, Richard Aldrich. He happened to stop by for a visit. I wondered how he felt, seeing me dressed like his late wife. He was charming, and remarked how like her I looked. When Dick Crenna, who portrayed him in the film, was introduced, Aldrich said amiably, "How nice to meet me!"

After a marathon pack-up, our company traveled to the South of France for the last leg of location shooting. We touched down in Nice on a perfect, sunny morning. The Mediterranean was sparkling, and the air held the scent of sun-warmed flowers, grass, and pines. I hadn't been in Europe since filming *The Sound of Music*, and I relished being back.

Emma, Kay, and I stayed on the top floor at the famous Hotel Negresco, overlooking the seafront. Zoë rejoined us, and my mother also flew in. Her visit to L.A. had been over a year ago, and she was longing to see Emma, who was now four and a half. Despite Pop's death the previous June, Mum was in surprisingly good form. She wasn't drinking much, and she seemed grateful for the change of scenery. We were shooting six days a week, but we could make a few excursions on Sundays. It was pleasant for us to spend time together.

Blake and I called each other daily, either late at night or first thing in the morning.

One evening, he asked, "Do you want to hear a really pretty song?"

Henry Mancini had been composing the music for *The Party*, and Blake said, "Listen . . . I hope this comes through over the phone."

The song was called "Nothing to Lose." It has a lovely lyric, written by Don Black, about there being nothing to lose, but much to gain, when a couple takes a chance on being together.

When the song finished, I said, "Darling, that is gorgeous!"

"It is, isn't it?" he replied. There was a pause. He cleared his throat. "Now . . . will you marry me?"

This came as a total surprise. We had only been seeing each other for a little over a year, and neither of us was yet divorced from our former spouses. To be truthful, I didn't know how I felt about getting married again—there was Emma to consider, and Blake's children—and as charismatic as Blake was, I wasn't yet certain that this was a relationship for the long term. I didn't feel I really knew him yet, and a part of me sensed a dark side that I might never know. He was so mercurial, so complicated in ways that I couldn't begin to fathom.

"Oh, Blake," I finally replied. "I love you for asking . . . May I think about it for a bit?"

"Yeah," he said. "But don't take too long."

OUR FILM COMPANY was besieged by the press in Nice. The journalists were part of a huge international junket that had been arranged by the studio to build anticipation for the film. They followed every move we made, which grew to be extremely wearing. I did publicity interviews for British and American television and radio, plus endless photographs, all between takes. Although I knew it was part of my job, eventually it became so distracting that I couldn't give the work my full attention, and I requested a reprieve. I think the studio recognized my dilemma, for they scaled back the promotional activities to a more manageable level.

On our last day in France, we shot a scene with Daniel and me on a raft in the bay at Cap d'Ail. The camera and crew were on another raft. The slightest swell caused both rafts to rock, although never at the same time.

The water was icy cold, and the weather was closing in. Between climbing in and out of the bay, and waiting for the sun to break through, or the camera to be reloaded, Dan's and my body temperatures began to drop. I turned blue, then dead white, and Dan was trembling from head to toe.

I asked for some brandy and hot coffee to help us stay warm. In no time at all, I became completely smashed—although upon reentering the icy water, I sobered up instantly. There were a number of takes, and I seesawed back and forth between tipsy and sober for the rest of the afternoon. I vaguely remember shouting, "Oh, shit on you all!" at one point, and the whole crew broke up with laughter.

Alas, we never finished the scene. The weather shut us down, and close-ups would have to be picked up later, back in Hollywood, against a rear projection screen. Bob was very depressed. I still have a mental image of him, hunched over on the camera raft under the gray sky, the last to leave and the absolute picture of despair.

BLAKE MET ME at the airport in Los Angeles, and we hugged all the way home. A two-week break in the shooting schedule allowed for the crew to regroup, and for me to rest a little and prepare myself for the next big onslaught of filming.

Blake had rented a house at the beach in Malibu for the months of July and August. Jennifer and Geoffrey were coming to visit for summer vacation, and he wanted to make it as pleasant as possible for us all. Going home along the Pacific Coast Highway in the evenings always relaxed me, and the sea air was refreshing after the long days in the dusty studio.

An excerpt from my diary:

Q-tip and Cobie [my poodles] in a catatonic state over Beatle. Massive amounts of dog shit in the yard in the mornings. Screen doors broken—pillows torn. Dog hair everywhere.

Strolls on the beach. Crabs, sand fleas. Beatle racing out. My dogs always running away, getting lost.

Talks with Blackie. Walks with Blackie. Nights with Blackie.

Emma browning. Cheeks aglow like a soft peach. Little girl in the sun all day, outdoors, loving it.

During our two-week "break," we never stopped rehearsing, but at least we laid off filming for a while. I mentioned to Bob how terrifying our shooting schedule was if I permitted myself to think of it. He said, "Don't. The only way to survive is to take it just one day at a time."

One of the hardest acting challenges for me was a drunken scene that occurs late in the film. I had no idea how to act drunk. In a moment of inspiration, I devised the idea of spinning around just before each take, in hopes that I'd be slightly off-balance and the dizziness would be reflected in my eyes. The scene took two days to shoot, and I spun so much that I ultimately grew used to the effect, and needed to spin more and more each time.

The end of the scene required an emotional breakdown. I worked all day long to sustain the mood— only to learn later that the film was damaged in the processing lab. To my dismay, the whole scene had to be reshot. As my mother used to say, "These things are sent to test us!"

My diary has a few entries that simply catalog the events on any given day. A typical example:

- Woke at 5:45 AM, at studio by 7:30 (did nails in car to save time)
- Makeup, wig, body make-up—into costume and on set by 9:20
- Between setups had interview for *News of the World*
- 11 o'clock photo session
- 2:30 make-up retouched, different wig on, into new costume
- Filmed scene—back to dressing room
- Patched make-up for different period in film. No good. Took make-up off completely. Bill started again.
- 5:20 PM back to set. Just one shot took seven takes. Heard a man snoring and discovered a lighting technician in the scaffolding had dropped off to sleep
- Finished work at 6:10 PM
- Analyst at 6:30
- Home at 8:00

The principal cast gradually dwindled as each major scene was completed, after which we took our second break in the filming, to rehearse the three biggest musical numbers.

My dad and Win came for a visit, and Geoff and Jenny arrived for their summer vacation. Although the marriage discussion had been set aside for the time being, Blake's and my relationship continued to deepen. But it was an adjustment for Emma to suddenly have two older "siblings," each of whom was understandably demanding attention. Blake went into overdrive trying to keep everyone occupied.

Another diary entry:

Blackie coming home with gifts for the children, a sun hat for me. Always buying some new kind of ice cream. Taking Dad for a drive up the coast—letting him try the new Mustang. Win embroidering, reading to Emma. Weekends so precious. Never enough time.

Traffic jams. Tourists at beaches. Hot. Humid. Work. Work. Work.

Discussions with Blackie. Tears of exhaustion with Blackie. Waking in the middle of the night. Touching hands—and backsides!

Geoff and Jenny, growing up, gaining a little

confidence in me. Jenny, making books and letters and pictures for Blackie. Loving him so. Geoff running to greet me in evenings when I get home.

Emma learns to swim, round and round in small circles, like a little tadpole. Great pride in her own achievement.

Emma goes to New York for 10 days. Blackie takes his children back to England. House is quiet. Very lonely, despite endless work. Sadness at thought that soon we'll be packing up at the beach. Talking about and tentatively planning a trip to Switzerland for Christmas. Can hardly wait.

EMMA BEGAN KINDERGARTEN at the Los Angeles Lycée Français, and she was none too pleased with it. She chafed at wearing a uniform, and conforming to the school's fairly strict rules, not to mention having to learn a new language. In addition, the twin boys sitting behind her in class were inclined to tease her. When one of them became ill and accidentally threw up all over her, she came home a basket case and plaintively asked, "Mum, how long until I graduate?"

I didn't have the heart to tell her it would be another twelve years.

WORK ON *STAR!* progressed. Of all the major musical numbers in the film, "Jenny" was the largest and most exhausting. Michael had conceived the sequence as a circus act, with trampolines and a flying trapeze. I worked for days with the professional acrobats that had been cast, trying to accomplish the "Risley" movements, in which the acrobats lay on their backs, spinning me on their feet and tossing me from one to the other.

Once again, I reached a breaking point, and told Michael I couldn't physically do what he wanted. He countered by saying, "If Shelah can do it, will you give it a try?"

Of course, Shelah did it brilliantly!

I became black-and-blue from all the acrobatics, and was terrified by the height of the rope ladder I had to climb. We must have shot a take of my somersaulting out of a safety net at least twenty times. It was a great relief when that number was finally complete.

Blake came down to the studios occasionally to pick me up after work. He was very circumspect around Bob Wise, because he knew how disconcerting it could be to have another director on set. One day, Bob really ran overtime, and I could see Blake getting more and more impatient. There was nothing to be done, as we had to finish.

Driving home with Emma in the car, Blake was very silent. I was silent because he was silent, and I was thinking that he could have been a little more sympathetic to my situation.

Finally, Emma's sweet voice piped up from the back seat of the car.

"Feeling a little uptight, Blackie?"

"Yesssss, Emma, I am," he replied through clenched teeth.

There was a small pause.

"Are you feeling anxious, or just tense?"

"Actually, Emma, a little of *both*."

Another pause.

Then Emma said innocently, "Have you ever tried Compoz, that gentle little blue pill that soothes and calms?"

It was a line from a TV ad that was running at the time.

The Rolls-Royce swerved to the side of the road. Blake exploded with laughter and stopped the car; I found myself weeping with gratitude. It was such a darling attempt on Emma's part to make everything right again. She waded in where I didn't have the guts to even try.

THE LAST SCENES we shot for *Star!* were "The Physician" and "Limehouse Blues." The latter was set in Chinatown, and was a dramatic ballet staged in a seedy "house of ill repute." Michael set "The Physician" in a harem, and that number begins with a shot of a large sheep, dyed orange, chewing lazily. The camera slowly pans across a long piece of yarn, pulled from the sheep by a group of exotic concubines, until it reaches me, knitting a sweater. As the cameras rolled, the sheep began to relieve itself. Somehow, the angle of the camera didn't reveal that, so the take progressed. By the time it reached me, I had collapsed with the giggles. Ah, show biz!

Originally, we had been scheduled to finish the picture sometime in September. That month rolled on; as did October, then November, then December. As Christmas loomed, I thought we'd never get away for the holiday we'd planned in Switzerland. Finally, we wrapped the film on the night of December 14.

Star! had taken eight months to shoot, at a cost of $14 million, which in those days was monumental. I had performed 17 musical numbers, and worn 125 different costumes, out of the 3,040 that Donald Brooks had created for the film. Boris Leven had designed and built 185 sets.

Throughout all the challenges of making the movie, Bob was his stalwart, kind, and patient self. Our relationship never suffered, and neither did my relationship with Michael and Shelah, who subsequently married. My friendship with them was one of the greatest gifts of this film for me.

I HAD ONE full day to try to deliver gifts, take Emma to the pediatrician, pack, and attend the wrap party for the film in the evening. Blake had gone ahead to Switzerland that morning, traveling with Ken and Kären Wales, in order to prepare the rental chalet we'd found for the holiday; Emma and I left the following day.

When we boarded the first leg of our flight, I was astonished to find a gorgeous bouquet of white lilacs waiting on my seat, with a loving note from Blake. We stopped in New York, where I delivered Emma to Tony before traveling on to Switzerland by myself. I was despondent about my daughter not being with me for Christmas, although I knew she would be joining us for the New Year.

Landing in Geneva, my mood was lifted by the view of snow-covered mountains and a brilliant sunrise. Blessed Europe, I thought. I experienced such a flood of emotions that I wanted to leap from the plane and kiss the earth.

Blake met me at the airport, and we journeyed up to the small mountain village of Gstaad. The rental chalet was gorgeous—all-natural wood, white stuccoed walls, and a country farmhouse feeling, with a puffy eiderdown duvet on every bed.

I rested, then unpacked, while Blake went back to Geneva to collect Geoff and Jenny, who had been on a later flight out of London. We all went out to dinner at a charming old hotel in the center of the village. On the way home, the stars were bright, and the snowy mountains were bathed in moonlight. There was even a little electric train puffing and whistling through town. Blake remarked, "My God, it looks like a Bing Crosby movie!"

The ensuing days were filled with Christmas preparations. The town was busy, with beautifully decorated store windows and people having snowball fights in the streets. Our group kept splitting up into various factions, and occasionally we would bump into each other in a shop. There was much calling out: "Don't come in here!" "Don't turn around!" "You mustn't peek!"

One evening, we went to dinner in town via horse-drawn sleigh. The kids had been dying for a ride, and it was a perfect night for it: cold and crystal clear. The horses steamed profusely, their harnesses jingling. We snuggled under blankets as they jogged along, and marveled at the wonder of it all.

Everyone took skiing lessons, except for Blake. He suffered from chronic back pain, having fractured his spine in his twenties during a miscalculated dive into a swimming pool. He appointed himself our official photographer. As he captured us all slipping and sliding on the slopes, he just about collapsed with laughter. It was a wonderful tonic to see him relaxing so much.

Blake, Geoff, Jenny, and I decorated the Christmas tree together. On Christmas Day, it snowed—huge, fat, white flakes, all day. After opening their gifts, the children built a snowman and went sledding.

At one point, Blake and I looked at each other and agreed without hesitation that this was possibly the most "Christmassy" Christmas we had ever known. I only wished Emma could have been with us.

Boxing Day was equally memorable. Blake and I drove to the nearby town of Château-d'Oex for lunch with David Niven, who was an old friend of Blake's, having been in the first *Pink Panther* film. The journey there was beautiful, and we would have been content to just drive in each other's company for hours. We met up with David at the train station, where he was also picking up Noël Coward and his longtime partner, Graham Payn, as well as Binkie Beaumont—who had produced *My Fair Lady* in London, and whom I hadn't seen for ages.

We followed David to his chalet, where his wife, children, and a nanny greeted us. We were later joined by Elizabeth Taylor and Richard Burton (who was dreadfully hungover). What a motley crew!

Elizabeth flashed an astonishingly large diamond ring that Richard had given her for Christmas, and remarked, "It's a bit of a giggle, isn't it?"

It all seemed rather decadent; lots of exclamations over the "*divine*" presents, and affirmations that "it's the loveliest thing I've ever *seen!*" Noël was his gracious and witty self. We chatted briefly about *Star!* He seemed immensely proud of his godson, Dan Massey, and said he was looking forward to seeing the film.

At lunch there was caviar, vodka, and endless bottles of wine. The talk was funny and bawdy and mostly theatrical, of course, with a good deal of reminiscing.

THAT EVENING, BLAKE received a call from Patty. She had filed for divorce in September, and we hadn't heard from her in a while. She was in a state of depression. Blake had told me that before and during their marriage she had attempted to take her own life several times. This made her a continual worry, especially to the children. Blake spoke to her for quite a while. Knowing how much I was missing Emma, I suspected Patty was feeling lost without Geoff and Jenny.

Emma finally arrived on New Year's Eve, accompanied by her new nanny, Rosemary, since Kay had recently married. Emma had grown—she seemed both assured and guarded, and was moody for much of the following week. I sensed it must have been difficult for her to embrace the culture of her dad's household and then transition to our quite different one in such a short period of time.

We saw in the New Year quietly. Blake and I had just turned in for the night when the phone rang. It was Patty again. She told Blake that she had taken a bottle of pills, and that she was saying goodbye. Blake covered the phone and whispered to me, "Go wake Ken. Tell him to call Patty's doctor, and ask him to go to her house right away."

Blake continued talking to Patty on the phone until he heard the doctor break through her door and take over. He handled the situation very calmly— obviously it wasn't new to him, but it certainly was for me. I felt wobbly and anxious for that sad lady who was obviously in such emotional pain.

AS THE END of our holiday approached, I found myself longing to stay in Gstaad. Phone calls came in from the States with business matters for both of us, and I felt intruded upon and unready to return to work. If Blake had said, "Let's just forget everything in America and live here," I would have done it like a shot. Although that wasn't possible, we fantasized what it might be like to have a chalet of our own one day.

As I struggled to sort out my feelings, I wrote a list of "Things I Will Always Remember About This Place":

The mountains, of course. Their towering nearness, and their edges razor-sharp in the crystalline air. Usually at the top of the highest ones there is a plume of snow, trailing softly into the sky like smoke. Last night we saw skiers coming down the mountain from a fondue party. Each one was carrying a flaming torch, and the line of lights crossed and re-crossed as they traversed slowly down the hill.

I'll remember the peace after everyone was asleep, when Blake and I would read, and the radio played soft, classical music, and the silliness of Jenny and me dancing in our long johns to "Sleeping Beauty." Blake and the children wrestling on the beds, among the big duvets, piled high. He took on all three of them, and they loved it, tumbling, puppy-like, never really getting hurt in the downy softness.

My heart aches at the thought of leaving.

We flew back via London, and spent a week there, as we needed to take Jenny and Geoff home to Patty, who was now in stable condition, and ready to have her children back again. I had not been in England for four years, and worried about what might be waiting for me there with respect to my family. My concerns were not unfounded.

When my stepfather died, I'd realized that Mum couldn't rattle around our family home—the Old Meuse—by herself anymore. Coincidentally, the local council wanted to buy the place and develop a housing estate on the land. The property was in my name, so with my mother's permission, I agreed to the sale, with the stipulation that a third of an acre be kept for her. We were in the planning stages of building Mum a new home on that smaller piece of land, and there was enough money left over from the sale to give both Mum and Auntie a bit of a financial boost.

Mum used her portion to purchase the cottage that Auntie had been renting. This was probably intended to be a loving gesture from an older sister to ensure the younger sister's security. At the same time, it also gave Mum the power to lord it over her sibling, which was typical of their relationship. I'd heard that Auntie was in tears because she was angry and frustrated by the games my mother had been playing. I also learned that her poor cat had just been killed by a car. While Blake was meeting with Patty, I headed down to Walton, stopping at the pet store in Harrods to buy a new kitten as a surprise for her.

My brother Don met me at the Old Meuse with his wife, Celia, and their young son, Rory. My old home was in a serious state of dilapidation; no central heating, only one of three bathrooms working, kitchen filthy. Squalid and damp, it looked as if it hadn't been cleaned for ten years. Clearly, it was essential that Mum move as soon as her new cottage was ready.

We all drove to Auntie's cottage, and I left the little kitten safely in the car, waiting for the right moment to give it to her.

Aunt Joan greeted me with "Don't come too

near me or I shall break down again! I've only just stopped crying . . ." She showed me her cottage, and gradually calmed a little. She had cooked us all lunch, and we were soon chatting, laughing, and swapping news.

After lunch, I mentioned the kitten. There was another emotional outburst: "I don't want it! I couldn't give it a good home, what's the *use*!" and then, "Where is it?" followed by great concern when she discovered that I had left it in the car. By the end of the day, she had talked herself into keeping the little creature.

In reflecting on the week, I realized that the saddest thing about my mother had been her total quiet about everything. Of all the family, she was the only one who hadn't complained, hadn't asked me for anything, except to inquire about plans for her new cottage. Her loneliness damn near broke my heart.

I had been doing everything I could for her, financially, for as long as I could remember; although physically I was far away, living in the States, as was Chris. Pop was gone, Donald was married, and Johnny was also married and living in Norway, working as a pilot.

I vowed to find some way, somehow, to be the daughter she needed me to be.

8

SINCE OUR FIRST meeting at my house in February of 1966, Blake had written the script for the film he had discussed with me, *Darling Lili.* He had coauthored it with William Peter Blatty, with whom he had collaborated on several other films, including *A Shot in the Dark*; *What Did You Do in the War, Daddy?*; and *Gunn. Darling Lili* centers on a British spy working for the Germans during World War I who falls in love with an American flier.

Rehearsals commenced in February of 1968, almost exactly two years to the day after Blake had pitched the project to me. At first, I ran between Paramount and 20th Century Fox, as I was also finishing looping for *Star!*

We began with hair and wardrobe tests, as usual. I would be wearing wigs, and there was the endless struggle to find the right style and color. Happily, the bulk of my costumes were being designed once again by the brilliant Donald Brooks.

Although the film is not a musical, I did have several songs to sing, as my character of Lili masqueraded as an entertainer. I really enjoyed the prerecording sessions; original songs composed by Henry Mancini with lyrics by the great Johnny Mercer. Both were Hollywood legends, and I felt honored to be working with them. Henry was easy in manner, with a terrific sense of humor. Musicians adored working with him, as did I. We only recorded one song a day—quite a change from the hectic schedule of *Star!*

On March 18, we began shooting. That evening, I wrote:

> I think I functioned in a fairly normal manner, and managed to conceal my extreme nerves at working with Blake, but inside I felt distant, unconnected and wary. What will working together do to our relationship?

Blake was obviously nervous, too, for that first day he paced endlessly and worked himself into a state. I eventually discovered that this was his modus operandi whenever he began work on a new project, whether directing or writing. Much like me, once he found his footing and felt at home with his concept and choices, he was able to settle down.

Blake was trying out a new technique called "video assist," which he was an early pioneer of, along with Jerry Lewis. A video camera was set on top of the film camera to record each scene simultaneously. In later years, it became integrated within the camera itself, which is how the equipment works today. The best thing about it was that it allowed the company to immediately see a scene that had just been shot, rather than waiting for the dailies to come back a day or so later. This saved an enormous amount of time, money, and film footage. It was the first time I'd had this kind of immediate feedback, and it was invaluable in terms of correcting a choice, an angle, a costume malfunction, and so on. *Darling Lili* is credited as being one of the first films to employ this technique, in addition to Blake's *The Party*.

Most of the early weeks of shooting were spent on the set of the Café Can-Can. I was filled with admiration for Blake's cinematic knowledge. He occasionally discarded the formal techniques of a master shot, and subsequent close angles, in favor of a more fluid kind of movement. The camera was constantly following the actors or shifting focus, which for me was very new. Our entire crew was enthusiastic about working this way—one day, they burst into applause at the creativity of a certain zoom lens shot.

Rock Hudson, who played Major Larrabee, Lili's American love interest, joined us in the third week of shooting. We had met briefly before filming began, but we didn't know each other well, and our first scene together required a passionate kiss—not easy when the director of the film happens to be your beau, and says, "That was fine, darling, but I *know* you can do it better!"

Rock turned out to be affable, funny, and a generous acting partner. That said, he was a private man, and we didn't see much of each other beyond the set.

Blake's and my physician, Dr. Herb Tanney, was not only a good friend and a superb diagnostician, he was also a wannabe actor. He once said to Blake that he'd love to have a walk-on role in a movie, to impress his five daughters. Herb was warm and cuddly, but not remotely photogenic, and he couldn't act his way out of a paper bag. Nevertheless, Blake gave him a walk-on in *Darling Lili*. In the years that followed, there wasn't a movie in which Tanney didn't appear; he became a sort of lucky mascot for Blake.

For this debut performance, Blake cast Herb as a "gypsy violinist," since he could actually play the violin. Herb had jokingly said to Blake that he should have his own dressing room, and to my surprise, Blake concurred. It was to be the first of many pranks that Blake played on Herb. The dressing room was the oldest trailer on the lot. It was a tiny wooden square on two wheels, and the prop department decorated it as tastelessly as possible, with cobwebs hanging from the walls and ceiling, a leopard-skin throw on the small sofa, and hideous bric-a-brac. Herb took it all in stride.

Just before we left for location shooting in Europe, we filmed a scene on a train where Lili becomes unglued. Blake wanted me to really cry, and I was having a hard time letting go. Knowing that I had an absolute phobia of loud explosions—gunshots, balloons bursting, fireworks—he had the foolish idea to shoot off a revolver unexpectedly, thinking it would so upset me that I'd weep authentically.

When the gun went off, I became icy with rage. I spun around and said, "Don't *do* that!" My anger did lead to tears, mostly from fright. Because he needed them for the scene, and I didn't want to publicly embarrass him, I allowed them to flow. That said, he shouldn't have done it, and he knew it. Later he apologized, and never played a trick like that again.

THE DIVORCE FROM Patty had by now gone through, and although Blake wasn't pressuring me further about getting married, he did pointedly remark that it was somewhat inappropriate for me to still be married to one man while seriously dating another. I knew he was right, and that it was time to take the next step forward. While I still wasn't ready to jump into another marriage, I talked with Tony, who had by now moved in with Gen, and we agreed to file for divorce.

Nevertheless, on the morning I was due to appear at the courthouse, I was an emotional basket case. I slipped into Emma's room to check on her. She was still asleep, and I crawled into her bed, fully clothed, and cuddled her. I'm not sure who was supposed to be comforting whom. I was so reluctant to hurt her, or Tony, or anyone else. Even though Tony wouldn't be in attendance, and I only had to show up with my lawyer and affirm my decision before a judge, I felt like a complete failure. It was one of the most miserable days of my life.

Five days later, Blake, Emma, her new nanny Rosemary, Ken, Kären, and I departed for Dublin, Ireland, where location shooting was to commence at the end of May. Though the film was set in France, Ireland had been chosen for its "unblemished" countryside—it had few visible television aerials or other modern contraptions, which would have damaged our World War I period look. We also needed the very talented Irish Air Force, who had been hired to perform the flight sequences.

We would be both living and filming at Carton House, a magnificent Georgian manor house originally built in the seventeenth century. Set on a thousand acres of gently rolling countryside in County Kildare, Carton has magnificent views from every room. Our company had rented the private estate to serve as the location for many of the interior and exterior scenes in the film, and also as housing for our family.

There were two dining rooms; endless bedrooms (including a "Chinese Boudoir" where Queen Victoria had once stayed); and a large kitchen with a vast fireplace and a cauldron on a swinging arm.

The massive property had beautifully manicured formal gardens; a medieval tower on a far hillside; and a huge lake with an island in the center of it, along with a boathouse, herons, swans, and ducks. There was also a working dairy decorated with delft tiles; stables with Gothic arches over the stalls; kennels, vegetable gardens, pens for breeding wild fowl, a bird sanctuary, and acres of beech woods. Hedgerows were filled with blossoming hawthorn trees, rhododendrons, primroses, bluebells, daisies, and daffodils. At the back of the house, there was a rose garden surrounded by neat box hedges. There was also a Gothic "folly" known as "Shell Cottage," since its interior walls were decorated with shells from all over the world.

During the first week or two at Carton, I almost forgot that the film company existed, and kept thinking I was on holiday. The days seemed to be a blend of beautiful fresh mornings, cloudy or sunny afternoons, and long twilight evenings. I roamed around with Emma, both of us wearing sturdy Wellington boots, inhaling the glorious country air. Sometimes a wall of rain crossed our view, as if a curtain were being drawn across the scene. I poured tea in silver servers for visitors and checked on fires and mealtimes, very much enjoying the game of being "Lady Muck."

It wasn't all tea and crumpets, though. Blake developed a painful strep throat, and lost his voice. A local physician prescribed antibiotics, which helped. This was the first I'd seen of many "health crises" that Blake continued to have over the ensuing years whenever a new project was beginning. There was no doubt that he was genuinely unwell each time, but I was starting to realize that he was also a serious hypochondriac.

Emma, on the other hand, was absolutely thriving during her summer vacation. Her cheeks were rosy from being outside all day. We had horses to ride, with a pony for Emma. With so much privacy on the large property, I didn't fear for her safety, and was happy to let her come and go.

One afternoon, Emma and I were out riding, and we ended up in the formal gardens at the back of the house. Blake had been resting in our bedroom—but hearing our repeated calls, he came out onto the balcony.

Suddenly, with a loud roar, six colorful World War I planes barreled down from the sky and flew low over Carton House. Those crazy Irish pilots flew around and around—banking and dipping, obviously "buzzing" their director. Standing on the balcony with his arms folded, Blake looked rather like Napoleon reviewing his troops. We waved and cheered, encouraging them to go around once more before the squadron finally disappeared into the dusk.

However, the work we were there to do was inevitable, and eventually the assistant director and members of the crew arrived for meetings and to begin preproduction.

I RECEIVED A letter from my dad saying he was on his own for a few days, as Win had gone to see Shad, who was now living in Yorkshire. It occurred to me that he might like to come over on a spur-of-the-moment visit. I phoned him just as he'd returned home from teaching, and he was eating scrambled eggs and cornflakes. It was one of his great pleasures to cook scrambled eggs, stir in some crispy cornflakes at the last minute, put the warm pan on his knees, and eat directly from it. "One-stop cooking," he always said. I invited Dad to pop over for the weekend, and he was all for it.

We had a grand few days together. Dad spent most of the weekend out and about, and even biked around the entire estate. At some point, he mentioned how appalling it was to him that one family could have owned so much—a grand manor house on a thousand acres, with outlying farms and holdings beyond that.

I said to him, "True, Dad . . . but at least in those days, every cottage was full, and everyone had a job. So many people maintained the estate, cared for the gardens and livestock, and provided for the larger community." Later, he returned to the subject and said, "I've been thinking about it, Chick, and you're absolutely right."

I hoped I might be able to treat my mother to a similar visit, but as she so often did, she declined to come.

LOCATION SHOOTING BEGAN at the Gaiety Theatre in Dublin. I went in ahead of time to work
with our choreographer, Hermes Pan, and to get
used to the Gaiety stage. Hermes had been Fred
Astaire's principal choreographer, and I was somewhat awed to be working with him, albeit in a
minor capacity.

Driving into the city, I was feeling a little lost
at being off the estate and out in the "big world"
again. I began to look around me, and suddenly
had a rush of memories. The houses, the people,
the villages, all vividly reminded me of touring
England in my early teens when I was performing
in vaudeville.

I wrote:

I noticed an ancient couple—hobbling and
bent, their arms linked, making their way slowly
and painfully to the shops. Another old woman
had her hand on her back as she walked, and
still another was buying a huge head of fish—
dead and gaping—from a street stall. I noticed
a young boy in a shiny, boot-black suit and an
old cap, stroking a weary cart horse, and a big,
shaggy dog, running alone with a pipe in its
mouth. I saw a man with a waistcoat and long
overcoat, but no shirt collar, tie or socks.

The biggest sense memory occurred when I arrived at the Gaiety. I picked my way through the front entrance, over a thousand electrical cables, through the main bar smelling of stale beer and cigarettes, through the pass door, into the "green room," and then on to the dark stage—and my past came up and hit me right between the eyes. There were the old footlights—colored celluloids broken, the orchestra pit with its surrounding brass rail, the center microphone that rose up out of the trap, the faded gold proscenium, the dusty, tasseled house curtain, and the three tiers out in front—circle, upper circle and balcony.

Suddenly I remembered Monday mornings and band calls—getting my orchestrations laid out on stage in time for rehearsal, placing them to the right of the band books already down ahead of mine, and waiting my turn. Unpacking the steamer trunks each week, and climbing endless stairs to the wardrobe room at the top of the theater in order to press my theatrical gowns. The halting, uneasy first performance on Monday nights, and the difficult 2nd "houses" on Saturdays. The smell of paint, turpentine, and dust, the depressing staleness—and the awful pretense of glamour.

Hermes remarked that I looked sad—and I was. Stunned, is maybe the word. It wasn't until I began rehearsing the song with him that I pulled out of my reverie and returned to the world of 1968.

At the Gaiety, we shot all the theater scenes in the film. We had about five hundred local extras for our audience, with marvelous faces full of character. Between takes, they sang Irish songs. When Blake appeared at the start of the day, they raised the roof with their cheers, then sang a rousing rendition of "For He's a Jolly Good Fellow." On my last day with them, they presented me with a bouquet of flowers and sang a song inviting me back to Ireland again one day.

When Rock arrived, we moved outdoors to film the dawn flyover of Larrabee's squadron, which was actually shot at sunset. The evening heat brought out a million little gnats, and within seconds, I was covered in them. They were attracted to the glue holding my wig in place, and were crawling all over my scalp and *biting*. I nearly went mad. I wanted to tear the hair from my head, but our light was fading, and it was essential to get the shot. I did my best to keep calm—even put a plastic bag over my wig to prevent any new invaders, and sat in a car between takes. But I was utterly miserable, and ready to scream. Rock, on the other hand, sailed through the scene without so much as a nibble. When the wig finally came off, I looked like I had the measles.

Another evening, Blake and I discovered about fifty huge bluebottle flies buzzing around our bedroom. Blake vowed to "get 'em"—and get 'em he did. He rolled up a newspaper tightly, and for the next half hour he proceeded to hurl it at the flies with unerring aim, and with lethal results. He leapt about from the bed to the chairs to the floor, throwing the paper straight up above him like an exploding rocket, or hurling it across the room like a boomerang. I was under the covers most of the time, as it seemed to be raining bluebottles. Eventually, the last fly bit the dust. My hero!

On June 5, we heard the terrible news of Senator Robert Kennedy's assassination. It was a somber time, as we reflected on the enormity of the Kennedy family's loss and what it meant for the United States. We felt very far from home.

Geoff and Jenny came for several visits, and my dad came again, this time with Win. Dad was a huge fan of cricket, rugby, and soccer, and Blake was passionate about American football. Occasionally they sparred about which was better. Dad attempted to teach Blake the principles of batting, and seeing them playing together was the first time I realized how genuinely fond of my dad Blake was. I suspected that Dad was the father Blake wished he'd had.

One miraculous Sunday, Blake and I had Carton all to ourselves. Emma was in London visiting Tony, and everyone else was out for the day.

In the morning we rode together, just the two of us, slowly walking the horses around the estate in the sunshine. At lunch, we had a hilarious episode. The old-fashioned clock on the mantelpiece over the fireplace struck two o'clock at 1 p.m.—it had never chimed correctly since we'd been there—so Blake vowed to fix it. He stopped the mechanism, slipped the hands around carefully, and it chimed perfectly each time: nine o'clock, ten o'clock, eleven o'clock, twelve . . . and at last, to one, whereupon again the clock struck *twice*. We then wondered what would happen at two o'clock, so we moved the hands forward—but it correctly struck two. Round we went again, laboriously waiting for each hour to chime. The room was filled with ding-dongs, and our ears were splitting. Finally, we reached one o'clock again—and again, two chimes. I was on the floor with laughter. Forevermore that clock struck two at one o'clock, though it was perfectly able to strike one at the half hour. We adored it so much that I bought it from the owners as a surprise gift for Blake's birthday.

That afternoon, we went for a walk to the bird sanctuary, passing through a gate that led to a path alongside the water. Suddenly, hundreds of ducks, mostly chicks, emerged from the reeds and floated down the river like a miniature armada. They came toward us, then hopped up onto the embankment in single file. They walked through tunnels in the high grass, staying close together—milling around us, gently nibbling our shoelaces, reaching up to see if we'd feed them. When they discovered we had no food, they did an about-face, as if at a given signal, and walked back along the same paths, to return to the water. I'll never forget the enraptured smile on Blake's face.

After dinner, we took a boat out onto the lake. We laughed at a swan who seemingly got his jollies from flapping into mad flight toward us, skimming the water like a jumbo jet, then calmly easing back in a few feet away. We felt so rested and happy that evening, and we vowed to try for another such day—though alas, we were so busy that no such opportunity presented itself again.

CHARLIE BLUHDORN, the film's producer, came over to check on the film's progress. He visited the set, chatted with Blake, saw the dailies, and talked to the production manager. His visit happened to coincide with a day when the crew was waiting for some clouds to appear to match something that had already been shot. Apparently, it seemed to Charlie that everyone was just lolling around in the brilliant sunshine, doing nothing. This resulted in his ordering the top brass, Bob Evans and Bernie Donnenfeld, to visit the set themselves—much to Blake's chagrin.

The following day, I returned from an invitation to tea at the local convent to discover that Bob Evans and Bernie Donnenfeld had arrived. They were in a heated conversation with Blake. We had intended to shoot the entire film on location in Ireland, but after the visit with the Paramount brass and because of the relentless weather challenges, Blake was forced to move the company to France. Just before we were to make the move, a series of student uprisings and strikes in Paris diverted us to Belgium instead.

Brussels was a total culture shock after Ireland. We stayed in a bizarre rented house full of stuffed animals—not the toy kind; the taxidermy kind. There was a fox, a pheasant, a cat on a chair, a dog by the fire, even a bird in a cage. Appalled, we crammed them all into a closet and shut the door.

Over the next three weeks, we shot many locations that served as suitable substitutes for Paris. During that time, *Star!* had a royal premiere in London. I had hoped to attend, and right up until the last minute I thought I might be able to fly in, but we were night shooting and I didn't make it. I felt simply awful about it—I knew I was letting down that company and disappointing my family, who were planning to be there—but there was nothing I could do. I was miserable, and the British press were none too pleased with me either.

The *Darling Lili* company was finally able to transfer to Paris, where we were to film some scenes at the Louvre. Blake had determined that one shot would be by the famed *Winged Victory* statue. Rock and I rehearsed the scene once, and then a long wait ensued—so long that we sensed something was wrong. We soon discovered what it was: blue smoke from the carbons in our arc lights had filled the room and was threatening the priceless art. Mayhem followed, as skylights that hadn't been used in years were frantically opened. The curator of the museum was called, and our work was suspended. André Malraux, the French minister of cultural affairs, was brought in, and we were forbidden to continue filming there.

We were all devastated. We were ready to shoot, the *Victory* had been brilliantly lit, and Rock and I were fully rehearsed. Finally, we were given five minutes by the authorities to get our shot, and get our lights off the premises. It could have been done—the scene lasts no more than a minute—but it wasn't our day. Two of the arcs began to flutter, and our five minutes went up in smoke, as it were. I was heartsick, and Blake was a wreck. In the end, we were given a small reprieve; we were told that if it was possible to light the shot with smaller, non-carbon lamps, we could go back and try it. We did—although Blake was none too happy with the result.

Another of our locations was the Villa Windsor in the Bois de Boulogne; home of the former King Edward VIII and Wallis Simpson, the American woman for whom he abdicated the throne. We only shot exteriors in the courtyard, but the Duke would occasionally step onto a balcony, and watch the proceedings. At one point, he came down for a brief visit, and we struck up a conversation about the riots in Paris. The Duke said to Blake and me, "Those students are throwing Molotov cocktails at our poor policemen. I wouldn't be a policeman for all the tea in China."

I couldn't help thinking, "Well, sir, you could never have been a policeman in the first place!"

One evening, Blake and I were returning to the Hôtel Le Bristol after a long, hot day of filming. Just as we arrived, the heavens opened. We stood by the car for a moment and let the summer rain wash over us. Then we leaned in and kissed each other, long and very sweetly—much to the delight of the front doorman.

GEOFF AND JENNY came to visit again, and all three children had a fine time together. In the evenings, I read them a favorite book from my childhood, *The Little Grey Men*, which they seemed to enjoy. They were, however, often unruly and left chaos in their wake—so one day, in desperation, I devised a game. If they managed to keep their rooms tidy, pick up their laundry, and brush their teeth, they'd win a prize. If not, they'd pay a forfeit.

"You have to play, too," Jenny said. When I asked her what I had to do for my side of the bargain, she replied, "You have to stop swearing so much."

I wasn't aware that I'd *been* swearing, but apparently the kids had noticed an uptick in my use of juicy adjectives. Needless to say, I was the first to lose the game. I asked Jenny what my forfeit should be.

"Write me a story," she said.

As I began to think about that story, I realized that I wanted it to be special—something meaningful and substantive for her. I remembered the charming Shell Cottage at Carton, and decided to write about a young orphan girl named Mandy, who discovers a similar abandoned dwelling, and tries to make it her own.

When I shyly mentioned the idea to Blake, he said, "That's really charming. Do it! And don't stop writing. Just let the pages build and build."

I started working on *Mandy* whenever I had a spare moment, and was surprised by how much I enjoyed the writing process.

THE DAY BEFORE Geoff and Jenny were scheduled to return home, Blake suggested that we accompany them back to London for the weekend.

"I think it would be easier on them," he said. "None of those awful goodbyes at the airport, and I can meet with Patty to discuss the kids. You've been wanting to see your mum and her new cottage . . . this might be a good moment."

I agreed that it sounded like a good idea.

I asked Rosemary and my assistant, Joan, to look

after Emma, and to take her to an ice cream parlor as a special treat. Emma seemed excited at the prospect.

Once in London, we checked into the Dorchester Hotel, where Geoff and Jenny were to spend the night with us. My arrival seemed to send my family into a tizzy. Don made plans to collect my mother, who was down at the coast in her holiday trailer. He arranged for her new cottage to be cleaned, and notified the architect and his wife, who began to organize a lunch for us all. I worried about everyone going to so much trouble, since I was only able to visit for a couple of hours.

In the car to Walton, I stared out at the rain. Hyde Park was awash, but I was so lost in my own thoughts that I hardly noticed the scenery. Geoff and Jenny had slept poorly due to a storm in the night, and they had looked tired and pale as I left. Blake would be meeting with Patty when he dropped them off, which made me feel strangely anxious, though I didn't really know why—something about the past intruding on the present—and visiting Walton, with all its attendant memories, was always unsettling.

When my car pulled up to Mum's new, as yet unfurnished cottage, the familiar driveway was totally waterlogged. I picked my way across a large plank leading to the front door, rain still pouring down. Mum, Auntie, Donald and his family, my former sister-in-law Jen (Walton) Gosney, and the architect and his wife were all there to greet me.

I had expected the cottage to feel small, but it was remarkably roomy, and I liked it immediately. There was central heating, and a nice kitchen with a separate dining area.

Staring out of the French windows, I could just see the old house further up the drive, behind the trees. It was sad to see it standing in the rain, run-down and unloved. I didn't want to go near it. I knew it would be dark, cold, and filthy inside, and filled with ghosts of the past. I didn't want to see my former bedroom, or the damp lounge where I'd sat alone, practicing my singing for so many hours. I hated the thought of the overgrown orchard behind the house, the untended rose arbor, and the abandoned tennis court. Presumably the planned council housing would replace it all. At least the new cottage was warm and bright, and promised a better existence for my mother. Perhaps, once a screen of trees and a new fence were installed, she wouldn't have to be reminded of her former life.

Eventually, everyone left except for Mum, Auntie, and Jen. We stood in the empty living room. A small fire made of leftover pieces of wood burned in the fireplace—the one cheerful thing in the drab early afternoon. I longed to sit down, but there was not enough room for us all on the stairs, and the floors were muddy.

All too soon, it was time for me to leave. I could tell that my mother was near tears; it was hard to know when we'd see each other again. I sensed that although she had her brand-new house, she had not yet found a brand-new life. She was still a lost and lonely lady—more so since Pop's death. No matter how much she occupied herself with the new cottage, it wouldn't be a home until she filled it with a new history. We clasped each other, me blinking furiously. Then Mum, Auntie, and Jen drove off to have their lunch with the architect and his wife. I was much relieved that she had company.

Back at the hotel, Blake shared that the meeting with Patty had gone well, although it had been a strain. When it came time for goodbyes, Geoff had nearly broken Blake's heart by whispering, "Am I being brave, Daddy?"

I spoke of my afternoon, my impressions of my old home and family, and found myself once again fighting back tears.

An hour or so later, we headed for the airport, but

with rain delays it was one-thirty in the morning when we arrived back at Le Bristol. As we climbed into bed, Blake turned out the light. We raised up on our elbows and kissed each other.

"Good night, darling. I love you," he said.

"I love you, too," I said, settling down. Then, as wave after wave of fatigue rolled over me and the world began to fall away, I said, "God—I feel as if I've been through about nine emotional blankets this weekend! What with family and fatigue and weather, and . . . well, the whole damn thing of just being in England!"

"Oh, that's right . . ." Blake murmured sleepily. "We *were* in England, weren't we?"

Rehearsing with Dick Van Dyke at The Walt Disney Studios for the "Jolly Holiday" sequence in *Mary Poppins*. © *Disney*

Enjoying tea with Walt Disney while doing publicity for *Mary Poppins*. © *Disney*

With Tony and Emma, not long after we first arrived in Los Angeles.
Julie Andrews Family Collection

A tough day at work with James Garner filming *The Americanization of Emily. Licensed by Warner Bros. Entertainment Inc. All rights reserved.*

L to R: Me, Saul Chaplin, Robert Wise, Marc Breaux, Ted McCord, and *The Sound of Music* camera crew in Salzburg, while shooting "I Have Confidence." © *Zoë Dominic*

With my sweet von Trapp family, taking a break on location in Salzburg. *The Sound of Music* © 1965 *Twentieth Century Fox. All rights reserved.*

Between takes with Chris Plummer on *The Sound of Music* set. Duane Chase had presented me with a bunch of dandelions! © *Zoë Dominic*

It was always special when Emma came to visit me on the set each day. © *Zoë Dominic*

Having fun with my chum Carol Burnett at Lincoln Center in 1971, during taping of "Wait Till the Sun Shines Nellie." *Michael Ochs / Michael Ochs Archives / Getty Images*

Doing some sightseeing in New York City with Auntie Joan. *Julie Andrews Family Collection*

With Max von Sydow and George Roy Hill on the set of *Hawaii* in Sturbridge, Massachusetts. *Courtesy of MGM Media Licensing.*

Cutting up with Paul Newman on the set of *Torn Curtain. Courtesy of Universal Studios Licensing LLC.*

A thoroughly modern threesome: Mary Tyler Moore, me, and Carol Channing during *Thoroughly Modern Millie. Courtesy of Universal Studios Licensing LLC.*

As Pierrot, in my dressing room, waiting to be summoned to the set for *Star!* © *Zoë Dominic*

Working on the staging for "Burlington Bertie" with my beloved Michael Kidd (*Star!*). © *Zoë Dominic*

I've always loved the freedom of recording in a studio. It allows me to concentrate solely on the music and lyrics. *Michael Ochs / Michael Ochs Archives / Getty Images*

A private moment with Blake on location during *Darling Lili*. © *Zoë Dominic*

Taking Emma to visit the stables at Carton House in Ireland, happy for our umbrellas and Wellington boots. © *Zoë Dominic*

With my dear dad, on one of his visits to Carton House while we were filming *Darling Lili*.
© *Zoë Dominic*

One of my favorite photos of Blake and me, taken by my dear friend Zöe Dominic in London, circa 1976. © *Zoë Dominic*

9

OUR FILM COMPANY made an unexpected return to Ireland, to reshoot some scenes in *Darling Lili* and to capture a few new shots that had been added. It was a delight to be back at Carton, which was now in early autumn splendor.

It happened to be my birthday while we were there. I was working with Zoë most of that day in a photo shoot, and unbeknownst to me, Blake had planned a surprise party; we were to have dinner in the grand dining room with about twenty guests, mostly members of the cast and crew. Ken's wife, Kären, garlanded the marble pillars with flowers, and the long table was bedecked with silver candelabra, the finest linen, and the best china, the way it must have been in days gone by.

Blake had arranged for three different groups of musicians to entertain us: a group of minstrels wandered around the table singing old Irish ballads while we dined; a more modern band played contemporary Irish songs during dessert; and later in the evening, another ensemble played popular favorites in the library as we took coffee and occasionally sang along. It was a wonderful evening, and I so appreciated the effort it had taken to pull it all together.

Location shooting finally wrapped, and we headed back to Los Angeles. Having spent the entire summer living together, it seemed unthinkable for Blake and me to go back to our separate homes. Blake moved into my newly renovated house in Hidden Valley, and that was that.

Filming resumed at the studios, and we shot the opening song, "Whistling in the Dark." Blake's concept was to shoot the song in one complete take, which required an enormous amount of rehearsal, special lighting effects, and disciplined camera work involving focus changes and cable-pulling. I danced with the camera, moving this way and that, which required that I hit my marks exactly and lip-sync without fault from start to finish. It took the whole day, but Blake and I went home that evening feeling we had achieved something quite special together. It was a beautiful piece of filmmaking on Blake's part.

Despite the tensions with the studio with respect to budget and schedule overages, Blake and I felt good about the film. We had so enjoyed working together. We agreed that, although we would not be mutually exclusive to each other, we would try to work together as often as possible. Our newly combined family, with the children's various comings and goings and their adjustments to our shared life, was also a priority. We began to look for other projects to collaborate on.

Although my agent had been discussing other film options for me with various different studios, most of the roles offered felt too close to *Mary Poppins*, and I was keen to avoid repetition. *Chitty Chitty Bang Bang* was one example. It was to star Dick Van Dyke, and Marc Breaux and Dee Dee Wood were choreographing. Songs were being written by the Sherman Brothers. As tempting as it was to work with them all again, I felt it might seem as though I were trying to recycle my *Poppins* image, so I regretfully declined.

For some time, there had been discussion of my doing a film for MGM called *Say It with Music*, featuring the songs of Irving Berlin, but nothing had come of it. Eventually, that project was swapped out for a film adaptation of the Broadway musical *She Loves Me*, which Blake and I were excited to work on together. Blake began to take preproduction meetings.

Star! had its Hollywood premiere on Halloween,

having opened in New York the week before. Alas, when the reviews came in, they ranged from lukewarm to negative. The reception was a huge blow. Everyone who had worked so hard on the film had given their very best, and we had all enjoyed the challenge. Despite the fact that large-scale movie musicals had begun to go out of style, I think audiences were expecting another *Sound of Music*, and were disappointed that this film was more of a biopic with music, rather than a musical per se. It also seemed that contemporary American audiences had little interest in Gertrude Lawrence. Although the film did poorly at the box office, I remain proud of the work, and I'm happy to say that in the years since, audiences seem to have found it again and are appreciating it more.

I did my best to take the film's failure in stride. I knew enough to realize that nonstop success in a career is impossible—you can't stay on a pedestal forever, and from that position, there's nowhere to go but down. Nobody sets out to make a failure, but you can never guarantee success either. I hoped that *Darling Lili* might fare better.

WE OPTED TO spend the winter holidays in Gstaad once again, in the same rental chalet that we'd had the year before. We flew via New York, where

Tony took Emma back to the heart of the big city for Christmas. I held it together, but I was fairly devastated after she had gone. Geoff and Jenny were to spend Christmas with Patty, and would join us for the New Year, as would Emma. Ken and Kären were with us, as was my brother Chris, who was still struggling with sobriety but made an effort to keep it together over the holidays.

On Christmas Day, we phoned our families, and I discovered that Emma had been in bed with the flu. She didn't want to leave her dad, and begged for more time with him now that she had recovered. I was disappointed, but I agreed to allow her to stay through the end of the holiday.

Patty then suddenly postponed Geoff and Jenny's arrival by several days, and was subsequently unreachable by phone. We ultimately gathered that she had been suffering from a deep depression. This made Blake worry about the kids, but they did eventually arrive, and after an initial period of guardedness and tension, they began to settle in. They wouldn't discuss the situation at home and changed the subject whenever we tried to approach it—but they gave Blake a cassette tape recorded by Patty, filled with paranoia, angry demands, and threats.

Some outrageous and untrue articles had appeared

in various supermarket tabloids, alleging that I was neglecting Emma and that she was distraught over my relationship with Blake. One even reported that Blake and I were indulging in "threesomes" with Rock Hudson. Patty had apparently taken the press at their word. She demanded that Jenny and Geoff's visits with Blake be limited, and that he no longer phone them from our house. Blake was outraged, but after some discussion we agreed that it would be best to take no action and wait until the drama subsided, which it did.

We were able to calm the children and give them a good second Christmas. Jenny and I put on mock ballet demonstrations for the guys, and Geoff reveled in snowball fights, sledding, and snuggles. By the end of the holiday, I found myself wishing that both kids could come and live with us. They were relaxed and seemed genuinely happy in those last precious days in Gstaad, and I so wanted to preserve that for them somehow.

But Geoff and Jenny returned to London, and we returned to Los Angeles, where another vitriolic article about me awaited us. The gossip columnist Joyce Haber claimed that I was having an affair with Sidney Poitier, and that I had been persuaded to terminate it for the sake of my "image" in the South. I had only met Sidney once, when he had presented me with the Academy Award, and I was appalled by the racism implied and the falsehoods generated in this mean-spirited article.

I ended up suing the tabloids in question and was awarded retractions in the same size and type as the original articles, along with a considerable sum of money, which I donated to charity.

I wrote in my diary:

How I wish we were back in Switzerland. I know now that it is where I really want to live. There is a solidarity to those glorious mountains— they aren't going to be swayed by anyone. I feel a sense of permanence there.

I HAD PROMISED Emma that if she remained unhappy at the Lycée, she could switch schools after the New Year, and I kept my word. She began first grade at University Elementary School, now called UCLA Lab School, at the end of January. She was instantly happy there, and began having regular playdates and sleepovers with new friends. The school's research into child development and progressive teaching practices was a model for others across the country. They recommended that Emma participate in their unicycle-riding program for physical education, and she quickly became a whiz at it. She spent hours after school wheeling around the garden, a small exclamation point of balance and coordination, which delighted me.

Blake, meanwhile, was having problems with the postproduction for *Darling Lili*. Bob Evans, the head of Paramount, was furious about the budget overages. He and Blake didn't have the best relationship to begin with, and when Bob took Blake to task over the issue, Blake lost his temper and challenged Bob to "step outside." Thankfully, Bob didn't take him up on the challenge, but tensions were high, and word began to get out that the film was in trouble.

To make matters worse, we learned that Geoff was struggling at school in London. He wanted desperately to come and live with his dad. Patty surprisingly agreed to Geoff's request. I admired her at that moment; it must have been hard to let her son go.

When Geoff arrived, he was in bad shape. He suffered from nightmares and often came thundering up the stairs to our bedroom in tears in the middle of the night. We found a good therapist, whom he began to see regularly.

My brother Chris was also a worry. He was clearly still on drugs, and he wasn't seeing the therapist we had provided for him. My own therapist (it seems we had as many therapists as family members!) asked the important question, "Do you want to help him *now*, or do you want to help him in the long run?"

"The latter, of course," I replied. He counseled me to give Chris a one-month ultimatum: get clean, get a job, and continue with therapy—or move out. The month passed with no change. With a heavy heart, I sent Chris packing, and he moved in with his girlfriend.

At the beginning of the summer, Blake and I took a much-needed break and made a quick trip to Florida. A beautiful Stephens motor yacht was going for a reasonable price in Fort Lauderdale, and we wanted to take a look at it. (*Tempest* had been better suited to a bachelor than an expanding family such as ours, and Blake had sold her.) The Stephens yacht was gorgeous, and Blake bought her on the spot. I had a small panic attack about the financial implications—I had no experience with this kind of indulgence, and it felt reckless— but Blake assured me that we would make it work somehow. Aptly, we named our new acquisition *Impulse*. She needed some repairs, so we left her in Florida and made plans to come back and spend time aboard with the children later in the summer.

On August 9, life in Los Angeles took a dark and terrifying turn. News reports relayed details of the horrific murders of Sharon Tate and four others by Charles Manson and his followers. The crimes were so mind-boggling that they challenged everyone's reality. Like many others in Los Angeles that week, we installed alarms and tall gates on the property, and took pains to make sure that we were safely locked in every night.

BLAKE AND I took the children for a summer holiday on Michigan's Lake Huron, where his aunt Thyrza owned a cabin. The kids fished from the dock, or lazily reclined in the dinghy, chatting for hours or writing stories. Blake and I did a lot of cleaning at the cabin to make it habitable, and it took a toll on us both physically. Blake's back began bothering him more than usual. Because of his chronic pain from the injury sustained in his youth, he had a regular prescription for Demerol. He began self-medicating rather liberally in the evenings, which worried me. When we talked about it, he admitted to being as concerned as I was about overuse and the possibility of getting hooked.

"I'll keep an eye on it," he promised.

When we received word that *Impulse* was in

working order, we headed to Florida for the last leg of our holiday. On our first evening aboard, Blake and I sat topside, watching lightning in the sky miles away, and an orange moon—a huge half cheese rising up, with black clouds striated across it. Airplane lights dotted the sky, and warning pylons flashed red across the water. It all felt strange and beautiful.

Blake looked up at the millions of stars and said, "Now you can't tell me that there isn't a God. Why all this?" Blake wasn't a religious man, but at that moment, all of life—the water, the stars, the boat, us—felt like a miracle.

Later, I wrote:

Relief, guilt, happiness—can this last? Is it really ours? Will *Impulse* suddenly be taken away? Well, perhaps it is like buying a second home. But why me? We've certainly worked hard, but my dad worked hard all his life and never got this kind of reward. Though hopefully he'll enjoy this too, one day.

We are supremely blessed to experience a gift like *Impulse* at this stage in our lifetimes. How lovely not to have to wait until we're too old to enjoy it.

The day after we returned home, I began rehearsals for a television special with Harry Belafonte, directed by Gower Champion. Gower and his wife, Marge, were longtime friends of Blake's—so much so that they had named their youngest son after him, and we often saw them socially. Michel Legrand arranged the music for the special, and it was a pleasure working with those three talented gentlemen. From the outset, Gower wanted something fresh and different; I did some calypso with Harry, and Harry leaned into more classical songs with me. It stretched us both in new directions, and everything about it felt playful and fun. It was a pleasure to go to work every day.

GEOFF BEGAN ATTENDING a new school that fall, very near to Emma's. The school informed us that Geoff struggled with learning differences that today would be diagnosed as dyslexia, and made recommendations as to how we could best support him. We also wanted to find an extracurricular activity that he might enjoy, and we settled on karate, which Blake had studied for years. We found a young man named Tom Bleecker who began to give Geoff lessons. Tom mentioned that he knew Bruce Lee, and Blake expressed interest in meeting the legendary martial arts master. Bruce came to the house one day and gave a demonstration for us. We lunched with him, and at one point we found ourselves talking about ballet. Bruce felt that dancers could benefit from the strength training of the martial arts.

"For instance, can Nureyev do this?" he said. Bruce pushed back his chair from the table, and from a sitting position, leapt high into the air with a side kick in just one move. He was so many feet above the ground that our jaws dropped.

BLAKE BEGAN A new campaign for us to get married. Because of the craziness of our lives, and my concerns for Geoff, Jenny, and Emma, I was still having trouble committing 100 percent. It was not that I didn't love Blake—I certainly did, and I couldn't imagine being with anyone else. But there was still that certain dangerous quality about him. I was aware that he abused pain medication at times, although he seemed to be keeping it under control. He was given to making impulsive decisions, and he was often excessive with spending. He was impatient—quick to anger, even. He was creatively brilliant, with six ideas a day, it seemed, and totally charismatic . . . but he often left me a little breathless. Having been married, and feeling so responsible for that marriage's failure, I didn't want to make any more mistakes by leaping into another one.

Blake countered: What was there to lose? We were already living in the same house, we were both divorced from our former spouses, we were sharing our lives in every way. No need to worry about happily ever after—why not simply take it one day at a time? He was very persistent, and finally demanded that I make a decision one way or the other. I realized that I couldn't procrastinate any longer. We made plans to wed on November 12, 1969.

Blake and I both wanted a quiet and intimate ceremony. Thinking that the children might feel conflicted about it, and hoping to focus entirely on each other in this special moment, we made a decision to be married in our garden while the children were at school. We would tell them about it, and have a celebratory family dinner, afterward.

Present at the ceremony were Blake's new assistant, Linda; Dr. Tanney and his wife; and Ken and Kären Wales. Ken's father was a minister, and we had asked him to marry us.

Although we hired a professional photographer, we gave Herb Tanney our video camera and asked him to film the proceedings from the little hill above our back garden. We also set a video camera on a tripod at a side angle, so that if anything failed, we'd have captured something one way or another.

It was a beautiful, sunny day. The garden looked immaculate, and the hillside waterfall was splashing gently. I was trembling with nerves and excitement. The minister stood with his back to the hill, and as he began to intone the wedding vows, Blake gazed into my eyes with such genuine affection that I was moved to tears.

Afterward, Herb came down from the hill, looking at the camera. "I'm not sure I got anything . . ." he said. "All I saw was black. Did I press the right button?"

Alas, he had not. We then discovered that someone had kicked the other video camera's plug out of the wall.

Blake turned to the minister and said, "Sir, would you mind marrying us again, so we can get it on film?"

Herb scrambled back up the hill, and we replugged the other camera. This time, Blake and I were able to focus on what the minister was actually saying. As he referenced "the spherical one-ness of the ring binding these two souls together," or some such hokeyness, I could see Blake's mouth beginning to twitch, and we both fought hard to stifle the giggles.

Needless to say, Herb didn't get any footage of the second ceremony either. Somewhere there may be a video from the side angle, but as I recall, it was so bad that we never edited it. Thankfully, our professional photographer managed to capture some suitable stills.

We had a little reception afterward, and then Emma and Geoffrey came home from school. To my delight, when we broke the news to them, Geoffrey flung himself into my arms and said, "Oh, *thank* you!" Emma was quiet, but she brightened later when we took them out to celebrate at Hamburger Hamlet.

Later, I wrote of the wedding:

Afterward, there was all the difference in the world between being married and not being married. How surprising to discover that it felt so good, and to realize that just a simple signed document could make me feel that way.

Our efforts to keep the wedding private had been successful, and it wasn't until a couple of days later that the news leaked out in the press. My parents knew, of course, and were happy for me, since they adored Blake. I was grateful for the lack of fuss surrounding the event, and any lingering anxieties I had about my decision were now put to rest.

TWO DAYS AFTER we were married, Blake and I flew to Oklahoma, where *Darling Lili* was being screened for a test audience. I waited in the motel bedroom while Blake and the producers assessed the preview cards, which in those days was how one measured an audience's response. The screening seemed to go well, but in truth, I was more focused on my desire to have a moment alone with Blake—to have some semblance of a honeymoon, even if it was only for one night at a motel.

It certainly wasn't the most romantic start to a marriage, but I knew we would be heading to Gstaad in December. We would be spending the first part of our time there alone, since Geoff and Jenny would be with Patty, and Emma would be with Tony. Maybe that would feel more like a honeymoon.

By the time we arrived in Switzerland, however, Blake and I were exhausted. I came down with a cold, and our week together was a bit of a washout. In addition to wanting time with my husband, I'd hoped to get on with writing *Mandy*, and to ski—but was unable to do any of it.

Geoff and Jenny joined us two days before Christmas, as did my friend Zoë. It was so good to see her again. I suddenly realized that I didn't have a close girlfriend in Los Angeles, someone I'd known all my life and could have meaningful conversations with. My work schedule, my marriage, and my children pulled so much of my focus, I didn't have a lot of time left to devote to a social life.

Emma arrived just after Christmas, and two days later, she came down with the flu, as did Ken and Kären. We no longer had a nanny, so I did my best Florence Nightingale impression.

On New Year's Day, Blake took Jenny sledding. I went into town to do some grocery shopping, and when I returned, he greeted me at the door on crutches. Before I could say a word, he opened his robe to reveal nothing but his underwear and a plaster cast from ankle to groin. He had torn a ligament while sledding. That evening it was dinner on trays for Ken, Kären, Emma, *and* Blake.

During the night, Blake was in considerable pain and could not sleep. I heard him get up, muttering that he was going to work on his screenplay, whereupon he stubbed his toe on the edge of the bed and let fly a stream of expletives. Seconds later, I heard an almighty shriek, and shot out of bed to see what had happened. Apparently, as he sat down at his desk, he had caught a vital part of his anatomy between his plaster cast and the wooden chair. Blake asked me to fetch a bread knife from the kitchen. With some trepidation, I delivered it to him and watched in horror as he proceeded to saw away at the top of the plaster, drawing blood and cursing all the while. It was a classic black comedy scene straight out of one of his films.

The following morning, Jenny woke with a fever. Blake sat at one end of the breakfast table, his leg sticking out sideways. Kären was still coughing, and Ken had developed a cold sore and could only talk out of one side of his mouth. We then heard a mysterious swooshing sound coming from Emma. She was swilling water around her mouth to soothe a loose tooth. When I handed Geoff an effervescent vitamin C, hoping to stall the inevitable day when *he* got the flu, he lifted the glass and intoned, "Good health to everyone."

Considering how few of us were still healthy, I collapsed with laughter. Needless to say, Geoff came down with the flu the next day. Thankfully, the great Swiss air and serene environment eventually restored the balance, and the holiday ended on an up note.

Blake and I began to fantasize about moving to Switzerland. We called Guy Gadbois to discuss it further, and he broke the news to us that *Impulse's* skipper had incurred astronomical expenses on the boat's "improvements," way beyond anything we had commissioned, and had also been sweetening the pot for himself. Blake was livid; I was heartsick. Our savings had been spent on purchasing that lovely yacht, and as owners, we were now liable for every expense incurred. Blake was so angry that he opted to let the bank claim her rather than pay another dime of upkeep. I understood his decision, and realized with great sadness that we would have to let *Impulse* go. I quietly chastised myself and Blake for being such fools as to allow selfish desire, lack of knowledge, and careless supervision to get us into such trouble.

10

BACK IN LOS ANGELES, Blake and I spent the first two months of the New Year writing. He was finishing the screenplay he had started in Switzerland, a western called *Wild Rovers*. I was trying to push forward with *Mandy*. While the children were at school, we would hunker down together in the living room. I'd curl up in a chair, Blake would sit at the dining room table, and we'd work on our respective projects while enjoying each other's company. Occasionally, I would quietly observe my new husband, typing and muttering to himself, and think how handsome he was.

Neither of us was much interested in the Hollywood social scene. Our idea of a good evening was having a quiet supper at home with a few friends, or taking the kids to one of their favorite local restaurants for family night, which we did every Wednesday.

In February, we received word that the new head honcho of MGM, James Aubrey, had canceled *She Loves Me*. When new management takes over a company, anything perceived as belonging to the previous regime often goes by the wayside. I was very disappointed, as I had genuinely been looking forward to the project. Blake took it in stride, as he was immersed in writing his western.

Soon after that, Chris was admitted to the hospital. He had been high on drugs and had attempted to fly from a window, landing on a car below. Miraculously, nothing was broken, but he was pretty banged up. Since he had moved out of my house, things had gotten progressively worse. I had received a string of unexpected bills: new cameras and lenses that he had charged to me and later sold for drugs. He was busted for possession twice, and I had bailed him out both times. He often called late at night, needing money and threatening to come over to the house, and would not take no for an answer. In the interest of "tough love," I decided not to visit him in the hospital, though I did cover his medical expenses.

In an effort to follow through on my commitment to care for my mother, I suggested that she come and visit me for a few weeks. Since Pop died, her time was more her own, which made it easier for her to travel, but in some ways she had also become more reclusive. While she was in Los Angeles, I took her to the doctor and dentist, which helped restore her to some semblance of health. Needless to say, Mum was very anxious about Chris, and we discussed his situation at length. I relayed to her the advice I'd been given, and I begged her to use the same tough love with him should the need arise. I think this approach was hard for her to comprehend. Mum never had the benefit of therapy, and she wasn't given to much introspection.

I FINALLY FINISHED my first complete draft of *Mandy*. Since I had written it all longhand, I gave it to my assistant, Joan, to type up, and sent a copy to my dad, asking if he would be kind enough to give it a quick proofread for me. I received a long list of corrections from him, which taught me a great deal about grammar, punctuation, and syntax. Blake lovingly drew four illustrations for the story in black-and-white, and I presented a leather-bound copy to Jenny— thinking that I had fulfilled my promise and that would be that.

My agent asked to read the manuscript, and unbeknownst to me, he submitted it to Harper & Row. I was astonished when he told me that the legendary Ursula Nordstrom, editor in chief of the children's division, liked the story enough to acquire it. Before I knew it, I was revising and editing in accordance with Ursula's suggestions, which took another year. It was a thrilling day indeed when the book was officially published on October 28, 1971. I opted to use "Julie Edwards" as my pen name, since if it hadn't been for Blake's encouragement, I never would have written the book in the first place. I'm proud to say that *Mandy* remains in print to this day.

FAMILY DRAMAS CONTINUED to plague us, alas. Blake's ex-wife, Patty, made another attempt on her life. This time, she was in a coma for ten days, and we were told that she might not pull through.

Blake and I sat with Geoff and told him the facts as gently as we could. Of course, Geoff was completely undone. We hugged and loved him up, and waited until he was calmer. We'd been sitting on our bed, and as we got up to go downstairs, this lanky, forlorn eleven-year-old suddenly said, "Carry me?" I was touched, realizing I was being asked to stand in for the mother he was so very concerned about.

"Oh . . . all right, you great lump!" I said, "Come on!" Though he was nearly as tall as me, I somehow managed to pick him up and stagger my way down the stairs, where we collapsed in a heap of giggles, which helped.

Thankfully, Patty made a full recovery, but Blake and I worried about the long-term impact of these experiences on Geoff, and also on Jenny, who was now thirteen and still living with her mother in London. She was attending boarding school during the week, but it was traumatizing for her nonetheless.

WHEN *DARLING LILI* opened, the reviews were tepid. Blake and I were disappointed, of course, and aware that this did not bode well for either of our careers, especially mine on the heels of the failure of *Star!* The reception didn't totally surprise us, since the film had been overhyped by the studio and made to sound like a splashy musical comedy, when in fact it was simply a romantic spy story with occasional songs that extended from plot and character.

Fortunately, Blake's western, *Wild Rovers*, had been picked up by MGM, so he had another project to focus on. At this point, I made a conscious decision to take a step back from work for a while and focus on family, as well as a few humanitarian causes that were becoming important to me. One was Hathaway Home, an esteemed residential center for boys with behavioral problems; another was the Committee of Responsibility, a group that consisted of concerned citizens, surgeons, and doctors. Its objective was to rescue children severely wounded in the Vietnam War and bring them to the United States for medical treatment. All services were donated, and Blake and I were very impressed by the sterling work the organization was doing. We signed on to help promote its activities, speaking about the group whenever possible in the press and on TV.

As was now routine, Emma went off to spend part of the summer with Tony, Gen, and Bridget. Their vacation included a spell on Alderney, where they would be staying in the little cottage, "Patmos," that Tony and I had purchased so many years ago. We still owned it, as we intended to give it to Emma one day. While I hated having to say goodbye to her, it was lovely to know that she would be on that sweet island and that the cottage was being used and enjoyed.

I accompanied Blake as he scouted locations

for *Wild Rovers* in Colorado and Arizona, during which time we also went to San Francisco for a few days for a very particular reason.

In his forty-eight years, Blake had never met nor spoken to his real father. Some months earlier, he had commissioned Ken Wales to begin a search to see whether the man was still alive, and if so, where he was living. Eventually Ken traced Don Crump to an assisted living community in San Francisco. Arrangements were made for a meeting between father and son, and I went with Blake for this monumental event.

Don opened the door to greet us. It was immediately clear that he was Blake's father. He was handsome, white-haired, slim—like his brother, Blake's uncle Owen. The two men embraced each other awkwardly, and we were ushered into the modest living room. I sat discreetly to one side and chatted with Don's wife, Ruth, so that father and son could converse privately, but the emotion, the chemistry, the power of things left unsaid, was palpable.

At some point during the conversation, Blake asked his father why he hadn't stayed in touch. Don replied that Lillian's vitriol had made it difficult, and that he had not wanted to cause further emotional upheaval to his son, particularly since

Blake had a stepfather and was settled into a new way of life. It seemed like a cop-out to Blake and to me, but those were different times.

When Lillian learned of the visit, she was angry with Blake; how could he have gone behind her back after all these years? Up to this point, she had controlled the narrative concerning Don, and Blake's initiative had upset her. Perhaps she was worried that Blake would develop a relationship with Don, and that her stories about her first husband might be revealed in a different light. On the contrary, after that initial meeting Blake chose not to pursue the relationship with Don further, beyond the occasional exchanged Christmas cards. Don must have felt the same way, for he didn't push for more communication either.

When we returned to L.A., Patty and Jenny arrived for the summer. Patty rented a house, and Geoff went to spend some time with his mother there, while Jenny came to stay with us. She initially seemed fragile and forlorn, but after a few days, she rallied. I was pleased to note that our relationship was still on solid footing.

Patty, however, called three times a day. I tried hard to keep my cool and be compassionate— but her conversations with Blake were endless and all about her own problems, or her struggles with Geoff, who wanted to come home to us. He was apparently acting out, getting to bed too late, watching too much television. One day, he and Patty had a fearful row and he packed his bags, which was fuel for further calls at all hours. When Geoff returned to us, Jenny went back to Patty's rental house, whereupon the phone calls continued. Eventually, Blake persuaded Patty to take a session with his analyst, and then Blake had a session of his own about the situation. The analyst advised Blake to make a clean break from his ex— saying that it was the only way she would get on with her life. He also told Blake that Jenny was hugely envious of Geoff's living with us, which I had already sensed, and could identify with, having often felt the same way about my brother John living with our dad.

Thankfully, Emma was still away and was spared most of the drama, but I knew she would be home soon. As much as I looked forward to seeing her, I worried about her coming back into such emotional chaos.

When she returned from her holiday with Tony, she was in good shape. She had grown, and lost another tooth, which gave her an adorable lisp. She seemed to have put everything connected with her two lives and two families into perspective. I sensed that she was feeling stronger in her own identity. She had brought a present for each of us—ties for Blake and Geoff, a belt for Jenny, and a pair of knitted gloves for me. She had chosen everything herself, and I thought it dear of her to do such a generous thing.

Not long after her return, my brother Chris came over to the house with his girlfriend. I had been nervous about seeing him, since we hadn't been together in some time. He was stoned, and asked for money. Emma and Geoff were adorable during his visit, keeping up chatter, showing off our new kitten, and helping to ease the tension. Later, Emma said, with amazing perceptiveness for a seven-and-a-half-year-old, "I thought you might need some help, Mummy."

AT THE END of the summer holiday, Jenny reluctantly returned to London with Patty. After she left, I had a sweet and simple opportunity to bond with Geoffrey. His favorite toy was a stuffed "Baloo" bear, from Walt Disney's film of *The Jungle Book*. Baloo meant more to him than anything in the world, largely because Blake would sit on Geoff's bed in the evenings, when settling him to sleep, and, using a funny voice, communicate "through" the bear. Over the years, the bear's nose had worn very thin, and Geoff asked if it could be mended. Although I'm a hopeless seamstress, some instinct made me step in and volunteer to do the job. The results were well worth it. Geoff was ecstatic when he discovered his newly patched Baloo. He came running in to give me a big hug, and later told Blake that he was seriously considering calling me "Mummy." Quite a reward for the small gesture of a mended nose.

ON MY THIRTY-FIFTH BIRTHDAY, Blake and I made an offer on a new house. Much as we adored Hidden Valley, with Emma and Geoff in residence and Jenny visiting often, it had become too small for us. We also had quite a menagerie—in addition to Blake's Great Dane, we had acquired a French spaniel and, more recently, a Scottish terrier. Then there were two cats, which quickly grew to four, due to Jenny's penchant for rescuing lost creatures, plus assorted fish, hamsters, and a canary (mine!).

Blake had found a beautiful house on Copley Place, a small cul-de-sac in Beverly Hills. It was a classic Mediterranean colonial, with stucco walls, terra-cotta roof tiles, and wrought-iron railings. There was even a multilevel reflection pool overlooking the Los Angeles Country Club golf course.

We had looked at a couple of other homes, but this one had everything we needed and then some, including offices for us both. Despite the fact that it was pricier than we'd hoped, we made an offer, which was accepted, though it would be several months before we closed on the property.

In November, Blake began shooting *Wild Rovers* in Arizona. I joined him there on our first wedding anniversary. It was great fun for me to be a visitor on the set, rather than "on duty." I watched as my husband gazed through his viewfinder to establish his framing, conferred with the actors, and joked with the crew. It was obvious that he was in his element. He was in full control, but he also trusted and empowered each member of his team, which was why people loved working with him.

Every morning, I'd accompany Blake to his Monument Valley location at the crack of dawn. I had long wanted to see the site where so many famous westerns had been filmed. While Blake set up his first shot of the day, I'd hang out near the catering truck, stuffing myself with warm bacon-and-egg sandwiches, chatting with the crew, and trying not to freeze in the biting cold air. The majestic panorama was extraordinary, and I thrilled as I watched the great actor William Holden racing his horse flat out across the desert, tracked by a camera on a fast-moving mobile crane, which Blake invited me to ride.

One evening, when I was back in L.A. and Blake was still on location, he phoned me in great excitement. Earlier that day, he had shot a horse-breaking sequence in the film. He sensed that he'd captured something special by employing occasional slow motion in following the wild herd, and the breaking of Holden's feisty black mare, all set against virgin snow.

Back in LA, when it came time for this sequence to be scored, Blake called from the studio.

"Can you drop everything and come over?" he said. "I want you to share this with me."

I hurried to MGM. On a vast recording stage, Jerry Goldsmith, the film's composer, stood before a full symphony orchestra. On the giant screen behind them, the horse-breaking sequence was cued up. Goldsmith raised his baton, the click track engaged on-screen, and he gave the downbeat. Wild mustangs thundering across the snowfields; two jubilant cowboys—Holden riding the bucking bronco, Ryan O'Neal doing cartwheels in the snow; and the Copeland-esque score soaring over all combined to create a small masterpiece of a scene. To this day, I watch it whenever I can. It remains one of my favorite pieces of Blake's filmmaking.

Alas, Blake's joy in making the film was supplanted by an editing process that can only be described as madness. James Aubrey had pulled MGM back from the brink of financial collapse since his takeover, but he was widely reviled for his cruel nature and the degree to which he controlled every aspect of a creative project. In the industry, he was referred to as "the smiling cobra."

From the beginning, Blake had had no intention of writing a typical western—he wanted to turn the genre on its ear, so to speak, and do something a little different. Geoff had inspired the film, having asked his dad to write a western—and he even played a small role in it. The story centers on an aging cowboy who mentors a younger colleague, almost in father-son fashion. There is also a secondary storyline about a ranch owner and his two very different sons, who compete for their father's attention.

I consider *Wild Rovers* to be the first of several films of Blake's that are particularly revealing of his character. The dialogue is often introspective, reflecting many of his philosophies of life—such as seizing the moment, rooting for the underdog, and having a conscience. It may also have been an attempt on his part to better understand fatherhood, since he'd never had a father of his own, or much of a mentor in his stepfather.

During postproduction, Aubrey turned Blake inside out and upside down in his attempts to force him to cut the film to his liking. Blake was riddled with anger and indecision. In those days, he didn't have "final cut"—the last word as to what ends up on-screen. He tried to compromise with Aubrey's demands, allowing one deletion in order to keep another scene he felt was essential.

Watching my husband go through these emotional contortions was agony. He would come home and tell me what Aubrey had insisted on, then brainstorm aloud as to what he could do to preserve the original intention of his movie. The final blow was when Aubrey cut a pivotal scene that changed the entire theme of the film, reducing Blake's intended Greek tragedy to a mere "cops and robbers" premise.

WILD ROVERS OPENED in America with Aubrey's ruinous cut, and it failed. Blake was devastated. His beloved baby had been butchered, both physically and by the press, and the entire experience challenged his reality. He took a nosedive into depression.

Surprisingly, Aubrey offered Blake an apology, along with another film, *The Carey Treatment*, as a sort of "consolation prize." For reasons I can only guess at, Blake took the bait. Perhaps there was some compulsion on his part to make things right, or perhaps he simply wanted to finally win out against the man who had caused him such pain. In any case, he plunged into writing and preproduction for the next film.

Around this time, we moved out of our beloved Hidden Valley house and into the one on Copley Place. I had mixed feelings: we couldn't really afford the upgrade, and things were further complicated by my having recently received an offer to do a television series for ABC to be made in England.

The night before the move, I went to check on the children in bed. Emma and Geoff were tucked in tight in their empty rooms—all pictures and toys having been packed for the morning. I prayed that Blake and I could see this time through for the children in a positive way. My familiar feelings of separation anxiety bubbled up as I remembered when my own parents moved to the Old Meuse; how scared I had been of a new bedroom, and the barn owl outside my window in the silver birch tree. I worried that the children wouldn't love the new house as much as the current one—then I realized that it was actually me who was afraid of that, and projecting it onto our kids.

Once the new house became ours, we made it our own and loved it. We restored it to its former glory by stripping away tacky wallpaper and linoleum to reveal lovely old murals and handmade tiles. Blake engraved a heart with our initials on a big tree in the courtyard. I began a tradition of gathering the family—and anyone else in the house—for English tea each afternoon, in the pretty conservatory overlooking the garden, which everyone seemed to enjoy.

Not long after we moved in, we were invited to a party at the home of a very powerful Hollywood agent. I can't remember why we chose to attend; we were so seldom partygoers. When we arrived at the house, we were confronted by a classic "scene" for those days, but one that I had yet to witness. A group of guests were doing lines of coke in the sunken living room. During dinner, the coke was passed around as dessert. When it was offered to Blake and me, we both declined.

The hosts began pushing me hard, curious to see how "Mary Poppins" would react. The peer pressure was intense.

Blake came to my aid. "She doesn't need any of that stuff," he said. "She's high enough on life as it is."

Mercifully, they backed down. When we left, there were bodies on the floor, leaning against the wall, totally wasted.

Back at home, I stood at my open kitchen window and looked out across the golf course, trying to make some sense of the surreal experience. Suddenly all the sprinklers came on. As they arced over the greens in the starry night, I felt the coolness of the air and smelled the water on the earth. It brought me back to reality and restored my equilibrium.

TROUBLE WITH MY brother Chris erupted once again.

He had married his girlfriend, and she had given birth to a baby daughter. Not long afterward, he was busted for selling drugs and went to jail, pending trial.

I had recently chanced to meet a California judge. I happened to mention that my brother was having problems, and he said, "If it ever gets out of hand, call me." In desperation, I took advantage of the judge's kind offer. He said he knew the justice who would be presiding over Chris's case, and would ask the court to consider deportation rather than a fifteen-year jail sentence. Chris was deported two weeks later, taking his wife and baby with him. I felt some relief that he was back in England, but also guilt that my mum was now saddled with his problems.

AT THE BEGINNING of the summer, Carol Burnett and I began rehearsals for another special together, this one to take place at New York's Lincoln Center. It had been almost ten years since our previous special, and we had always wanted to do another. In fact, we'd hoped to do a whole series of them—but we had both been rather busy. Carol was now doing her very popular television series, and we hadn't seen much of each other beyond the occasional family dinner. Happily, ours was a friendship that always seemed to pick up where it had left off.

For this special, we did a long medley of popular songs from the sixties, and a silly homage to Martha Graham. We ended the show with something we'd always wanted to do: a rousing version of "Wait Till the Sun Shines Nellie," dressed in sou'westers, hats, and rain boots. We taped three complete shows back to back in one day, enjoying every minute—and it rained, much to Carol's delight.

When the special was done, Blake and I traveled with the kids to Europe, where they would be joining their other parents for summer vacation.

The scene at the London airport resembled a Noël Coward farce. Patty brought Jenny, who brought her dog to show Blake. Tony, Gen, and Bridget were also there, to meet Emma. There was a confusion of kisses and cars, gifts and greetings; definitely messy, and no one knew what the hell anyone else was doing.

We spent the week in London, during which I visited my family in Walton. Blake came to fetch me one afternoon. I showed him my mother's new cottage, and despite my misgivings about seeing it again, I also took him over to the Old Meuse, wanting to give him a glimpse of my childhood. We wandered through waist-high weeds where once there had been a wide and generous path to the empty house, which was still standing.

Everything was damp and covered with dust. Blake saw my old bedroom, the kitchen, and the music room, and we went into the garage that had once been my aunt's dance studio. It was still

filled with memorabilia, including an old traveling trunk of mine and a wartime rationing card.
Blake didn't say much, but I was grateful that he
was with me, to keep me rooted in the present
and remind me how very far I'd come since those
early days.

After we said goodbye to my family, Blake took
me to dinner at Hampton Court. We wandered at
dusk in the gardens of the palace and looked at the
glorious Long Water, the fountains and avenues
and beautiful flowers. The Thames was running
high by the towpath just beyond the boundary
wall. Blessed river; it still holds such fascination
for me.

Emma stayed on in London with her dad, who
was designing Ken Russell's film version of *The Boy
Friend*. Geoff was with his mother and Jenny for
a spell, so Blake and I traveled on to Switzerland.
It was high summer in Gstaad, and very hot. The
grasses were green and lush, and geraniums and
petunias spilled out of every window box.

There was a tacit understanding between us that
we hoped to find our own chalet. I was concerned
about the expense, and said as much to Blake.

"Imagine what and who that money could help,"
I said.

"And we do help, and we will again, hon," he

replied. "But that shouldn't prevent us from enjoying ourselves as well."

Despite my concerns about whether we could, or should, afford it, I have to admit I was a willing co-conspirator with Blake when it came to things that we both wanted. Plus, as long as there was work on the horizon, we felt we could somehow justify it.

Seeing Gstaad in the summer confirmed our love for the place. But our real estate agent said there was nothing on the market, with the exception of "one unfinished chalet on the wrong side of the tracks, far from the chic side of town." "Unfinished" and "far from chic" was music to our ears, and we asked to see it.

It was owned by a tiny, eccentric English lady. With fluttering eyelashes, she informed Blake that her reason for selling was that she had to move to a lower elevation due to asthma arising from "a disappointment in love."

The chalet didn't have much land, but it had a magnificent view on all sides, and best of all, an unfinished third floor that offered us the chance to design it to our taste. We made an offer on the spot.

Wanting more time to ourselves, we decided to travel back to the U.S. by sea. I was feeling a real reluctance to go home, to return to all the responsibilities of work, children, and a household. I ached to hold on to the feelings of escape, of being alone with Blake, of peace and reflection.

We flew to Paris for one night and stayed at the Hôtel Le Bristol, where we had been based during *Darling Lili* three years before. The same familiar doorman was there to greet us. Smiling broadly, he exclaimed, "Ah! The couple who kissed in the rain!"

The next day, we boarded the *Queen Elizabeth II* at Le Havre. It was my first ocean crossing, and I was ecstatic. We had a beautiful suite with a balcony, and an attentive steward who brought us breakfast every morning.

We had both intended to write on the journey. Blake spent most of the day curled up in his bathrobe, absorbed in another screenplay, but it was taking me longer to get started. Before moving to the Copley house, I had stumbled upon an idea for another children's book. I had been looking in a thesaurus and had discovered a list of mythical creatures that I had never heard of. They had fantastical names, like Gyascutus, Sidewinder, and Swamp Gaboon. One word in particular jumped out at me: Whangdoodle.

Looking it up, I discovered the definition to

be "a humorous, mythical creature of fanciful and undefined nature."

"Well, I can define it!" I thought. "I'm going to write a book called *The Last of the Really Great Whangdoodles*."

Until this point, however, I had not put pen to paper. But I had been thinking about it, and I had a vague idea of my outline. I finally began scribbling.

Each day on the *QEII*, Blake and I worked side by side, partook of a late lunch, then read each other what we had written thus far. We took naps, then walked around the ship's perimeter in the fresh sea air, had dinner, and tumbled into bed.

Blake had said that on our last evening, he would take me to the casino. He saved it until the end of our cruise, knowing that with his addictive personality, if he visited any earlier, he might gamble away every penny we had. I had never gambled before, so Blake took me to the craps table, and showed me how to play. I won a little money, and immediately set half aside for housekeeping funds, which made him chuckle.

"The whole point of gambling is to take a risk," he said. "Play it again! Bet it all!" He goaded and encouraged my every throw, whipping me into a frenzy of enthusiasm, and I kept winning. At bedtime, I was so wired that I couldn't sleep. While my husband was serenely out for the count, I lay with eyes wide open, heart racing, adrenaline pumping. I haven't gambled since—but the details of that night, the colorful, spinning wheel, the dice clattering into place, and most of all, Blake's wicked delight, remain as vivid to me now as they were then.

11

Blake traveled to Boston in late August to begin work on *The Carey Treatment*. The film was to star James Coburn and Jennifer O'Neill. Blake had also cast his daughter, Jenny, now fourteen, in a good supporting role.

I joined him as quickly as I could, sensing that trouble with James Aubrey was already afoot. Aubrey had shortened the film's production schedule, and had begun editing footage while shooting was still under way.

One evening, Aubrey's producer and right-hand man tried to introduce Jenny to cocaine. When Blake found out, he went off the rails. I had never seen him so angry. He paced up and down our hotel suite, venting his desperation, then went to the window and pounded his fists against it so hard that I feared he would break the glass and throw himself out. While he raged, I sat in the middle of the bed, wondering what to do. Some instinct made me realize that Blake needed to work it out himself. I stayed very quiet, simply being present, and he finally calmed down.

The following day, guys from the Teamsters union knocked on the door to our suite.

"We hear you're having some problems, boss. Want us to deal with it?" they asked. Blake told me it was a tempting invitation, but something made him say, "Thank you . . . but no."

Time and again, Blake tried to ease himself out of his contract with MGM.

"I've gotta get away from Hollywood," he said to me. "The studio system is so corrupt." His agents and lawyers advised him to hold on, hold out, but the stress took a serious toll. It even landed him in the hospital for a weekend.

In the end, Blake didn't participate in editing the film, knowing that Aubrey would have butchered it anyway. He even requested that MGM remove his name from the project, but the request was denied.

One evening at dusk, he was driving home from Beverly Hills, thinking about Aubrey and deeply preoccupied, when a jogger appeared. Blake swerved, missing him by inches. Glancing in his rearview mirror, he realized that the jogger was in fact James Aubrey. Afterward, Blake said that had he hit Aubrey, no one would have believed it was an accident. The near miss shook him to the core.

MY HUSBAND BEGAN self-medicating again. From late in the afternoon onward, he became more and more emotionally unavailable, making conversation difficult. He was often unapproachable when writing—the whole family recognized when he was preoccupied with a new screenplay—but this was different. I agonized as to whether and how to confront him. God knows what I was so afraid of—did I doubt my instincts? I certainly had no knowledge of what resources existed at the time, such as twelve-step or other treatment programs, or even what to ask of him in that respect.

Finally, during a quiet moment, I said, "Blake—there's something we need to discuss." I conveyed my concern about his drug use, and what toll it might ultimately take on our marriage and our children. To my surprise, he did not disagree. He vowed once again to cut back, and seemed for a while to do so.

THE INVITATION TO do a television series for ABC was still on the table, but the filming location had now transitioned from London to Los Angeles. The offer had come from Sir Lew Grade, who had been my agent during the vaudeville years, but was now a prominent television producer, working both in

England and the States. I hadn't had much luck with television in the past, and I didn't relish the long commitment of a series. It was to be twenty-three shows per year, with a guarantee that Sir Lew would produce a film of Blake's—which hopefully I would participate in—for each year the series was on the air. It was a very good deal, and we needed the money, but I worried about being unavailable to the kids for such an extended time.

I wrote:

There is so much that is still unresolved. Should I accept the television show? Will Blake's work on *The Carey Treatment* be totally wasted or will he salvage some dignity for himself? Will next year bring much-needed finances for either of us? Will we make it to Gstaad at Christmas? I don't know, but I do know this: that whatever happens, I want to experience it beside my husband.

We did make it to Gstaad. Ken and Kären traveled with us; the children would be following in a few days' time, giving us a chance to prepare the new chalet for everyone to move into.

We stayed at our previous rental for the first week, but made a beeline for our new chalet the moment we arrived. We opened all the shutters and let the sunlight flood in. The wooden floors gave out a warm yellow glow. A musty smell emanated from the bathrooms, and there were dead flies lying around. Nevertheless, we planned to move in, camping-style, as soon as possible. It said much about lovely Gstaad that we were so happy to be there.

We rented a VW bus, and began stocking our new home. We bought a refrigerator and a vacuum cleaner, and a local friend lent us a dining table and chairs, along with a huge old sideboard. We put up beds and took dustcovers off some old chairs that had been left in the house. We ordered carpets and bought lamps and bedside tables. We tried to keep expenses down, but it seemed there were so many little things we needed. Thankfully, I had brought linens, crockery, and cutlery from the States.

One day, I spotted a young man and woman walking up the small valley in front of our chalet. They introduced themselves as brother and sister, Gottfried and Annemarie Von Siebenthal, who lived across the way. Their family owned the local home-and-hardware store in town, and they wished to welcome us to the village. Their ancestry dated back to the 1100s, making theirs among the oldest and most distinguished families in town. Little could I guess that the family would become our most enduring friends in Gstaad.

I wrote:

I swear the people here have some secret to life. I envy them. I'd like to know the country the way they do. To be strong, physically, to be in tune with one's body. Oh, for a year to get in shape here. To write—or sing—daily, rather than just grabbing time when possible.

My sorrow is that I don't know if I'll ever have the guts to take that precious time. Life passes by so quickly—there is so much to be done. I feel that the past two years have been good for me. There has been reflection, and a deliberate focus on family, but no professional work. Now I feel almost ready to contribute again.

The TV situation is something I churn over in my guts daily. It would certainly force me to be creative and practice and keep in shape. And it will bring us the money we need to help pay for the chalet and the house in L.A. But a TV series will take me away from the real things I yearn for—nature, the children, writing. I must somehow make it a means to an end.

The kids arrived, and were in good form. They took daily skiing lessons and pitched in at the new chalet. One day, Blake and I decided to try cross-country skiing. The clothing required light jackets and bloomers, ending at the knees, with long socks and square-toed shoes. We dressed in identical navy-blue outfits, feeling ridiculous.

We set off in our car, one snow-chain loose and clanking away. I looked down at my lap and suddenly said to Blake, "Do your trousers have flies?"

"No . . ."

"Well, mine do!"

We swapped trousers while still in the car.

Another day, I went downhill skiing. There was a perfect moment when Emma, a red-clad demon on the snow, caught up with me halfway down the mountain. I heard her whistling and calling, and saw her cheerful face, smiling and shouting encouragement. As I continued to plow laboriously down the hill, she danced along beside me like a busy gnat on the surface of a river. For five perfect seconds, we skied together in harmony; true happiness for us both.

Real life kept interfering, however. Jenny went back to her mother in London, and the television show kept rearing its head. I worried about the short amount of rehearsal and taping time allocated—

only a week per hour-long episode. What would happen to the children? My writing? What if other creative projects were offered?

Blake gave me good advice. "Look, honey, here's the bottom line. You haven't made a film in two years. I've always said, when in doubt, play your best hand. Right now, your best hand is television. They want you very much, and they're willing to pay you well. If you choose to do the series, I'll stay home and write, and look after the kids. We'll reverse roles."

His words encouraged me to finally commit to the series, a variety show to be called *The Julie Andrews Hour*. Two American producers flew in to Gstaad for three days to have meetings about it all.

I wrote:

When they read me the press release for the show, it was a shock. It is happening. I just wish it could be done without all the ballyhoo and pre-publicity. With such a build-up, it seems the risk of failure looms large.

I looked about the sweet chalet today, trying to impress the view on my mind. At least this is something solid and real and worth working hard for.

Blake began painting, usually a very good sign. But these subjects were slightly scary to me; they were surrealistic creatures, a combination of circus animals and prehistoric monsters, against a Dada-esque landscape. I suggested that he was painting out his demons from the past months, and he agreed.

I spent the last days in Gstaad getting back to work on my *Whangdoodle* book. I read chapters to the children. There were many questions from them, much imagining and wondering, and eagerness for me to hurry up and finish. What a compliment!

We decided to travel back to L.A. via London, so that in addition to having more meetings about the television show, I would have a chance to see my family. As we left our chalet, a wonderful thing happened. Standing by the farm in the snow next to our house were two chimney sweeps, with long wire brushes coiled in a ring on their shoulders, old-fashioned stovepipe trousers, and peaked caps.

I said to Blake, "*That* is a good omen."

I'm not usually superstitious, but chimney sweeps have always been considered a symbol of good luck in England, as a certain song lyric in *Mary Poppins* will attest. I hoped it was a positive sign.

IN LONDON, BLAKE and I met with Sir Lew Grade about the TV series, and discussed what our subsequent first movie might be.

Sir Lew bubbled with enthusiasm—he was in love with life, his wife, his job. But he was also yearning for knowledge of the movie business. He and Blake swapped ideas, and got on like a house on fire. It was a tremendous relief, and Blake became steadily more enthusiastic.

When we got back to the hotel, we met up with my dad, Win, my stepsister Shad, and my brother John. We all had dinner together, talking and laughing through every course. It was a memorable evening, made all the more so by the fact that Blake was in great form, too.

The following night, we did the same thing with the other side of my family. Although Mum and Auntie were, as usual, uptight with each other, the dinner went almost as well. Two rare and successful events with my family, back to back.

Just as Mum and Auntie were leaving, Mum thrust six somewhat crumpled new handkerchiefs into my hand, in an embarrassed sort of way, and wouldn't listen to my thanks. I realized she must have waited all evening for that one private moment to give them to me. I became teary with some emotion I couldn't explain. The fact that she had gone to the trouble of purchasing a small gift for me—something she so seldom did—and that she had shopped for and chosen handkerchiefs, moved me deeply. It was a quick gesture of love, and we so rarely shared that kind of intimacy.

On the flight back to L.A., I wrote:

We are not excited about going home. So much hard work awaits us there. It's going to be a difficult year—a very difficult one. I'll be working non-stop, and not spending as much time with the children or Blake as I'd like. Now, one starts to pay the price for all "goodies" received by signing the TV contract.

If we slip back into all the drama of last year, or allow the stress level to get to us again, it will be a terrible shame. It was such a good holiday—and I feel as if I've emerged from it fresh and new-born. Somehow, Blake and I must preserve that feeling.

It had taken me almost two years to make up my mind to do the television series. Initially, Blake's and my role-swapping made me anxious. As I headed out the door for work, I'd say, "Now, remember, Geoff's got a dentist appointment today, and Emma gets picked up at three . . ."

"Relax, honey," Blake would reply. "It's all taken care of."

In the evening, I would come home exhausted and say, "Let me tell you about my hard day at work."

He'd say, "Let me tell you about *your* kids and what they got up to."

The truth is, the house had never been better run. But Blake was also trying to write, and he did eventually need some help with the chores. So, in mid-February, an eighteen-year-old Irish lad whom we had never met came to live with us.

Young Tony Adams had originally come over to the States as a tutor for the children of John Boorman, who was directing the film *Deliverance* with Burt Reynolds. When filming was completed, Burt employed Tony at his ranch. Blake and I had dinner with Burt one evening, and when we mentioned that we were looking for someone, he recommended Tony. We hired him sight unseen.

Tony arrived at the Copley house two days shy of his nineteenth birthday. He was a raw country lad with a thick Irish brogue and bad teeth, but he quickly proved to be invaluable. He drove the kids to and from school and various appointments, went shopping, took care of the cars, and did household chores. Geoffrey was initially wary of him, but Emma took to him immediately, and he soon became a member of the family.

Two weeks after Tony arrived, Blake had his wisdom teeth pulled. The dentist said to him, "Be careful not to get a dry socket." Of course, Blake promptly got a dry socket, and was in excruciating pain. I was discovering that in addition to being a hypochondriac, my new husband was inclined to develop any ailment suggested to him.

MY TV SHOW was to be taped at the ABC facilities at Prospect and Talmadge, a run-down neighborhood in Los Feliz, just east of Hollywood, about an hour from home. Scenic construction began, writers were hired, and we held daily script and production meetings, all under the loving guidance of our producer, Nick Vanoff. During this pre-production period, I tried to keep some mornings free for writing *Whangdoodles*, knowing that once taping for the series officially began, I would be too busy to continue.

Blake suggested we make a small documentary about preparing for the series, to air just before its launch. We shot it at a shabby but comfortable beach house situated on the bluffs in Malibu that we had rented for the summer.

"If you're going to work this hard, you're going to

need somewhere to crash on the weekends," Blake had said. The house soon became a godsend as our daily pressures escalated.

In July, Jenny came to live with us permanently. Blake and I had been growing increasingly anxious about her, since her life in London had deteriorated to an almost Dickensian level. Patty agreed that Jenny would be happier living in Los Angeles, with more stability. Adjustments had to be made to every aspect of our lives; a school needed to be found for her, space in our home allocated, and Geoff and Emma had to adapt to her being with us full-time, as did I. I quickly learned that being a stepmother takes a lot of patience and maturity. I had to allow for the time and attention my stepchildren needed from their dad, and also understand his guilts and his need to make up for lost time with them. Both kids tested Blake and me, and poor Emma was often the "odd man out." I hoped that she had the emotional foundation to know that my heart was with her, even though my attentions were sometimes elsewhere. Fortunately, she hero-worshiped Jenny, who was six years older, which helped.

One day, when I was passing Emma's room, the door was open, and she was standing in front of her full-length mirror, with both hands on her flat, nine-year-old chest. Unaware that I was watching, she viewed herself right and left, then declared quietly, "Hah! Coming along *just* fine!" I found it adorable, and Emma and I often quote that phrase to this day.

I HAD BEEN thinking about a theme song for my series, and I'd come up with a little melody that I hoped might work. My friend Leslie Bricusse was in town, and I dared to ask him to listen to it and perhaps write a lyric. He showed up a day later with a gentleman named Ian Fraser—a musical director, conductor, and arranger who had worked with Leslie for many years. Ian played piano, and Leslie sang the lyric he had magically written overnight. My song sounded a million times better with Leslie's lyric and Ian's talented arrangement. I instantly wished that Ian could be part of the series, but alas, he was heading to New York to work on a Broadway show.

Shooting for *The Julie Andrews Hour* began in early September. We had a phenomenal creative team—wonderful writers, and the great Nelson Riddle and his orchestra supporting me onstage. Nelson was widely renowned in the industry for his work with Frank Sinatra, Ella Fitzgerald, Nat King Cole, and Judy Garland, to name just a few. His agreeing to do my show was a gift, and I relished working with him. I was also blessed to have a truly stellar lineup of guests: Steve Lawrence and Eydie Gormé, "Mama Cass" Elliot, Donald O'Connor, Sammy Davis Jr., Jimmy Stewart, Henry Mancini, and Peggy Lee, among many others. Rich Little and Alice Ghostley were regulars.

The schedule, however, was grueling. We had merely five days to complete each episode. On Mondays, we had a script read-through, and set the songs so they could be immediately orchestrated by Nelson. On Tuesdays, we learned the dance moves with our choreographer, Tony Charmoli, and staged the comedy sketches. Wednesdays were devoted to rehearsal, and prerecording in the evenings. Thursdays were spent marking everything in the studio to be ready for Friday's taping. That last day usually began at the crack of dawn, and went into the wee hours of Saturday morning. Every three or four weeks, we were given a week off from shooting, during which time there were more production meetings and wardrobe fittings in order to try to stay ahead of ourselves.

The rented beach house was my salvation. We spent every weekend we could there. Blake painted in an outside studio that faced the ocean, and I pressed ahead with *Whangdoodles*. We took long walks, and had cookouts on the beach. Emma made friends with the children next door. They had horses, and she frequently rode bareback with them across the sand and surf. The house was old and scruffy, but indestructible—which was great with three kids. We fell in love with the area; the perfect combination of sea and countryside.

But mostly, I worked. It quickly became obvious to Nelson and to me that the amount of music each show required was overwhelming, and we had too little time to do it justice. With wall-to-wall music in every episode, we were both floundering. Miraculously, I received word that Ian Fraser's Broadway show had not materialized, and he was able to come aboard to assist with the orchestral layouts and arrangements. The difference was palpable to everyone. Ian and I became close friends. More than that, he quickly became my most trusted musical advisor.

Every episode of the series was more like an hour-long "special"—one that would normally take six weeks or more to shoot. But we did have fun, in spite of the hard work. Ian made me try things musically that I never thought I could accomplish, and I attempted a number of other things I hadn't tried before, with varying degrees of success—roller-skating, performing Shakespeare, doing imitations, all in a supportive, nurturing environment under the leadership of our excellent director, Bill Davis.

Now that I was "back in circulation," so to speak, I began to have some challenges with enthusiastic fans. They followed my car when I was dropping the kids off at school, or when I drove to private appointments, such as sessions with my analyst.

One evening, the family and I were at dinner when I saw a pale face among the bushes in our back garden.

"There's someone out there," I gasped. Blake went to check and confronted a timid and morti-fied young lady, who had merely wanted a glimpse of what our family life was like after hours. I found it difficult to balance my appreciation for the fans' affection and loyalty, which was always so generously given, with my natural desire to maintain a modicum of privacy and to protect my family.

THANKS TO THE weekends at the beach house, I finally finished the first draft of *The Last of the Really Great Whangdoodles*. There was still a lot of correcting to do, but the bulk of the work was done, and Harper & Row had agreed to publish it, as they had *Mandy*. Every member of the family presented me with a rose, and Emma made a drawing for me, all of which touched me deeply.

I sent the manuscript to my dad, asking if he would pass his eye over it, as he had for my first book. He returned it to me with suggested corrections that amounted to half as many words as I had written for the entire manuscript. I was initially disappointed that he had found so much fault with my writing—but then I realized what a supremely generous and loving gesture it had been to take the care and time to so improve my literary efforts.

Work on the series continued apace, and there were decisions to be made regarding the film that Blake and I were scheduled to make for Sir Lew the following year, during the hiatus from the TV show. It was to be a romantic thriller called *The Tamarind Seed*, and Blake had adapted the screenplay from a novel by Evelyn Anthony. We were to film in Europe and the Caribbean, which fit in nicely with Blake's growing disenchantment with Hollywood—but not with my obligation to the series, which had a possible option for a second season.

In addition, Blake began to complain about my working such long hours. One morning I got home at 6 a.m.; another morning at 4. Blake accused me of staying late out of perfectionism, but with working those hours, I was more focused on survival than perfection. I was deeply hurt. How could I abandon the work before it was finished? I longed to be home as much as he wanted me there, and I felt miserably torn between my professional and familial obligations. I reminded him that he had encouraged me to do the series in the first place, and that we were in this together. It didn't help much. I guess he hadn't fully considered how much of my time would be consumed by this work.

Finally, the pressure became too much, and I blew my stack. I said to Blake and my agents that I wanted out of the commitment; doing the series wasn't worth the stress. Of course, it was impossible to quit—I was under contract, and in truth it would have gone against my nature to do so.

I wrote in my diary:

I am longing to take a break from the television show. We are planning a brief Christmas in Gstaad in our newly-renovated chalet, and in the spring, after the last eight episodes are in the can, there is the film to be made. If the series is not renewed, will we move to Europe permanently? I wonder.

As I predicted, it has been a terribly tough year.

The day before we left for Gstaad, I worked at the studio from 8:30 a.m. to 6 a.m. the following morning. I ached in every bone.

Although the chalet was still in a state of renovation, it was heavenly to be there, and I soon rallied. On New Year's Day, Blake and I took a walk, and talked about the year ahead; about being apart while I taped the last eight episodes of the series in L.A. and he prepped the film in England. As always, I felt depressed at the prospect of leaving Switzerland.

I STRUGGLED THROUGH the last of the TV shows. We still had the rented beach house for the weekends, and the kids and I tried to make our days there cheerful, but I missed Blake terribly.

On the last day of taping, there was a wrap party. Nick Vanoff screened irreverent outtakes, and Ian and Nelson presented me with a private album of my solo songs from the show.

The Julie Andrews Hour was nominated for ten Emmy Awards and won seven, but it was not picked up for a second season. The general feeling was that one had to "put on a suit and tie" to watch the show, which didn't garner us a mass audience. I've never been more relieved.

Fortunately, Sir Lew Grade still wanted to

continue our collaboration. In lieu of doing another season of the series, he offered Blake and me six television specials, to be shot at his studios in London. Because of our contractual terms—one film per year that we worked for him—this would guarantee us at least one more movie after *The Tamarind Seed* concluded. I wasn't consciously choosing to work exclusively with Blake, but this was such a convenient and lucrative contract . . . and it kept our whole family together, which we greatly appreciated.

SINCE WE WERE now going to be in England for at least a year, we rented out the Copley house with an option to buy. I organized the packing of books, files, clothes, toys—trying to be ruthless about what to give away and what to keep in storage. Thank God for Tony Adams, who was a tower of strength throughout the process and kept us all in good spirits with his great sense of humor.

Meanwhile, in London, Blake moved into a service flat on Upper Grosvenor Street, directly across from the American Embassy, and began preproduction for *The Tamarind Seed*.

The week before I was to join Blake was madness. I made arrangements for all our animals to be re-homed. Emma and Jenny were both sick, and

I discovered that Geoff, now thirteen, had been smoking pot, and had to confront him about it.

Geoff and Jenny would be finishing their terms at school and spending some time with Patty, who, ironically, had moved back to Los Angeles to be closer to them. They were to join us in Europe in a few months' time. We made plans to hire a summer tutor for Emma, who would be accompanying me, so that she could catch up with the schooling she would miss due to our travels.

Jenny had her sixteenth birthday just days before our departure. It was our last weekend at the beach house. We decorated the place in yellow and white, with big baskets of daisies. Blake flew in as a surprise, and Jenny screamed with delight and burst into tears of joy at the sight of him. She had sixteen guests, and everyone had a grand time. It was a lovely farewell to a great home.

12

THE FIRST THING I noticed upon arrival in London was the daffodils in Hyde Park—hundreds of them, cheery and bright. But the apartment that Blake had rented was unbelievably small. Once Emma and I arrived, it was bursting at the seams with our personal belongings, office supplies, and more. The ceilings were low, and the place was always filled with people—Tony Adams assisting Blake with preproduction, drivers waiting in the kitchen, Blake's secretary working in the dining area. There were endless phone calls and doorbells. Emma was a ten-year-old angel. One day she made sixteen cups of tea for various visitors and production staff. We mostly took meals at home, just the three of us, in the kitchen late at night.

I wrote:

I am so torn between countries, times, emotions, memories. This next project will be a way station—we're on our way to something; to new feelings, new thoughts. I liken us to pilgrims, crossing the water, beginning anew. It will be good for us, shake us up. But I feel a bit useless here. The past year required that I give out so much of myself, and now I'm a little lost.

Blake was dashing around, scouting locations and seeing to all the business of *The Tamarind Seed*. We did makeup and hair tests, and I met Omar Sharif, with whom I would be costarring. I liked him immediately—he seemed gentle and fun.

Finally, we departed for Barbados, where we would be living and filming for the month of May. The Caribbean island was hot, and *very* humid, but quite beautiful. We stayed in an exotic beach house that was almost entirely open to the elements, with few walls or windows. Bougainvillea climbed the trees, and bizarre-looking cacti were grafted onto the trunks. The beach was pristine, and the ocean beyond it a clear aquamarine blue. During our first weeks there, we swam every morning. We dined in the lovely outdoor dining area and watched beautiful birds with odd-sounding names. Emma did her best to adjust to a new place, a new schedule, and her new tutor, though I sensed that she was beginning to feel the strain of so much traveling and so many moves. Blake set up the production offices and prepared for filming to begin.

On our first day of shooting, I developed a sunburn, as did several other members of our company. It was clear that filming in the Caribbean was going to pose a challenge in terms of keeping freckles at bay and looking cool and graceful on-screen.

That said, it was very pleasant to be working with Blake again. He was always at his best on a film set, and he was clearly enjoying the experience of working with a British crew. He seemed very much at ease, tending to each day's work in baggy shorts and a big sun hat. For me, the more leisurely pace of making a film was a welcome change after the rush and compromise of the TV show.

Omar was easy to work with, although he had a rather endearing, almost Inspector Clouseau–like clumsiness. Being a chain smoker, he often dropped ash on my costumes, and once he accidentally stood on the hem of my dress and tore it. But none of that mattered, because of his charm.

One evening, we were filming a fairly intimate scene, and we heard a loud "clackety-clackety-clack."

"Cut!" Blake yelled.

Giant crabs, the size of dinner plates, were

scuttling up from the beach by the dozens, their pincers held aggressively aloft. They climbed walls and trees, and the crew had to use brooms to sweep them out of range of the camera.

"Everybody wants to be in show biz!" Blake joked. Crab-management became standard procedure during night shoots.

When I wasn't filming, I continued to work my way through my dad's copious notes for *Whangdoodles*. Blake generously offered to help, and we spent most evenings and every Sunday working together on the final revisions for the manuscript.

LOCATION SHOOTING FOR *The Tamarind Seed* moved to Paris, and we found ourselves back at our beloved Hôtel Le Bristol. By now, Emma had finished her work with her tutor, and had pulled up to grade level, but I was still concerned about her. She seemed to be a mess of nerves, and was frequently queasy and anxious. As she was about to head off to her dad for the last two months of summer, I tried to spend as much time with her as I could, taking her on excursions in Paris—shopping, sightseeing, visiting museums. I loved spending time with her, and in spite of all the upheaval in our lives, I sensed that she felt the same way. By the time she left for New York, she seemed more like her old self.

Geoff, however, had joined us in Barbados and was a worry. He was just thirteen, but he was now six-foot-one, and had started drinking and smoking. It's hard to do much finger-wagging when you're looking up at someone and he is looking down at you. Like most teenagers, he was moody: one day he wanted to return to L.A., the next, he changed his mind. I suspected that the same things that had been bothering Emma were bothering him: our moves, the upheavals, the prospect of a new school. Finally, Blake gave Geoff a job as a gofer on the film, which was a good idea. Geoff embraced the hard labor, and enjoyed working alongside the crew and being "one of the guys."

TONY ADAMS HAD been scouting somewhere else for us to live in London, and finally found what appeared to be a nice townhouse in Chester Square. Once we moved in, however, it turned out to be anything but. On our first night there, we had no curtains and no running water. The following morning, within five minutes of the water being fixed, a pipe burst and our kitchen became a swimming pool, with a little fountain spraying out of the cutlery drawer and a big one coming from behind the refrigerator.

Tony converted the basement of the new house

into a room for himself and a giant office. One morning, he didn't appear for breakfast, and we went down to check on him. Thank God we did; the pilot light in the old water heater had gone out, and carbon monoxide had been leaking into Tony's room. Seeing that he was unconscious from the fumes, we quickly called a doctor, and moved him to a different location, where he soon recovered.

We acquired a black Scottish terrier named Haggis, an Abyssinian cat, and a canary. Despite my best efforts and those of everyone else, Haggis never became house-trained, and she relieved herself everywhere. Somehow, in the midst of this chaos, I rehearsed and recorded a Christmas album with Ian. Though incongruous to be singing Christmas songs in August, it was lovely to be working with a full orchestra again, and Ian's arrangements were beautiful. I've always had a fondness for Christmas music, especially my dad's favorite carol—"In the Bleak Midwinter."

There's a tradition among orchestral musicians that after a piece concludes, if they like what a soloist has done, they tap their music stands with their bows or the floor with their feet. I could sense when we began recording that the London studio orchestra musicians we were working with were curious as to how Hollywood might have affected me, or whether I could still cut the mustard vocally. It made me very proud to receive that special tapping accolade after I'd sung something they appreciated. As always, it was a pleasure working with Ian. By now we had developed such an easy rapport—almost a communion of sorts. Whatever vocal choices I made, he was right there with me musically. Sometimes, when we'd completed a song, we'd share a smile of mutual respect and admiration, and no words were needed.

WHEN *THE TAMARIND SEED* finally wrapped, Geoff, Tony, Blake, and I escaped to Gstaad, where we spent the better part of August. Jenny joined us there. I reveled in the smell of hay, the flowers, the clouds tumbling over the mountaintops, the sound of cowbells in the fields. I loved walking out on the balcony first thing in the morning, taking great lungfuls of fresh air, and watching the crows fly home to roost in the evenings. It felt like paradise.

BLAKE AND I began to talk about having a child together. Up to this point, our relationship had been consumed by work and making a combined family of our existing children. Now, with nearly four years of marriage behind us, and the prospect of a new life in Europe together, it seemed the right moment to consider growing our family. I was soon to be thirty-eight, and Blake was fifty-one, so we knew time was of the essence.

We fantasized what a child of ours might look like. Blake joked, "With our luck, it'll have my bat-wing ears and your bandy legs!"

"We'll love it anyway," I countered.

Our existing children, meanwhile, were still adapting to our relocation. Jenny returned to Patty in Los Angeles after her summer holiday in order to graduate from the high school she had been attending there. Geoff and Emma were to attend the American School in London in the fall.

ONCE BACK IN London, looping, dubbing, and scoring began on *The Tamarind Seed*. I saw a rough cut of the film, and was struck yet again by the three separate aspects of my husband's talent—writing, directing, and editing. He always claimed he was a writer first and foremost, but when directing or editing his work, he had no problem "killing his darlings." His editing for *The Tamarind Seed* was tight, stylish, and enhanced the complicated story. It seemed that the break from Hollywood had done him good.

Emma and Geoff started school, and Emma

made friends with an American girl her age who lived on the opposite side of Chester Square. The two spent many happy evenings playing together in the central fenced-in garden. Then, to Emma's great delight, Tony, Gen, and Bridget came to live in London for several months, while Tony worked on Sidney Lumet's film adaptation of *Murder on the Orient Express*. Bridget enrolled in Emma's class at the American School. It was the first time Emma had had her entire family in the same city for any length of time. She began to spend weeknights with Blake and me, and weekends with the other side of her family. She was the happiest I'd seen her in a while. Geoff was finding the rigors of the new school challenging, but he, too, made friends and enjoyed being in the school play.

I FILMED THE first two of the British TV specials for Sir Lew almost back to back: *Julie on Sesame Street*, with Perry Como and the Muppets, and *Julie's Christmas Special*, with Peggy Lee and Peter Ustinov.

During the taping of the Christmas special, Blake went back to L.A. for two weeks on business, and the exact date of his return to London kept changing. One day, I was standing in mounds of fake snow singing "Hark! The Herald Angels Sing" when I suddenly spotted him behind the camera. I was in the middle of a take, and unsure what to do. I longed to hug him, but didn't want to break the shot, which was going well. I teared up; he teared up. When I finished the song, I ran into his arms with such force that I just about knocked him flat.

BETWEEN THE TWO specials, I gave a concert at the Royal Albert Hall with André Previn conducting the London Symphony Orchestra and the London Symphony Chorus. The program was entirely Christmas music, and André combined orchestrations from an album we'd made together years ago and my more recent one with Ian Fraser. The concert felt very important to me, because I'd never sung with the London Symphony before, nor appeared at Albert Hall. I was very nervous and I wanted to sing better than I ever had before. I had been vocalizing daily throughout my time in Gstaad to get in shape, and André and I worked hard in the weeks leading up to the concert itself.

On performance day, we rehearsed in the huge hall, which seats more than five thousand. The Symphony Chorus was in attendance, and it is almost impossible to describe my thrill in hearing their massed voices, about one hundred and fifty of them in all. At times, they sang in the quietest whisper; at other times, they expanded into full-throated glory. Singing with so many consummate musicians, one cannot help but strive to be better than one's best. Once I was onstage among them, my nerves were replaced by intense concentration and the sheer pleasure of singing with such an esteemed orchestra and choir.

We finished the concert with André's arrangement of "Jingle Bells," which at one point required me to sing in 4/4 time while the accompaniment was in 6/8—something I had seldom attempted. I ended the song by climbing to a high, quiet note, which I sustained for as long as possible. It was followed by a decisive closing chord from the orchestra, and the sold-out audience gave it a rousing ovation. I felt it was one of the best evenings of song that I'd ever given.

THE CHILDREN WERE to spend the first part of the winter holidays with their other parents, so we invited the grandparents to join us in Gstaad: Blake's mother and stepfather, my dad and Win, and Blake's sweet aged aunt Thyrza. Hilarious scenes ensued.

"Okay, everybody, into the car!" we'd yell, followed by slow-motion shuffles that took forever.

At one point, when Thyrza was taking an especially long time, my dad teased, "For God's sake, Thyrza, stop leaping about!"

There was competition between the older men. They bickered over the chocolate dish, each blaming the other when it was empty. But they also swam together in the local public pool, and generally enjoyed themselves and each other.

In the New Year, we headed back to London to tape the next television special, *Julie and Dick at Covent Garden*, which brought Dick Van Dyke and me back together for the first time since *Mary Poppins*. Carl Reiner was to costar, and Blake directed this special. Working with Dick again was lovely, and we fell back into an easy rapport. However, the underlying concept for the show was ill-conceived and the production was fraught with problems, not the least of which were union issues having to do with Blake being American. The end result was disappointing, and we got less than stellar reviews.

SADLY, BLAKE AND I were having no luck conceiving a baby. After five months of temperature-taking and dashed hopes, I threw the thermometer away. We knew that André Previn and his new wife, Mia Farrow, had recently adopted a daughter from Vietnam, and we began discussing the possibility of adoption ourselves. Mia told us what an easy process it had been for them, and how quickly they had received their child. We would have welcomed a child from anywhere in the world, but André and Mia's experience felt propitious. I drafted a letter to their contact in Saigon, conveying our interest.

By now, Blake was busy writing the second film for Sir Lew, a remake of a charming movie originally called *Rachel and the Stranger*, which had starred William Holden and Loretta Young, and in which I would play a leading role. He was also in discussions for a possible television series based on the *Pink Panther* films. In addition, we were in preproduction for the fourth and final special for Sir Lew, *Julie and Jackie: How Sweet It Is*, starring Jackie Gleason.

The house was full of children and production staff, all needing answers, and our business manager was urging us to pare back on expenses. Blake's employment status was suddenly in jeopardy due to the new Labour government changing its position on noncitizens working in the UK. Americans were fleeing the country left and right, and we were warned that we, too, might have to leave England temporarily, at least until the new fiscal year began.

Blake began to work himself into a state about all

this. His back was bothering him, and the tension made us both so ratty that I finally snapped. For only the second time in our marriage—the first being my attempt to cancel the TV series—I threw down the gauntlet.

"This madness has to stop!" I said. "I don't want to do this film. I want to move to Gstaad as we planned. We *have* to simplify our lives!"

Blake looked at me for a beat.

"You're right," he said. Then, in typical fashion, he turned on a dime. "I have an idea. Don't do a thing until I get back. I need to see Sir Lew."

While he was gone, Ian came over to rehearse songs with me. I was still in a frazzled state when the doorbell rang. I flung it open testily, only to discover a lady from the adoption agency, who had arrived unannounced to screen us as prospective parents. It was my turn to do an about-face.

"Oh! *Do* come in, how lovely that you're here!" I gushed with as much charm as I could muster.

I made cups of tea and chatted nonstop, trying desperately to convey how well run my house was and what good parents we would be. I must have gotten away with it, for she seemed fairly satisfied when she left.

When Blake returned, he was grinning like the Cheshire cat.

"You're off the hook!" he said. "Sir Lew wasn't thrilled with *Rachel* anyway, so I told him I could persuade you to forgo it. I pitched a new *Pink Panther* film instead of the TV series. We're going into production immediately."

This was not exactly what I'd had in mind. Although I was grateful to be relieved of my obligation, I had been hoping that we'd move to Gstaad for a time of peace and quiet and reassessment. I did know, however, that we badly needed the financial boost. So the London house remained home base, and the chaos escalated.

Per the new government regulations, we did leave the country for a few days, and for a couple of weeks after that we were not allowed an "official" residence in London. Jenny was visiting, so we moved into a hotel with fifty suitcases, three children, and the canary. Emma went to the Hampstead Heath Fair with her dad and returned with a bowlful of goldfish. Blake began writing the screenplay for *The Return of the Pink Panther*, which would star Peter Sellers, as had the original film. Tony Adams was promoted to associate producer.

Finally, we were given permission to move back to the depressing Chester Square house. Since our lease was ending soon, we decided to search for a

more suitable place to live once Blake's film concluded shooting in September.

The basement became a production office once
again. Haggis the dog had been with the vet for
house-training, and she returned, only to desecrate
the carpet immediately. Because the dog was back,
the cat developed nervous gastroenteritis. I began
rehearsals and taping for the last television special,
while Blake cast his film, traveled to France to scout
locations, and took endless production meetings—
during which time he also came down with a
cold and broke his toe. So much for simplifying
our lives.

IN THE MIDDLE of all this madness, we received
some exciting news: we had been approved as
adoptive parents by the orphanage in Vietnam. I
was beyond thrilled; our baby would be arriving in
a few months' time!

When we broke the news to the children, they
were mostly generous in their support, although
Emma, not yet twelve, was a little anxious about
the prospect of having yet another sibling. It occurred to me that it might help for her to meet the
Previns' daughter, Lark. Mia and André very kindly
agreed to a visit at their home in the country
village of Leigh.

I picked Emma up early from school. In the car on the way to the Previns' house, she was irritable, saying she thought the day would be a waste of time. But within an hour of our arrival, she was helping to make Lark a snack and pushing her around in the pram. I was greatly relieved. The following day, Blake and I settled on the name "Amy Leigh" for our new daughter. (In her mid-teens, however, Amy decided she preferred to be called Amelia, which she has been called ever since.)

Our elation was short-lived, for word arrived from Saigon that little Amelia had contracted viral pneumonia and was in an oxygen tent. We were warned that she might not survive, and that even if she did pull through, her arrival would be delayed until she was well enough to travel. After yearning for this baby for so long, it was unimaginable that we might lose her, and with the war still escalating, we couldn't fly to Vietnam to visit her. We felt so helpless, and so very far away. Blake suggested that the entire family focus healing energy in Amelia's direction. She was in our thoughts, day and night.

A week later, Blake, Emma, Geoff, and I traveled to Casablanca. The new *Panther* film was to be shot on location there, as well as in Marrakech, France, and Switzerland.

Casablanca in 1974 was not as I'd imagined. No Bogart, no Bergman—nothing romantic at all, in fact. Every time we ate a meal, we prayed that the dreaded "tourista" would pass us by, but members of the film company began to drop like ninepins, including Geoff, and of course, Blake. Somehow, I avoided the worst of it, mostly by eating yogurt, bananas, and peanut butter for weeks on end. Emma escaped it altogether by leaving to spend the rest of the summer with Tony, Gen, and Bridget on Long Island.

Marrakech was more lush and pleasant, although it was difficult to reconcile the incredible wealth on display in our hotel with the extreme poverty outside. The heat was tremendous, and filming was slow and arduous, particularly when a huge sandstorm brought everything to a halt.

While the company was in Marrakech, I traveled to New York and Washington, DC, for three days to do publicity for *The Last of the Really Great Whangdoodles*, which had finally been published. The initial reviews were not entirely favorable, but happily the book developed a good word-of-mouth following, and went into subsequent printings. Since its main theme is the power of the imagination, I had made a conscious decision not to have the book illustrated, in the hopes that readers would use their own imaginations to conjure the Whangdoodle and all the other fantastical creatures for themselves. I am always moved when I receive letters from children with marvelous renderings of the characters, or maps of Whangdoodleland that have been class projects.

At last, it was time for Blake's film company to move on to Switzerland. They would be shooting in Gstaad for a week, and it was heavenly to be there again. Blake and Peter Sellers were having a ball, often reducing each other to helpless giggles over the scenes they were creating together.

The final leg of location shooting was in Nice, France. While I hated to leave Gstaad, I could not have anticipated the lovely month that lay in store. The film called for a few scenes to be shot aboard a yacht, the *Hidalgo*, and Blake had decided we should stay on board in lieu of a hotel. I felt guilty about the fact that my husband had to work so hard every day while I lounged about, but I sensed he was not unhappy. *The Tamarind Seed* had opened to mixed reviews, but they were favorable enough to ensure a decent run, and the *Panther* film was progressing well. The work was stimulating, and the weather was excellent, which kept the company on schedule. I finally had all the rest and peace of mind I had ever wanted, and I wallowed in it.

In the evenings, we motored out to the little bay of Villefranche, and enjoyed being gently rocked on the after-dinner journey back to Nice. My dad and Win joined us for eight days, and we made an overnight trip to Corsica, engaging in long philosophical discussions on the way. They took walks, wrote postcards, and swam daily. One afternoon, the motorized dinghy we used to get to shore wouldn't start, so Dad and our captain rowed to the harbor to collect Blake. I was reminded of the days when Dad took Johnny and me rowing on the Thames, and it was grand to see him in such good form.

To our immense relief, we received word that little Amelia's health was improving, though it would still be a while before she would be well enough to travel. Blake also received a telegram from Jennifer, revealing that she was in a serious relationship with Tom Bleecker, the man who had been Geoff's karate teacher and had subsequently worked as Blake's personal assistant. The relationship between Blake and Tom had not ended well, and this new situation with Jennifer worried Blake dreadfully, especially given that Jenny was only seventeen and Tom was eleven years her senior. Blake asked Jenny to come to Nice so they could discuss the matter in person. When she arrived, she was initially defensive, but eventually, with what we sensed might be some relief, she promised she would wait at least a year before moving in with, or marrying, Tom.

When shooting in Nice wrapped, we returned to London. Our search for a better house had resulted in our renting another one in Chester Square—smaller than the one we'd been living in, but clean, bright, and cheerful. Blake resumed filming at the studio, and I set about organizing the monumental move from one side of the square to the other. When all the furniture had been transferred, Blake took Haggis across to the new place, while I went through every room in the empty house for one final check.

As I rounded the last flight of stairs, I found a surprise on the landing: a substantial pile of dog poop, sporting a toothpick with a paper flag. Upon it was written, "Have a nice trip!"

13

LITTLE AMELIA WAS finally deemed able to travel. Her visa application was filed, a Vietnamese passport granted, and it seemed she could be with us within a couple of weeks. I could barely contain my excitement. I set about shopping for baby furniture and equipment, and began to interview nannies, quickly settling on a lovely woman from South Africa by the name of Avril. She had been a professional nurse, and was warm and easygoing.

Emma came back from her summer vacation in relatively good form, although the transition home after having spent time with her dad was always emotional for her. She liked the new house, and busied herself with helping me and Avril set up the nursery.

I was at the hairdresser when I received word to call our lawyer immediately—it was urgent. I knew it must be about Amelia, and my heart skipped a beat.

"She'll be here the day after tomorrow," he declared.

I phoned Blake immediately, but he had already heard the news, and was as thrilled as I was.

There was so much to do that I almost came to a standstill, until I began making lists. More shopping for baby gear, along with a fold-away bed for the nurse who would be bringing her from Saigon and staying with us for a few days. Avril moved in, with diapers and baby food in tow. Furniture was delivered and installed, baby clothes unpacked and laundered, and everything was made ready for the new arrival.

On August 3, 1974, I wrote:

Up at 6:30. Quick breakfast, hug and kiss to Blackie. Everyone excited. Tony and I headed to airport. Plane delayed into Paris, and Amelia and nurse had missed the connection. Orly airport supposedly in chaos. Where could they be? And on what flight?

Went to Air France lounge. Found out that baby and nurse might be on a British Airways flight already arrived. Then "Message for Mrs. Blake Edwards!" was announced on the PA system, and suddenly there they were!

Amelia is adorable. Big smiles for me, and I

fell in love at first sight. She is so pretty. Huge eyes and a watchful gaze. Susan, the nurse, so dedicated, so tired. All the way from Saigon. A miracle.

Blake came home early, and Amelia smiled for him too. We propped her up against pillows on our couch, and she was so tiny that she almost disappeared but for those wide, watchful eyes. Em and Geoff so interested, observing Amelia and asking questions. Avril taking charge of her domain on the top floor. Pediatrician came by and pronounced Amelia OK, though with a bad case of scabies and serious congestion in her chest and nose.

Special moment at bedtime tonight, hugging Blake, both of us knowing our little one was finally safe and asleep upstairs. Happy day.

Two nights later, Blake came down with acute appendicitis. Tony Adams and I took him to St. Mary's Hospital, where we were met by an ancient Harley Street surgeon with an unsettling tremor in his hands. Surgery was scheduled immediately, whereupon the whole scene took on the black humor of a Blake Edwards movie. The anesthetist was called in and the operating room prepared— everyone seeming a little boozy from dinner. Blake was dosed up with Valium, and Tony and I followed his gurney down endless sloping hallways, while he yelled, "Gung ho, Ben Casey!"

The cart rattled around corners, in and out of elevators, and nearly got away from the attendant altogether. It finally shot through the rubberized operating room doors and came to rest amid a pile of cardboard supply boxes.

Apparently, the operation had been very necessary, as Blake's appendix was on the verge of rupturing. But I couldn't help thinking how Freudian it was for Blake to have "labored" with such intense stomach pains and endured abdominal surgery a mere two days after our new baby had arrived.

I spent Amelia's first days with us dashing between home and the hospital, and totally lost my voice in the process. Amelia needed X-rays and blood tests, which Avril took charge of. Tony Adams did his best to manage the press, who had heard of Amelia's arrival and kept ringing our doorbell. Everyone coped as best they could with the myriad emotions of having a new baby in the house and Blake being in the hospital.

My husband finally came home five days later, on the same evening that President Nixon resigned from office in the wake of the Watergate scandal. Sitting in London and watching Nixon's bizarre resignation

Giving Jenny her first copy of *Mandy*, the book I wrote for her. *Wally Fong/Shutterstock.com*

Taking a walk through the snow on our first visit to Gstaad, Switzerland. © *Zoë Dominic*

With Jenny and Geoff in Gstaad, reenacting *Sleeping Beauty* in our long johns! *Julie Andrews Family Collection*

Getting a bear hug from Geoff in Gstaad. *Julie Andrews Family Collection*

Blake's and my wedding in the garden of the Hidden Valley house, November 12, 1969. *Julie Andrews Family Collection*

Rehearsing with André Previn for the Christmas Concert at the Albert Hall in London, 1973. © *Zoë Dominic*

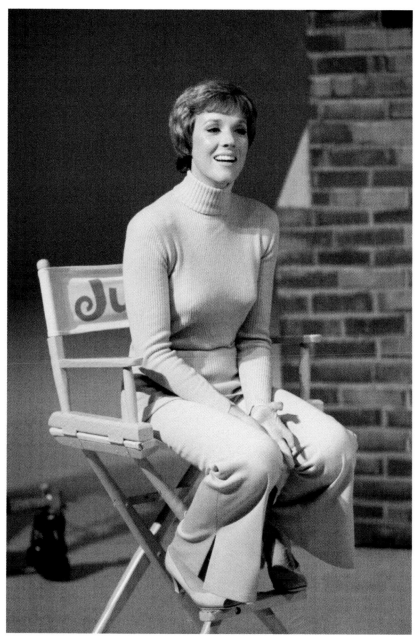

On the set of *The Julie Andrews Hour*, my television series. © *American Broadcast Companies, Inc. All rights reserved.*

Relaxing with the brilliant and adorable Dudley Moore while filming *10*.
© *Zoë Dominic*

With Omar Sharif and Blake on location in Barbados for *The Tamarind Seed*. © *John Jay / mptvimages.com*

Theadora Van Runkle's famous red dress in *S.O.B.* Licensed by *Warner Bros. Entertainment Inc. All Rights reserved*.

Riding a golf cart to the studio commissary with Richard Mulligan and Blake during
S.O.B. Julie Andrews Family Collection

Performing at the Budokan arena in Tokyo, Japan, 1977. © *Zoë Dominic*

Playing with Amelia on our balcony in Switzerland. *Julie Andrews Family Collection*

Cuddling Joanna by the beach in Malibu. *Julie Andrews Family Collection*

Making friends on the street in Saigon (Ho Chi Minh City), Vietnam, while traveling with Operation California, now known as Operation USA. *Julie Andrews Family Collection*

With Blake in my "Victoria" costume on the set of *Victor/Victoria* at Pinewood Studios in London. © *Zoë Dominic*

As "Victor," with James Garner, just before the first kiss in *Victor/Victoria*. Licensed by Warner Bros. Entertainment Inc. All rights reserved.

Me and the other "guys"—Robert Preston, Tony Adams, and Blake—on the set of *Victor/Victoria*. Licensed by Warner Bros. Entertainment Inc. All rights reserved.

A family portrait we took as a birthday gift for Blake. Standing, L to R: Amelia, Geoff, Emma. Seated on the grass, L to R: Joanna, Jennifer. *Julie Andrews Family Collection*

Our *That's Life!* family, L to R: Jenny, Jack Lemmon, me, Emma, Chris Lemmon.
Julie Andrews Family Collection

Loving the music while in performance at the London Palladium, 1976. © *Zoë Dominic*

speech, followed by the swearing in of President Ford, was surreal. With all the drama in our lives and in the news, it seemed to me that the world had gone quite mad. I wondered what the future held in store for our newest family member.

BLAKE AND I had another series of long discussions about the advisability of moving to Gstaad sooner rather than later; of "holing up" there, so to speak, to gather our resources—physical, emotional, and financial. Our business manager and lawyers had been advising us to establish official residency in Switzerland, as it could significantly ease our complicated visa and tax issues. Since most of our work seemed now to be based in Europe, and given that Blake and I had long fantasized about living in Gstaad, it seemed the right thing to do. Blake still had editing to complete on the *Panther* film, so we debated whether to move right away, or wait until Christmas to do so. Relocating before the holidays meant he would need to commute, yet it didn't make sense to have the children start the fall term at school, only to uproot them again. So, toward the end of August, as Blake headed back to work at the studios, I began organizing a move to Gstaad for Avril, the children, and myself. I hoped it would be the haven of peace and quiet we needed, and that it would provide Amelia with a healthy beginning to her life with us. Since Switzerland was only an hour's flight from London, Blake promised to join us most weekends.

Living in Gstaad, however, required securing additional rooms for our entourage, including the tutor who would soon be joining us to homeschool Geoffrey, since the town lacked an English-speaking high school that could accommodate his needs. Luckily, a tiny chalet across the road from ours was available for rent. When the tutor arrived, she set up one of the rooms as their classroom, and Geoff seemed to welcome the discipline and security of working with her.

Happily, there was a small international elementary and middle school for Emma in the neighboring village of Saanen. It was run by a Canadian family, had a fine reputation, and classes were held in English. The school day was unusually long, however—from eight in the morning until five-thirty in the afternoon—and I worried whether Emma would have the necessary endurance. She was nervous, but within a few days, she was gamely walking down the hill in the mornings to greet the school bus.

Emma was also increasingly tender with Amelia, and I recognized the generosity of heart it must have taken for her to embrace so many big changes in our lives. I found myself surrendering to the joy and happiness of being focused almost exclusively on my children, and of living in Switzerland at long last, with no departure date in sight.

Blake, on the other hand, was not as happy with the new arrangements. He was still experiencing physical discomfort post-surgery, and traveling back and forth between Gstaad and London wasn't as easy as we'd hoped. There were constant business calls whenever he was home, and he was often tired and grumpy. I prayed things would settle down soon, and that he would eventually come to feel the same way I did about living there.

Thankfully, Amelia was adjusting nicely. Her lungs and skin had cleared, and she was putting on weight. On arrival, although she was five months old, she had barely weighed ten pounds, but within a month or two of good nutrition, hygiene, and love, she had begun to blossom. At times she giggled and chatted; at other times she was silent and serene, albeit with that ever-watchful gaze.

I began to notice, however, that she seemed reluctant to truly bond. Whenever I held or attempted to cuddle her, she arched her back and pulled away. She also had a habit of banging her head against her mattress rhythmically to self-soothe, especially when trying to sleep. I reached out to our pediatrician, and to Susan, the nurse who had brought Amelia to us, and learned that this was fairly typical behavior for a child adopted from an orphanage.

"You have to realize," Susan said, "that at any given moment there were at least a hundred children in one room, half of whom were wet, hungry, and crying. The distraction is intense, and head-banging is the baby's way of trying to carve out her own identity, to establish her sense of self in that chaotic space."

It helped a great deal to know this, and I began to realize that Amelia's reluctance to bond stemmed from an understandable lack of trust. I eventually found other ways to comfort her; stroking her back, or rubbing her little feet.

Once Blake's editing on the *Panther* film was complete, he joined us in Gstaad for an extended period. During this time, he was able to reflect on all that had happened in the previous months; the crises of *Wild Rovers* and *The Carey Treatment*, the relocation to England and our crazy existence there, and now this latest move to Switzerland. He began to channel his feelings into a screenplay set in Hollywood, which was clearly cathartic for him. He called the project *S.O.B.*—short for "Standard Operational Bullshit." I could hear him clacking away on the typewriter in the attic, chuckling and mumbling lines of dialogue. When he came downstairs for meals, he seemed highly pleased with himself and couldn't wait to get back to it.

I was, as always, astonished by his facility when writing. I doubt he would have called it that—but to me, ideas seemed to just pour out of him. When I asked him how he did it, he said, "I go down many avenues in my mind. I follow an idea and try to top it, and top it again, until I can't go any further. Then I see if there's an alternative idea. Eventually the best one takes over." He always felt that he could tell a better story through comedy; he could reach the audience with a dark or meaningful theme that they didn't initially recognize because they were laughing so hard. He also said that sometimes he felt he had a muse on his shoulder, who told him what to write. I related to that, having often had a similar feeling myself when in need of guidance.

Ever mercurial, Blake didn't settle into one mood for long. We learned that Jennifer had not kept the promise she'd made in France, and had moved in with Tom Bleecker in L.A. The news hit Blake hard, since it meant he would have to withdraw financial support, as he had warned her that he would. He felt as though he'd gained one daughter but lost his firstborn, and he was such an emotional basket case that he developed chest pains and went to see the local doctor. Blake knew they were probably psychosomatic—and mercifully, they were—but I was grateful that he checked.

I accompanied him to London for a few days to see a rough cut of *The Return of the Pink Panther*. Even in its unfinished form, the film was hilarious, and I dared to hope that it could be very successful.

Returning to Gstaad, I was overwhelmed by the happy feeling of coming home. Emma, however, seemed a little "off"—she was tearful and anxious. I feared that, despite her affection for Amelia, the baby had been taking a little too much of our focus, and that perhaps my being away had left her feeling a bit neglected.

The following day, Emma came home from school looking flushed and sporting a golf-ball–sized lump on one side of her neck. It turned out she had mononucleosis. She was confined to bed with a high fever for several weeks, during which time she became horribly depressed. I read *Jane Eyre* aloud to her, and brought her games, coloring books, and other activities—but mostly she just wanted to sleep. Being a nurse, Avril was a huge help, giving Emma alcohol rubs to bring down her fevers.

One evening, Emma's new teacher from school came to visit her and have dinner with us. My heart melted as I watched Emma prepare for her guest. She sat up in bed, swollen and pale, with a clean nightgown, hair brushed, hands folded on her lap, and the most wonderful look of expectancy on her face. I was so grateful for the kindness of the teacher in paying such close personal attention to her new student.

Geoff, however, was no longer enjoying being in Gstaad. He asked if he could return to California and attend school there, now that he was fifteen. This was quite a blow. Blake and I said we would give it some thought, and in the ensuing days, found ourselves in tense conversations. Then Blake suddenly claimed that he himself felt claustrophobic living in Gstaad, and out of touch with the rest of the world. He said he couldn't work or paint—and yet, daily, I saw so much evidence to the contrary. I knew him well enough by now to recognize how much he thrived on change and stimulation. When I asked him what he would like to do about it, he didn't seem to have any answers, other than "Well, *you* wanted to live here!"

Each time Blake sounded off about his distress, it seemed to relieve the pressure somewhat and he would improve for a few days. I came to realize that he needed to vent regularly, to manage the emotional chaos he always carried inside him, which had been inflamed by the various challenges with our three older children, the arrival of our new baby, our many moves, and the pressures of his work. I soldiered on, trying to stay in the day and hoping against hope that he would one day come to feel the way I did about being based in Switzerland. Little did I know what a logistical and financial challenge our Swiss residency would ultimately become, especially since it required that at least one of us spend an extended amount of time there per year, and limited time elsewhere. Had I been able to see into the future, I might have tried to find a different solution. But we were committed, so I focused on being grateful for every moment in that beautiful haven.

When Emma was well enough, she began attending school again, but she wasn't yet herself. She was anxious, and seesawed between anger and depression, frequently complaining of headaches and queasiness, and talking about wanting to go and live with her dad in New York. Given all the recent changes, I could hardly blame her, but I tried my best to stand still about it, and I asked her to do the same. I had always suspected that there might come a day when she would wish to go live with Tony. Being the child of divorced parents myself, I understood only too well. I just prayed that she wouldn't have to spread her wings too soon.

THE HOLIDAYS CAME and went, and in early 1975, we turned our attention to the next television special for Sir Lew, to be called *Julie: My Favourite Things*. Blake was to direct, and we began coming up with ideas based on that title. The Muppets were to be my special guests.

We shot in February, at Elstree Studios in London. Emma stayed in Gstaad for the first two weeks with Avril, Amelia, and Geoff; but unbeknownst to me, Blake had arranged for a surprise visit. I was shooting a scene in front of a giant jar of peanut butter—definitely one of my favorite things!— when suddenly, my adorable daughter emerged from behind it, riding her unicycle. She circled me once, waved, and cycled offstage. I was simply thrilled to see her, and she stayed with me until taping for the show was complete.

We spent a delightful day filming at the estate of the great artist Sir Henry Moore. I have always adored his beautiful sculptures, and Blake had asked him whether we might borrow one as a set piece for me to sing to. Sir Henry was reluctant to send a piece out to Elstree, and suggested instead that we come and film at his estate in Hertfordshire.

I will never forget shaking Sir Henry's hand as I greeted him. He was a diminutive man, yet his gentle strength made me wish my hand could have rested in his, safe from the problems of the world, forever. He took us around his property, showing us the giant studios in which he worked; one for stone, one for wood, and one for clay. There was also a library that housed his lithographs. Sir Henry invited us to tea in his cottage, and I noticed that in the center of his coffee table there was a large bowl overflowing with oddly shaped objects: stones, fossils, bones.

"People send me things from all over the world," Sir Henry explained. "I use them as inspiration for my work."

The plan was for me to sing Harold Arlen's "Out of This World," while gazing at a massive Moore sculpture in the Sheep Meadow on his property. It took Blake forever to choose his setup, since every angle was so superb. Although the scene was unfortunately cut from the final televised special—it seems I have too many favorite things!—that day has stayed with me. Thankfully, I received a copy of the scene on tape, which I cherish.

NOT LONG AFTER Amelia came into our lives, Blake and I had discussed the fact that it might be good for her to have a sibling from Vietnam, but we had decided to wait at least a year or two. The situation in Saigon was becoming increasingly urgent, however, as the Viet Cong had pushed further south and were now threatening to overwhelm the capital. We realized we had to act sooner rather than later. I wrote another letter to the orphanage, to convey our interest in adopting a second child. This time we received an almost immediate response that we should gather our documents as quickly as possible.

When I mentioned it to Emma, she didn't seem surprised. "Oh, all right," she sighed. "As long as I don't have to babysit."

We had always wanted Amelia to be an American citizen, and we had recently received word that her California adoption papers were ready; the first step in that process. Blake and I traveled with the family back to Los Angeles, dropping Emma off in New York to visit Tony for the Easter break. We took a bungalow at the Beverly Hills Hotel.

Within a few days, Saigon came under direct attack. President Ford announced that the U.S. government would evacuate orphans on military aircraft in a series of flights that became known as

"Operation Babylift." On the first mission, there was a devastating crash shortly after takeoff that killed 138 people, including 78 children. We were horrified to learn that babies and caregivers from Amelia's orphanage had been on board, and we feared that Susan MacDonald, the lovely lady who had brought Amelia to us, had been killed. Mercifully, we caught a glimpse of her on the news.

We cabled our contacts in Saigon, and five days later received word that our new baby was in fact already in the U.S., having come in on a subsequent airlift with more than three hundred other babies, all on one visa. We were asked to wait twelve hours or so until all children had been accounted for. Mia and André were also adopting another baby at the same time, and the agency then asked if we could possibly take care of their child for a few days, since the Previns were still in England and their travel visas had not yet been processed. We agreed to do so.

On April 11, 1975, Joanna Lynne Edwards joined our family.

I wrote:

What a day! Our second baby is *here*—in the Beverly Hills Hotel. Asleep, clean, fed, warm—and safe. We got word this morning that a

woman named Christie would be bringing her
in. Christie was in the horrendous plane crash,
and we were told she is pretty close to a breakdown. Apparently, she had very bravely turned
around and gone straight back to Vietnam to
accompany the next group of babies traveling
out, which included our Joanna. We offered to
put Christie up for the weekend to give her
some TLC. She seems bone-weary, dazed and
clearly in shock, but trying to hide it. Hope we
can help her.

Joanna is only three months old and weighs
about nine pounds. She is very alert—a personality baby. She smiles a lot and "talks" up a storm.
She has no hair at all. Her head was shaved on
arrival in the U.S. to accommodate an IV due
to a bronchial infection, but the first thing Blake
said when he saw her was, "I think she's beautiful." Already I wouldn't swap her for anything.

Christie was clearly coping with post-traumatic
stress disorder, and I asked my analyst how best to
support her. He suggested we offer lots of tactile
activities—things that wouldn't require too much
communication on her part. A trip to the hairdresser, a massage, a walk on the beach, to help her
reconnect with herself.

Alas, we had little chance to do much for her, since the next day we received word that the Previns' baby was in San Francisco and ready to be picked up. Tony Adams accompanied Christie on a quick round-trip to collect her, and our Beverly Hills Hotel bungalow suddenly became a nursery, overflowing with babies and caregivers. The following day, the orphanage in Saigon summoned Christie back. As she departed, I found it hard not to weep at the courage and dedication it must have taken for her to return to the horrors there.

The Previns' baby was not well. She had severe dysentery and an ear infection. The poor child worsened as the day went on, her little knees drawing up in pain, and she cried nonstop. Our pediatrician very kindly made a house call, and promptly admitted the baby to UCLA Medical Center, where she rapidly began to improve under their excellent care.

Both our babies needed a visa to exit the U.S., and another to enter Switzerland. Joanna had no passport or birth certificate, and if Saigon fell, which was looking increasingly likely, Amelia's Vietnamese passport would become obsolete. Our lawyer managed to obtain a laissez-passer travel permit for Joanna from the Vietnamese Embassy and an entry visa from the Swiss Consulate, and we hightailed it back to Switzerland.

Almost immediately, we received news that Saigon was falling. I rushed to the Vietnamese Embassy, over an hour away, in Bern, to obtain a passport for Joanna before it became impossible to do so. Everyone there seemed amazed that Jo had reached us without any travel documents or identity papers. The slightly pompous consul told me I would have to return with a notarized letter explaining everything, and photocopies of any adoption-related documents. I politely asked what would happen if Saigon fell before I could get back to Bern. Wouldn't the embassy close?

"Oh, madame," he replied condescendingly. "We will *always* be here."

Two days later, Saigon did indeed fall to the North. I was just departing for Bern once again when I received a call from the embassy saying they had closed. We had missed getting Joanna her passport by one day, and now Amelia's was no longer valid. The only option for the time being was to continue applying for laissez-passers whenever we traveled.

Blake had gone back to Los Angeles for the press opening of *Return of the Pink Panther*, so Avril and I took turns caring for the babies individually during the nights, getting up for feedings and diaper changes and so forth. The day before Blake and Tony were due to return to Gstaad, we set about decorating the house in pink to welcome them. We made a huge banner to string across the balcony, Geoff and Emma made posters, we put pink flowers and candles throughout the house, and I put a stuffed Pink Panther, along with pink Kleenex and soap, in Blake's bathroom.

Just before their arrival, we all dressed in pink. Blake had chartered an air taxi service to bring him and Tony up from Geneva to the small airport in our neighboring village of Saanen.

That evening, I wrote:

Drove to the airport and there was the plane, landing quickly and smoothly. A skylark was singing over the field in the hot sun; even the plane did not disturb its song.

The miracle has happened—my Blackie is home and safe, our children are home and safe, and for this moment, all seems right in my world.

14

*T*HE *RETURN OF THE PINK PANTHER* was a smash hit, breaking box office records in America. The European opening was scheduled for early fall, and plans were made for a press gala in Gstaad at that time, since some of the film had been shot there. Blake and Tony were suddenly engaged in phone calls and trips to London to discuss the possibility of a sequel.

Emma departed to spend the rest of the summer with her dad, and Blake, Tony, Avril, Geoff, the babies, and I headed to Los Angeles, where we would be spending the next two months in a rental house in Malibu while Blake worked on the *Panther* sequel. We also needed to research high schools for Geoff for the fall, since he was still adamant about moving back to California. It had never occurred to me that the children might not be happy in Gstaad, and I was terribly concerned about the family being separated. Patty was still emotionally unstable, so having Geoff live with her was not an option. Thankfully, Blake's uncle Owen and his wife Lucille generously offered to help by allowing Geoff to live with them for a few months until we had a clearer sense of next steps.

When we arrived in Los Angeles, we discovered that all was not well between Jenny and Tom. Blake very quickly found himself in the middle of that situation, and in endless discussions with Patty. Then I received word that Emma had contracted chicken pox while traveling with her dad, and we began to notice that something was amiss with Tony Adams, now twenty-two. He complained of back problems, and had developed stomach ulcers, for which he had been given prescription pain meds. Blake and I wondered if he was abusing them.

Blake was still self-medicating every now and then when his back acted up, and Tony was clearly influenced by everything that Blake did. He had begun to dress like Blake, drive a similar car, and even use similar expressions. Although Tony was still the generous soul he had always been, Blake asked a great deal of him, and the promotion had obviously added pressure. Blake suggested that Tony take a couple of weeks off, which he did. It occurred to me that my husband was not unhappy to have someone else to point fingers at with respect to substance abuse—but I didn't mention these feelings to him.

Emma, now twelve, rejoined us at the end of August. She had spent the summer in Santa Fe, New Mexico, where her dad had been designing an opera, and though she had recovered from the chicken pox, she returned home with an ear infection and an orphaned kitten she had found in the desert. I was so happy to see her, but she was strung out about saying goodbye to her dad and trying not to cry. It was painful to know that she was hurting so much.

Our worries about Jenny and Geoff escalated. Tom Bleecker sent a letter informing us that, despite their recent relationship troubles, he and Jenny intended to be married in the fall. Jenny had just turned eighteen. Geoff, not yet sixteen, was still smoking and drinking, and Blake and I were deeply concerned about leaving him with Owen and Lucille Crump, as had been arranged. We prayed that the school we had found for him, his therapist, and the Crumps could "hold" him for the time being, but we knew we couldn't impose on them for too long.

Emma was entering eighth grade, the highest level at her school in Switzerland, and there were no English-speaking high school options other than boarding schools near Gstaad. Thanks to the success of the *Panther* film, Blake was now receiving a number of good offers for other film projects in Hollywood. It was becoming apparent that my dream of making Switzerland our permanent home might not be possible for much longer.

Blake and I began discussing plans to reestablish a base in the United States once the new *Panther* sequel finished shooting the following summer. In order to maintain the official residency we had established in Switzerland, we would have to divide our time between Europe and the States for a while, and do our best to make it all work somehow. As luck would have it, we found a piece of land adjacent to the rental property we had loved so much on the bluffs in Malibu. It included an old 1935 ranch house, and we put a down payment on it.

For now, though, work was calling us back to Europe. We had the *Pink Panther* gala weekend in Gstaad ahead of us, and Blake was on deadline to deliver the script for *The Pink Panther Strikes Again*, the sequel that was to start shooting in the New Year.

The Gstaad tourist bureau and United Artists went all out for the gala weekend, which took place at the Palace Hotel. There was pink swag everywhere, and huge pink paw prints led up the road to the Palace and spilled over the side of the hill. It poured with rain for most of the weekend, but everyone was in a festive mood.

The screening of the film was preceded by entertainment from the local brass band and an alpenhorn demonstration. Attendees gathered for dinner under a tent on the hotel grounds, where Henry Mancini conducted an orchestra. I sang "Moon River" directly to Blake, and was surprised to see him tear up.

EMMA BEGAN HER last year at the local school, and Blake pushed forward with his next *Panther* script. As the exquisite Swiss autumn days unfolded, I focused on the babies and made it a point to enjoy as much of the outdoors as possible, especially on Sundays.

A diary entry from the time:

Went for a lovely walk this afternoon with Avril, Em and the babes. Em and Avril each had a back-pack with one little girl strapped inside. Getting tiny Joanna strapped into Em's backpack was hilarious—at one time, the webbing under Jo's chin was too tight, and she was grinning good-naturedly while slowly turning purple. Later, Em stopped to drink at a water trough, and Jo found herself staring at the sky, arms and legs pointing to all four corners, eyes wide with astonishment. Where had the earth gone? All very sweet, lots of giggles, and lovely fresh afternoon air.

The children and I remained in Gstaad throughout the autumn. The film company procured a small rental house in London for Blake and Tony, since we had by now given up the house in Chester Square and they needed a base for preproduction on *The Pink Panther Strikes Again.*

Just after Christmas, we learned that Jennifer and Tom had indeed gotten married, and that Jennifer was pregnant. There were also rumbles of trouble with Geoff, who had been suspended from school for two weeks. Blake flew out to L.A. to meet with Owen and Lucille, who conveyed that they couldn't manage Geoff's ongoing struggles much longer. It was now inevitable that we would have to move back to Los Angeles as soon as our work in Europe was complete.

Blake commenced shooting at Shepperton Studios in England, and I commuted back and forth between London and Gstaad. Blake had hired a new secretary by the name of Francine Taylor, and on my first day there I overheard her muttering to herself about a gentleman who had been trying to circumvent her to get to Blake for some insignificant reason.

"He is *not* going to get past *me!*" she said tartly, and I realized that Blake was in good hands.

Almost immediately, Blake began having trouble with Peter Sellers. Peter had recently been diagnosed with a heart problem, the medication for which appeared to be affecting his mood and energy. As the days unfolded, he was chronically late for work in the mornings, asked for lunch breaks to begin early, and couldn't wait to be dismissed in the evenings. He frequently phoned in sick, forcing Blake to shoot around him when possible, or fold the company for the day for insurance purposes. It was tough on company morale, especially so early in the production schedule, and very disturbing for Blake, since he had enjoyed working with Peter for so many years.

When Blake confronted him, Peter threatened to quit the film, or sue. Blake talked him down, but the détente would only last a day or two before problems flared up again. Blake confessed to me how difficult it was to do comedy with someone so depressed. He began to look for ways to build the comedy *around* Peter, rather than having it emanate *from* him.

MUM AND AUNTIE made a visit to Gstaad, and it was not what I would call successful. Mum was now sixty-five, but looked a good deal older. She had gained a lot of weight, and was breathless from her years of smoking. Auntie was five years younger, and had long suffered from rheumatoid arthritis, which had worsened considerably.

I wrote:

Took Mum and Auntie to the top of the mountain for a late lunch as it was such a gorgeous day. Mum seemed uptight, and it was hard to tiptoe through the sulks and icy remarks. Hard to tell who's the worst of the two ladies. They are both bitchy behind each other's backs. Auntie is perhaps the more subversive and devious of the two. Mum is more out front and just plain bad-tempered. Incredible that their sibling rivalry has lasted sixty years, yet they cannot live without each other.

I hated to admit it, but it was a relief when they returned home.

I had been receiving offers for quite some time to make an appearance at Caesars Palace in Las Vegas. Initially, I'd postponed a decision—but Caesars was persistent, and given that our expenses now included the new property in Malibu, it made sense for me to seriously consider it. It had always been important to me that I contribute to the family coffers when I could, so I finally accepted the offer to do sixteen performances there in August.

I knew, however, that I couldn't just open "cold"—I needed to create an act worthy of such a high-powered venue, and put in a considerable amount of time rehearsing and trying it out. A perfect solution presented itself: while Blake continued filming, I would premiere the act at the famed Palladium in London, where I had first appeared as Cinderella at age seventeen.

I pulled myself up by the bootstraps and embarked upon a serious regime of exercise and singing practice. I recalled Richard Burton telling me that, in his younger years, he had gone to the Welsh mountains to orate from Shakespeare as a means of improving his voice and lung capacity. It occurred to me that I had mountains right outside my door. Since it was "off-season," I thought I could safely attempt my own version of Richard's exercise.

Each day, I walked a full circle, up the hill from our chalet, across the fields behind it, down along the brook, and back to the chalet. It was a good stretch, and my legs grew stronger while I vocalized along the way.

One day, I was practicing "The Sound of Music," which I would be performing in my act. I was rounding the last curve, singing flat out, when suddenly a group of Japanese tourists, cameras around their necks, crested the hill in front of me. They recognized me, and looked simply stunned. I dashed for home, mortified.

On one of my trips to London to visit Blake, he and I went to see Shirley MacLaine, whose act was currently the toast of the town at the Palladium. We went backstage afterward and showered her with praise and admiration. I asked Shirley if she had any secrets to help me overcome the anxiety I still felt whenever I made a first entrance in concert. It was one thing to hide behind a "character" in a play or musical, but when appearing as myself, I often felt awkward and self-conscious.

"Julie," she said, "I just choose a persona to play. Will I be the gracious hostess, the comedienne, the vivacious dancer . . . ? It's all part of the act, and once you've decided on your role, it's a lot easier." I vowed to remember her words.

On my next trip to London, I met with Ian Fraser, who would be arranging and conducting. The more music we went through, the more I realized just how much singing I would have to sustain, and the old familiar panic arose as to whether I would be able to cut it every night—and twice nightly in Vegas—without losing my voice. I realized that the only thing I could do was to be so well prepared and in such good shape that I'd have a reserve of energy that hopefully never needed tapping.

We spent the Easter break in Gstaad, and then Blake and Tony departed for Munich for location filming and I soon joined them.

Dad and Win visited us in Munich, and it was lovely to have enough time to spoil them a little. Emma flew in for a long weekend as well. She and I spent a glorious day accompanying Blake and Tony location scouting in Salzburg.

That evening, I wrote:

Salzburg was fabulous—a beautiful day, and I felt the grandest feeling; something to do with coming back to Austria a happier person than when I was last here. Who would have guessed that I'd come back one day with Blake and Em? We had a delicious lunch at the Goldener Hirsch, looked at the gardens and churches, then took a horse-drawn carriage through the old town. Emma loved it, as did I.

While I was having fun being a tourist, Blake was still struggling with Peter Sellers. One night in Munich, Peter stayed out until dawn with his leading lady and didn't show up on set until the afternoon. Blake was furious, but didn't confront him, since he knew it would only lead to sulking on Sellers's part and cost even more time. Omar Sharif flew in to play a small role as a courtesy to Blake, and Blake confided to me what a joy and relief it was "to have a pro on the set."

Emma and I traveled back to Gstaad via Paris, where I met with the great Hubert de Givenchy, who had agreed to design the costumes for my act at the Palladium. He was a lovely man—tall, elegant, beautiful to look at, and beautiful in spirit. It was, however, incredibly hot in his studio and I was dripping with perspiration, standing in my bra and panties between fittings, feeling lumpy and embarrassed with staff members coming in and out—but no one seemed to mind. At the end of the afternoon, Givenchy presented me with a folder with chosen designs and fabrics in it, to take home to study.

In May, I began rehearsals in London with the choreographer Paddy Stone, whom I'd known for years. It was great having Paddy and Ian on board, and I was struck by how sensational Ian's contribution was going to be—wonderful ideas for the arrangements, beautiful structure and chords. I missed my kids terribly, but it would only be a few weeks, and they came in for occasional weekend visits.

The days flew by, and suddenly we were loading in to the Palladium. Our orchestra call was held in the sweltering upstairs bar, as the stage was needed for hanging lights and rigging. I put on my first theatrical makeup in about fifteen years and tried on all the gowns. My favorite was made of chiffon, in shades of ombré peach. It needed some earrings and possibly a necklace, but we had yet to find something suitable.

A package arrived from Blake. To my astonishment, it contained a necklace and earrings that we had admired together at Asprey's a few months before. They were made of the palest angel coral, and they matched the dress perfectly. I was simply gobsmacked.

We did a dress rehearsal before an invited audience mostly comprised of *Pink Panther* company and crew members and their spouses. It was a mess. The quick changes barely worked, and the playback to which I occasionally lip-synced during the more strenuous choreography broke down completely. I ad-libbed, and did one number with a handheld mic while dancing my head off. It was unbearably hot, and I worried about perspiration stains on my gowns.

On opening night, June 9, I wrote:

Woke hoarse and weary from the dress rehearsal. It was the hottest day of the year. I headed to the theater and was devastated by how tired my voice sounded—like bringing something back from the deep. Worked out a little, tried to eat an egg. Nerves really giving me hell. Practiced gently, sprayed my throat.

At curtain time, I was in a semi-hypnotic, semi-terrorized daze as I walked onto the stage. Suddenly, the audience was on its feet, clapping, yelling, a standing ovation/welcome home. I was deeply touched, and felt the challenge to rise to the occasion and give them a performance worthy of their generosity.

The voice warmed up, mercifully, but sweat ran off my nose, and in my eyes. The wonderful audience helped and encouraged. Tons of flowers in the dressing room, and a long hand-drawn mural of the alps from Em and the children, which I displayed on my dressing room wall. Em and Blackie were the last two people I thought of before I walked on stage.

The London press were kind, but I knew that my act needed more polishing for Vegas. I did fourteen performances, sometimes two a day, and really felt how much effort it took to pull it off. Michael Kidd flew in to watch the last two performances, and I was grateful when he agreed to help me further improve the act.

The day after we opened, Blake took me aside and delivered the astounding news that Avril and Tony Adams had secretly been married six months prior, and were expecting a baby in January. I couldn't understand why they'd felt the need to hide it from us. It seemed like such a breach of trust. Avril brought Emma and the babies to London for the last couple of performances and things were strained between us. But life seesawed on, and eventually, she began to help us search for a replacement nanny.

Blake finally finished shooting his film, and we began the marathon pack-up to return to Los Angeles. There was much to deal with—Jennifer had given birth to a baby daughter, Kayti. Geoff would be moving in with us again at a new rental house while we were waiting for construction at our property on the bluff to be completed. A school had to be found for Emma. Avril's friend Charley, who had subbed for her in the past, had agreed to replace her, and the babies now had a new nanny to adjust to. I started rehearsals with Michael Kidd for the Vegas version of my act.

Michael and I began to address some of the problems with the show. I knew that Vegas demanded more razzle-dazzle than most venues, and I was aware that my act was currently a little too white-bread. It needed a serious goosing.

Michael knew about my struggles with respect to making a stage entrance. He suggested that we "fool" the audience into believing that there was a special pre-show demonstration by members of the Queen's Guard, brought to Vegas courtesy of Caesars Palace. The guards would march onstage, immaculately clad in their traditional military attire, including swords, belts, and bearskin hats. What no one would spot was that I was one of them, unrecognizable under my tall, fuzzy hat. The number would then begin to go awry, and after some choreographed confusion I would be knocked to the floor, my hat would fall off, and I would be revealed, laughing and already onstage, without having to make that dreaded first entrance.

I worried about making such a fool of myself, and Ian downright hated the idea. But Michael was persistent, and between that and Shirley MacLaine's advice to act the role of confident performer, I gave it a shot—and it worked.

Michael also conceived a truly brilliant moment in the middle of the act where we needed another lift. He had me lip-sync to Johnny Cash's recording of "One Piece at a Time," about assembling a Cadillac from parts stolen off the assembly line. The audience loved hearing Johnny Cash's voice emanating from my mouth. My dancers and I, piece by piece, assembled a mock Caddy, using a railroad flat and adding the "parts" referenced in the song by having the dancers assume certain positions. The number was a great success, and was just what my squeaky-clean little act needed.

Blake, Emma, and I were given the honeymoon suite at Caesars Palace: purple, pink, and red with gold-spattered mirrored ceilings. At least it was air-conditioned, and had a piano. As was her wont, Emma pitched in, sending out dry cleaning, answering phones and doorbells, ordering room service, and running errands.

For the next two days, my company and I worked out sound problems, improved dialogue, and continued to shuffle songs into a better order. Costumes and orchestrations arrived. People busied themselves all over the place. I had a hundred questions that no one had the time to answer. The hardest part was the dance rehearsals, during which I became more winded than usual and totally parched, due to the heat and dryness of the desert climate.

On the morning of our opening, I went down to the theater early and wearily put on theatrical makeup. The thought of what lay ahead of me was daunting beyond words. The previous act had concluded the night before, and my set had been installed overnight. There was much drilling and hammering. Lights were being hung and focused, and everywhere I looked I saw exhausted people, working hard. I tried all my costume changes, then began a four-hour tech run-through. I forgot lyrics and pieces of dialogue, prerecorded cues never came on, click tracks were missing or late. The stage floor covering kept curling up because it was so new.

Once we finished the run-through, I showered and put on fresh makeup. The dressing room was full of flowers, and Emma had written me an enchanting poem. The curtain wasn't until 10:30 p.m. I tried to jump-start my tired mind into action, pacing around the dressing room and going through the entire act in my head until it was time to go onstage.

After the performance, I wrote:

Very hard to judge the audience reaction—something to do with the sound coming from front of house. The tapes and cues worked. I couldn't see anything except the front row, but Blackie told me later that the audience was on its feet, stomping and cheering. Unlike London, which I went through in a totally hypnotic state, I was aware of every moment. I thought my legs would give out, really thought I couldn't move them another step—but Blake said it didn't show. I was SO hot. The usual agonizing sweat, eyes stinging from cold cream and new eyelash glue.

Crush backstage afterwards. I changed and went to the restaurant here, where all guests were gathered: Diana Ross, Vikki Carr, Burt Reynolds, Hank Mancini, Joe Layton. Later, I could not sleep. I watched a sad Hepburn/ Tracy movie on TV and bawled my eyes out. I'm sure I was just letting go.

For the next week, I did two shows every day, the second one starting after midnight. The act grew steadily better, but I was living like a hermit in order to conserve my voice and energy. I never set foot outside the hotel, and barely knew whether it was day or night. I slept late; did a slow, careful workout; ate a light meal; did some gentle vocalizing; and headed down to the theater. There, I'd put on makeup and begin the process of hyping myself up.

Before going on, I was never certain I would get through both performances. Between shows, I experienced an odd depression. I was tearful and had no idea why. One evening, in an attempt to understand it, I wrote the following:

OK—write it down. Pin it, like a fly on the wall. That small dot, tiny and black at my core, threatens to grow and explode inside me.

Depression.

Where does it come from? I feel it lingering, lurking, never far from the surface, and oh, it is black. I keep thinking that it's chemical, menopausal perhaps, but it's been waiting around for years, I think; a stalking shadow from my vaudeville days? I want to catch it, look at it, wipe it clean. It is to do with the deepest me.

When the week was finally over, I knew without a doubt that I couldn't do Vegas again. Looking back on it now, I realize that the heat, the carnival atmosphere, the incredible effort to be a "show-stopping phenomenon" twice nightly, was, for me, soul-killing. It wasn't where I wanted to be at this

stage in my working life. I didn't feel authentic—
I just felt alone, and more exposed than I had
ever been before. There was none of the creative
collaboration of a film or stage musical, and no
real satisfaction in the work itself. I was never
more happy to return to the soft, moist beach air
of Malibu.

15

IT WAS NOW early September of 1976. We were
still in the rented house, but would soon be
moving to our new home on the bluff, which was
nearing completion. I had a little time for reflection, and it occurred to me that it had been ages
since all the family had been in one place for any
length of time. We seemed to be forever flinging
things together, living in a chaos of professional
and financial obligations, which showed no sign of
abating anytime soon, since we were still attempting to honor our residency in Gstaad while also
maintaining a base in Los Angeles so the children
could attend school there.

Emma began her freshman year at Brentwood
School. To my delight, she settled in quickly and
happily. Geoff, now nearly seventeen, moved back
in with us and secured a temporary job on *The
Pink Panther Strikes Again* in the Los Angeles editing department, which he seemed to enjoy. Amelia
and Joanna, now two and a half and one and

a half, adored Charley, and were continuing to blossom.

On Christmas, which we spent in Gstaad once again, I wrote:

Oh, what a lovely day. Really perfect—everyone seemingly content, peaceful, happy. And all my dear ones around me. Blackie, in a happy, cheeky frame of mind. Emma radiant, giving, discovering the pleasure in doing just that. And the little ones, enchanted by the tree and presents, and not letting so many people over-stimulate them. Super lunch, lazy afternoon. Great turkey dinner. Bed. Happy.

The joys of that holiday notwithstanding, the first six months of 1977 were a time I would not care to revisit. Our two home bases, in California and in Switzerland, were aggravating our financial pressures. Geoff's editing job had ended, and he totaled his car; my dad suffered a minor stroke, and though he didn't seem to have any permanent damage from it, I was worried about him. Then my mother fell down her stairs in England, fracturing two ribs. Blake and I brought her to Los Angeles to recuperate, and tried to persuade her to consider staying in L.A., but she preferred to return to Walton.

Two days before we were due to move into our new home, we received an early morning call from the Malibu sheriff. Our house was on fire.

A neighbor had spotted flames and contacted the fire department. Had they arrived five seconds later, the windows would have blown out and the whole house would have burned to the ground. The kitchen was destroyed, but luckily the rest of the house was saved, although it was blackened with soot. Later, the fire chief told us that it looked like arson. We'd had a few run-ins with a disgruntled workman and suspected it might be him, but never found out for sure. It was a devastating blow.

We cleaned and repainted as best we could, and set up a makeshift kitchen in the lounge. Everything was in chaos—boxes everywhere still needed to be unpacked, air-conditioning filters needed to be cleaned, and Blake came down with the flu . . . but at least we were able to move in.

We hired a French couple to help with the new house, and headed to Gstaad for the Easter break, praying everything would hold in our absence. The onslaught of the previous weeks had taken a toll, and we all had a hard time decompressing. Then we received a disturbing call from my dad. Win, now fifty-seven, had apparently gone off for a bicycle ride the previous afternoon and had not been seen since. Dad had notified the police, and they had been searching all night without success. Blake and I headed to England on the next available flight.

We drove straight from Heathrow Airport to Dad's house in Ockley. Dad looked tearful and pale. My brother John was there, along with a few of Dad's closest friends. Somehow, the press had gotten word of Win's disappearance, and they were swarming about, but the local police did their best to keep them at bay as much as possible. Search parties with police dogs were organized for the afternoon and evening. I made soup and endless cups of tea for the myriad visitors. Still no sign of Win.

Blake booked a room at the Dorchester Hotel in London, and I stayed in Ockley with Dad. The following day, more search parties were organized. Divers explored the nearby lake, and a helicopter search was under way. Dad was by now truly despondent. He told me that Win had seemed "odd" before she left, almost as if she had wanted to say something to him. The doctor came by to monitor Dad's blood pressure, and the local vicar paid a visit. Johnny had to get back to work, so he reluctantly headed home to the Midlands, and

Blake brought in food for dinner. He, Dad, and I ate together quietly and somberly.

At 9 p.m., there was a knock at the door. I answered it, thinking it was another visitor, or the press. It was Win.

"Hi, Ju!" she said with acutely forced cheer. She was pale and swaying, held up by two friends, who had apparently found her sitting by the roadside about ten miles out of town.

My dad completely broke down. He flung his arms around Win, sobbing with relief. She was terribly dehydrated and couldn't stop shivering. There was blood all over her clothes and arms, and her stockings were torn. Most of all, she seemed to be suffering from some sort of amnesia. She thought it was Tuesday, when in fact it was Friday, and couldn't articulate where she had been or what had happened to her.

The doctor arrived and took Win upstairs for an exam and to attend to her needs. When he finally came down, he informed us that she had attempted suicide by taking an overdose of pills and slashing her wrists with a broken bottle. She had been in the woods for four days and was suffering from exposure. An ambulance was called, and Win was taken to the local hospital. Blake headed back to the hotel; I spent another night with Dad.

After everyone had gone, Dad let go again, with huge, heartrending sobs. It seemed as if he couldn't stop, but when I held him, he pulled away, saying, "No—you mustn't be too kind." He seemed wracked with guilt of some sort, which I struggled to understand.

The following morning, Dad brought a cup of tea up to my bedroom. It had been a short night, and I'd been awake and watchful for most of it. Dad sat on the edge of my bed and we chatted. He began to unburden himself, revealing to me that he, too, had once considered suicide, when he felt "less than a man." It was surprising to me that the man whom I had always seen as a pillar of quiet strength had at times felt vulnerable and weak. I did my best to be a good listener, but my heart ached for him.

Blake returned, and there were some lighter moments later in the day. I considered it a monumental achievement when Dad roared with genuine laughter at some anecdote Blake shared about the children. Eventually, Dad went to visit Win at the hospital. While he was there, the vicar paid another visit to the house, and Blake and I had a long discussion with him. He was concerned that Win hadn't been receiving enough love, kindness, and respect. I realized that in recent years, despite his generosity of spirit, Dad could occasionally be a little inconsiderate—even patronizing—toward Win, which must have stoked her feelings of inferiority.

Johnny and Shad arrived the following afternoon, with John's daughter, Jayne, and Shad's adorable new baby, Sonia, in tow. They immediately went off to visit Win.

I had been hoping that Blake and I could return to Gstaad, but I sensed that Dad was still deeply anxious and nearing an "explosion" of sorts. I worried about his blood pressure and his not being able to care for Win properly once she was released from the hospital, nor she for him. Blake and I agreed that it would be best to bring both of them to Los Angeles, where they could stay with us for a couple of weeks and receive top-notch medical care and emotional support.

When we proposed it to Dad, he seemed hugely relieved, but he made one stipulation—he would go, provided it was all right with Win. We then visited Win at the hospital, and she seemed just as willing and relieved as Dad was. She said that she hadn't had a complete physical in over twenty years.

Once in Los Angeles, Dad and Win saw Dr. Tanney, and also took several sessions with a good therapist, both independently and as a couple.

Little by little, they began to find each other again. I noticed them holding hands and being affectionate with one another, which I hadn't seen for quite some time. When they finally headed back to England, they were in much better shape physically and emotionally.

Blake and I traveled back to Gstaad, leaving Emma and Geoff in the care of the new French couple. The babies and Charley greeted us joyfully with bunches of Swiss flowers. I focused on getting back in vocal shape, as I now had several concerts lined up in the States beginning in August, culminating in a tour of Japan in late September. My act needed "retooling" once again, since Vegas had been such an anomaly, and I wanted to shift the focus back to music. We opted to make it a solo concert with limited choreography and no dancers.

Much to my dismay, Ian would not be the musical director for these particular concerts. As brilliant a conductor and composer as he was, and as dear a friend to me, he was always a bit of a terrier, and he had butted heads with my team. It was decided that the venerable conductor and arranger Jack Elliott would take Ian's place this time around. Jack was hugely talented, but initially I missed the instant and easy communication that I always had with Ian. Jack and I watched episodes from my television series and various specials, and listened to recordings, which gave him a better sense of my style and what I was capable of vocally.

Blake was producing these concerts for me, and was also in negotiations for yet another *Pink Panther* sequel. But Peter Sellers was acting up again, making unreasonable contractual demands, and the studio finally told Blake it was up to him to get Peter on board. Blake devised a plan; we would head to the South of France, where Peter had bought a house with his new wife, an actress by the name of Lynne Frederick. We would vacation in Saint-Tropez for a week, during which time Blake would meet and work with Peter.

Within two days, we were en route to Nice, with Emma, the babies, Charley, Tony Adams, and Blake's assistant, Francine. Once again, we stayed on a chartered yacht. I shuddered to think of the horrendous expense, but Blake assured me that the film company was willing to cover it, as they were eager to get the problems with Sellers sorted out. Thus began what was, for me, Emma, and the babies, a marvelous vacation—and for Blake, Tony, Charley, and Francine, a working one.

Blake took daily meetings with Sellers, and the situation with him became even more crazy. Peter was hustling all sides, telling Blake one thing and the producers another. Lawyers and managers flew in and became embroiled in the discussions.

The rest of us were having a terrific time kicking back, but Blake was under tremendous pressure and growing more and more irritable. He and Peter seemed destined to continue their "merry dance"— part competitive, part love/hate, yet dependent upon one another for so many reasons.

On our last day aboard, Blake and I took a moment for ourselves and went to admire some of the other yachts in the marina. We were stunned to discover our beloved *Impulse* moored among them. She looked dilapidated and uncared-for, and I could swear I heard her groaning at her rope ties. It made us both very emotional to see her, and we left quickly, having lost our appetite for window-shopping.

UPON OUR RETURN to Los Angeles, I began rehearsals for the three concert dates at American venues and the Japanese tour. I met daily with Jack Elliott, and little by little we began to lay out the act. Every day felt like three steps forward, two back, as we tried new material, worked out sequencing, then abandoned that material to try something else. I began to really worry that the act wouldn't be ready in time for the concert dates. Michael Kidd came in to consult once again, and to work with me on the staging. In his continued efforts to help me conquer my first entrance discomfort, he urged me to stride onto the stage and make a sweeping curtsy, with arms wide, as if to say, "Welcome, everyone! I'm thrilled you're here, and we're going to have a lovely evening." The body language carried me through, and I began to feel more confident. There were costume meetings and fittings, and promo spots to be taped for the various venues. Zoë flew in to take publicity shots, and there were interviews with press outlets.

The daily commute to town from our new house by the beach—which was still very much a work-in-progress—was long, but weekends there made the effort worthwhile. Emma was summering with her dad again on Long Island, but I did my best on days off to put in as much time as I could with Amelia and Joanna, swimming with them in the pool and playing together in the garden.

The girls were developing such enchantingly different personalities. Amelia was poised and radiantly beautiful. Now three and a half, she was already a serious fashionista, standing in front of her closet each morning to contemplate the perfect outfit for her day. Joanna, on the other hand, was a feisty and funny two-year-old, with her socks forever around her ankles and scrapes galore.

On one of our walks around the garden, I asked both girls what they might like to plant if I gave them each a little plot of their own.

Amelia instantly replied, "Strawberries!"

Joanna pondered a moment, then said, "Ratatouille."

IN LATE AUGUST, I flew to New York for the first of the American concerts, which was to take place in Westchester. I wrote:

> I think I earned my whole week's salary today. Kept thinking of the old adage, "Well, you wanted to be in showbiz!"
>
> Our run-through began at 3:30. Photographers were out front shooting everything and seeing all the little disasters—and there were many. The orchestra needed more rehearsal. Some numbers we didn't even get to, like the final medley. Then Michael Kidd announced that my 20's dress didn't work, and I should do that medley in the full skirt, which is virtually impossible to move in. A lady was waiting to do a television interview. She was rather hostile, and kept asking weird questions about failure,

and my "image," and why did I bother to work when I didn't need to, etc. I wanted to reply, "What makes you think I don't need to?"

It rained, and the highways were flooded, so the show began late. I went on just after 10, a basket-case of nerves, convinced I'd had a small stroke because I could not remember my dialogue. Lo and behold, the audience was welcoming—and it helped so much.

I got through everything, though the orchestra fell apart at one point. But in spite of the gown, and the rain, and being under-rehearsed, the audience wouldn't let me go.

We did five performances in Westchester. Emma came to the final one with Tony, Gen, Bridget, and Tony's parents, who were visiting from England, and with whom I had remained close. I was weary, and quite nervous, especially about Tony seeing the show, with his vast knowledge of theater. But when they came backstage after the performance, it seemed they'd all enjoyed themselves. It was great to see my Emma, radiant and proud, smelling of sun and swimming pool and shampoo.

A FEW DAYS LATER, I departed for Michigan and four performances there at the Pine Knob Music

Theatre—a fifteen-thousand-seat amphitheater just north of Detroit. I shared the bill with Henry Mancini. The concerts went relatively well, but the lights were incredibly bright, to the point where I couldn't see where to walk or even the first row. It was disorienting, as was the sound. The night air seemed to make the orchestra feel distant, leaving only my voice booming back at me through the monitors. Standing in the bright spotlight, I attracted a host of fans from the insect world, ending up with a moth in my bra, another in my eye, and one in my mouth. Since I was mid-song, I pocketed the latter in my cheek and eventually swallowed it at a discreet moment. Yuck.

Back in Los Angeles, I performed at the Greek Theatre, another open-air venue, in the Hollywood Hills. Because it was on home turf, there were many friends in the audience who came backstage afterward—Richard Crenna, Bob Wise, Saul and Betty Chaplin, and Blake's assistant, Francine, who was now going to be assisting me in Japan. Between the guests and the packing up required for our tour, it was a very late night for us all. Poor Emma had only four hours of sleep, and had to go to school the next day.

Blake developed a bad virus of some sort, rendering him unable to travel, and the French couple suddenly gave notice. This left me in a bind, as I knew that after the tour, I would only have two weeks left on my visa before having to return to Switzerland until the New Year. Charley and the babies would be joining me there, and Blake would be heading to London to start work on *Revenge of the Pink Panther.*

Even though it meant she would miss a few weeks of school, I had already decided to bring Emma with me to Japan, reasoning that visiting that country and culture would be a valuable educational experience. I had no idea, however, what I was going to do once the tour ended, and she had to return to school in L.A. for the remainder of the fall term.

I discussed the problem with my analyst, who asked whether there wasn't a kind aunt or cousin who might come and stay for a spell during my forced absence. I suddenly remembered that my former sister-in-law, Jen Gosney, had long wanted to visit the States. Like Emma, Jen's daughter, Clare, was fourteen, and the cousins were very close. Jen was open to the suggestion of spending time in America. She happened to be going through a divorce, and it seemed we would all benefit from the plan. It was a huge relief.

EMMA, FRANCINE, AND I traveled to Tokyo accompanied by my concert team: a core group of six musicians—violin, woodwinds, trumpet, guitar, bass, and drums—plus our conductor, Jack Elliott. They had all been on the road with me, and would continue to be folded into the resident orchestra of each venue we played. Our tour manager, Gerry Nutting, doubled as our lighting designer, working alongside our sound engineer.

There followed a memorable two weeks, which may best be expressed in a series of installments from my diaries of the tour:

Arrived at Tokyo Airport, where to our surprise, hundreds of fans had turned out to greet me. They swarmed so hard and so close, pressing flowers and gifts upon us, that we nearly went to our knees three times and were sweating with panic by the time we reached our cars. Emma is being a trojan and I'm so glad to have her with me.

* * *

Took a vast press conference today. Our lovely translator, Saito, was kept busy interpreting the many odd questions that came up: "What is

my philosophy or religion about my work and/
or life?" "How do I raise my children?" "What
attracts me most about my husband?" "Do I
dream, and if so, is it in color or black and
white?" I couldn't outguess the thinking behind
these questions. I finally surmised that the inter-
viewers wanted to approve of me as a wife and
mother. They seemed to like it when I said that
I put my husband and family first. Lots of questions about my books, and a children's choir
sang "The Sound of Music" and "Do Re Mi."

* * *

Blackie, Tony and Geoff have arrived. Hooray!
Geoff will be helping out backstage.

Did my first concert in Tokyo this evening at
the Budokan arena. We filled to capacity. The
sound system was excellent, and for such a vast
place, it was quite an intimate feeling. The stage
was six or seven feet high, built that way, I'm
told, because enthusiastic fans were inclined to
rush at and even climb on it, and indeed at
the end of my show, people were jumping up
against the structure trying to throw or place
their gifts and flowers on deck.

The audience was mostly very young . . .

teenagers and people in their early 20's. (I gather older people don't go out to the theatre much. I wonder when one becomes an older person?) The minute I turned to say something to Jack, the applause died immediately, as if no one wanted to miss a single word I said.

The string musicians have a different way of bowing here. They seldom lift the bow to breathe, but rather "slide" up and down to notes, presumably because their own music is played that way. Dick Dennis, our resident first violin, was a tower of strength in rehearsal, giving them pointers for a more western sound. The musicians are industrious, and no doubt they will soon be perfect.

The dressing room facilities were awful. A ladies' loo with no make-up lights, so God knows how my face looked—I just sort of guessed. While I was making up, I kept hearing great crashes, screams and yells. I discovered I was dressing next to another hall where Kendo artists were practicing for a tournament. They finished their practice as I emerged from my dressing room heading for the stage, and we blinked at each other for a moment. The incongruity of their attire—complete with long capes, padded breastplates, head gear and bamboo sticks—compared to my elegant evening gown was farcical.

In general, it was a successful evening and the audience loved the "Do Re Mi" singalong, clapping and stomping and joining in when I sang it in Japanese.

* * *

We are in Osaka. The Festival Hall is a lovely theater. The concert looked pretty and was a huge success. It was hot and humid, but I did enjoy myself. The evening was recorded by RCA and I sang well.

Blake seems depressed. His back is out and he has been swallowing Demerols at an alarming rate. I have a hunch he'd love to get out of the madness of the next *Panther* film with Peter, yet he's committed. I understand his mood, but Em is finding it hard, as he is inclined to be snippy. Blake says he will go home in two days, which makes me sad.

* * *

Blake and I have suddenly realized we won't see each other for about a month. I'm trying to be calm about it all, and I don't understand why he's being difficult. Too much pressure, and business and chaos, I guess—yet we've created it all.

I feel myself opening and warming to the pleasures of the tour, and I want to be able to grow and examine where performing still fits in my life, yet I feel stifled by all these other problems.

* * *

Saw Blackie and Tony off at the station this morning, where they took the Bullet Train back to Tokyo for their flight home. I tried not to weep, but it was hard. Afterwards, I drove to Kyoto with Em and some of my gang. Mr. Yokoyama, our producer, had invited us to a very special place for lunch—the Okochi-Sanso Villa.

The exquisite pagoda-like inn was set on a hill. There was a wrap-around balcony one floor up, and as we went on to the lawn below for sweetmeats and a tea ceremony, a familiar voice said, "Well, what took you so long?"

I looked up, and Blackie was standing on the veranda, legs wide, arms folded, looking pleased with himself. I couldn't believe my eyes. It seemed like some sort of magic, since I'd seen him depart on the train.

"I couldn't leave you," he said. "We are more important than any of the other bullshit."

Apparently the first stop on the Bullet Train was Kyoto, and Blake suddenly said to Tony, "I've got to get off." They did just that, and found their way to the inn. Saito, who had been escorting them, and who was normally totally circumspect, became quite emotional, saying, "This is the most romantic thing I've ever seen!"

We had a fantastic Japanese meal in the tranquil, exquisite surroundings—Fall colors just beginning to set in.

* * *

Blake has come down with another virus that seems to have beaten him to a pulp. I stayed with him all day today, while Emma went with my gang to Hiroshima. She was stunned by the visit. Geoff, too. Good.

It's been decided that my gang and I will go to Sapporo tomorrow for the one concert there and meet up with Blake in Tokyo on Tuesday.

* * *

A "hard work" show in Sapporo, and a really obvious language barrier.

One funny thing happened: Geoff had been given the job of paging my microphone cord so I didn't trip over any slack wire. I walked across the stage and suddenly couldn't go any further. Looking into the wings, I saw that Geoff had fallen asleep. I gave the cord an almighty yank and he woke with a start, almost falling off his stool!

* * *

Back in Tokyo. Played the Budokan again. Blake still having a hard time. Claims that I've "changed" on this tour. I have no idea what he means. Maybe it's his flu—or the drugs. Or maybe he's just feeling redundant, because I'm working and there's little for him to do. I went to the concert hall feeling low, but gave one hell of a concert to the lovely, packed audience.

* * *

Went with Tony Adams, Em and Gerry to hear the 16-track tapes made of the second Osaka concert. They were surprisingly good—could almost release them untouched.

Blake in another dark mood today, saying that we never get a moment alone together. He suggests that Em and I meet him in England and go to Gstaad for 2-3 weeks before heading back to L.A. in time for Jen Gosney to take over with Em. God, it's difficult.

* * *

Gave a party tonight for my gang. A good time to say thank you—but it also turned out to be a pre-birthday party for me, since Blake and Tony are now leaving tomorrow. We had delicious eats and lots of disco dancing later. Geoff asked me to dance, and Blackie and I had a rare slow dance together.

* * *

Said goodbye to my mate and Tony, then flew with Emma and the gang to Fukuoka City. Saw Mount Fuji from the airplane, with the volcano steaming on top. I would so love to come back and really explore this beautiful country.

The gymnasium where the concert was held is vast. Oddly, the sound there was probably the best of the tour. I did a sort of floating, easy show, feeling somewhat removed, but everyone said it was great. The orchestra played "Happy Birthday" after "The Sound of Music" finale, and each member presented me with a carnation. I was deeply touched.

* * *

Journeyed back to Tokyo. Found lots of loving notes from Blackie, and a suitcase of his for me to bring into London. Thank you, darling. The room is a mess. So many gifts, luggage muddled and untidy.

* * *

Last concert tonight. I had a lump in my throat when I sang, "I'd Rather Leave While I'm in Love." The dearest moment of the evening was when my sweet musicians shuffled into my dressing room after the show and presented me with a white bomber jacket, with "Julie—1977 Japanese Tour" inscribed on the back.

* * *

Last night, Emma and I began the marathon pack-up. Suddenly, the hotel began to shake. It was an earthquake, and we were on the 39th floor. We could feel the building swaying and hear the empty hangers banging against each other in the closet. As Emma and I ran toward each other, I thought, "This is it."

Afterwards, we kept our bedroom doors open so we could see each other and vowed to meet in the hall between our rooms if it happened again, which it did—a second, bigger one. We were terrified, but thankfully there were no more tremors after that. Somehow, I managed to sleep through the night, which was a testament to my fatigue.

The next morning, I phoned each of the eight guys on my team to say thank you and goodbye, and signed endless photos and programs for fans. I sorted through and packed the piles of gifts from each venue we had visited. Finally, dear Saito took us to the airport, where a few loyal fans were waving banners saying, "Julie! Come back soon!" We flew across Siberia, with a brief layover in Moscow. After the lightness and beauty of Japan, everything seemed dour, dirty, and bleak.

London seemed equally bleak. We piled into the Hilton at midnight, UK time, and Blake was banging on the door the following morning at seven-thirty, having just arrived from Los Angeles, in much better spirits than when he left Japan.

16

WHILE IN LONDON, I visited with my mother and Aunt Joan. The visit with Mum was brief, as she was leaving for a vacation at the coast with a gentleman friend whom she seldom mentioned but who I gathered was often in residence. Mum looked terrible, and never removed her sunglasses.

Auntie and I had a long chat. She was angry, lonely, paranoid, in physical pain—and hating herself. She ranted on about her church and the deceit of her friends, about her ambivalent feelings toward Mum. Finally, I asked her what she intended to do about it all. She had no answers. In one heartbreaking moment, I asked her how she'd feel if she never saw Mummy again, since they so obviously rubbed each other the wrong way. She thought about it—it really stopped her—then answered, ". . . but you see, the *real* Barbara, the Barbara I used to love, is still in there somewhere." I guessed that she missed the big sister that took care of her long ago. It made me deeply sad.

I met with Jen Gosney to firm up the plans for her stay with Emma in L.A. Emma visited with Clare; both girls were excited at the prospect of living together for a stretch. Blake, Emma, and I then headed for Gstaad, where Charley and the babies were waiting for us. They had grown yet again, and Joanna was beginning to form sentences.

Peter and Lynne Sellers were in town, and they took Blake and me to dinner. I was struck by how young Lynne was, and wondered what she saw in Peter. He still appeared to be acutely depressed. They had seen a chalet for sale that belonged to good friends of ours, and had fallen in love with it. I felt mixed emotions about the prospect of having them as neighbors, and I voiced my concerns to Blake.

"If it gives Peter one day of true happiness," he said, "then it'll be worth it."

A week later, we headed back to London, where Blake began preproduction for *Revenge of the Pink Panther*. Emma and I picked up Clare Gosney, and the three of us boarded the flight for Los Angeles. Jen would be joining us there in two weeks' time.

When Emma returned to school, Clare was sitting in alongside her. Once Jen arrived, I headed back to London. It was heartbreaking to leave

Emma, but I was reassured by how very happy she seemed to have Clare and Jen there, and she didn't know that I planned to fly back later in the month to surprise her for her birthday.

There followed a packed few weeks, during which I taped another special with the Muppets, and visited the set where Blake had begun filming.

Once again, Blake was having trouble with Sellers. Peter was becoming more and more eccentric— he was moody and paranoid, superstitious about the color purple, and holding regular conversations with his dead mother. One night, after a particularly difficult day during which Blake only achieved one shot, Peter telephoned to say that he had good news. He had spoken to God, who had told him how to solve the problem of the scene they had been working on.

"Fine," Blake tactfully replied. "Show me tomorrow."

When Peter demonstrated God's plan for the scene, Blake said it was so appalling that he couldn't help but respond, "Peter, the next time you speak to God, tell him to stay the hell out of show business."

I BOARDED A flight back to L.A. for Emma's fifteenth birthday. When I arrived at the beach house, Emma and Clare were out seeing a movie. Jen made me tea, and then wrapped me from head to toe in gift paper. I sat on Emma's bed and waited for her to find me. Her immediate words were quite matter of fact:

"Mum! What are you doing here?" Then she burst into happy tears.

I spent an all-too-short week with her. Jen and Clare's presence hadn't sustained her as much as I'd hoped, and she confided in me that she was blue and had developed a phobia of earthquakes, which kept her awake at night. I did my best to boost her spirits and help her understand why we had to be apart, but in truth, I was as blue as Emma was, though trying very hard not to show it. I've always felt that if my kids were OK, I was OK, but in this case, my hands were tied by the complications of our residency in Europe, which only allowed me to spend a certain amount of time per year in the U.S. I realized yet again what Blake and I had gotten ourselves into, and worried about the impact of so many extended separations.

THE WHOLE FAMILY regrouped for the winter holidays in Gstaad, along with Avril and Tony, who now had two babies. Shooting for *Revenge of the Pink Panther* was scheduled to resume in the New

Year, in Hong Kong. I took Emma and Clare back to school in L.A., then joined Blake on location. Since Gstaad was still our "official" home base, it made sense for Amelia and Joanna to remain there with Charley. Avril and her babies stayed on there as well, since Tony was working with Blake. Geoff was also in Hong Kong, working once again with the editing department. Much as I wished my family could all be together, I tried my best to ensure that everyone was safe and secure, even when at opposite ends of the earth—but my head was beginning to feel a little like a whirligig spinning in the wind.

The *Panther* company was staying at the famed Peninsula Hotel, which still had an air of old colonialism. I visited the set and suddenly felt a twinge of concern about the degree to which Blake seemed interested in Lynne Sellers. With a wife's intuition, I sensed there might be a touch more going on than compassion for her situation with Peter.

Given how attractive Blake was, women would often throw themselves at him. It had never amounted to anything, but he had a soft spot for what I called "willow ladies"—lonely, fragile, and usually very pretty young women, who seemed to lack a central core. I always tried to wait it out, and they'd eventually fade into the mist. I hoped this would be a similar situation.

Emma and Clare came for a visit, and I took them sightseeing. We saw the floating village of Aberdeen, the beautiful resort community of Repulse Bay, and the Tiger Balm gardens, where the girls bought out the gift shop. Later, they slathered themselves with the aromatic ointment to such an extent that it's a wonder the hotel didn't need fumigation! When shooting wrapped in Hong Kong, Blake, Tony, Geoff, and the film company returned to London to continue filming there. I traveled with Emma and Clare back to L.A., where they resumed their schooling with Jen in residence once again, then I returned to Gstaad.

Our beloved Charley was soon to leave us to resume her work as an obstetrics nurse. It was essential that I get back to Amelia and Joanna, now four and three years old, to help manage the transition to a new nanny. The stress of Charley's departure took a toll on both girls, but for Amelia it was especially difficult. She was anxious and angry. I had come to understand that abandonment was a huge issue for her, given her background, and this had clearly triggered those feelings. I did my best to put in as much time as possible with both girls, taking them swimming at the local pool, playing games, reading to them, and having lots of cuddles, but it never seemed to be enough.

One evening, at the dinner table, Amelia suddenly announced, "I know exactly what heaven looks like." I asked her if she'd care to explain. "It's like a square handkerchief, and on every corner, there's a beautiful arch and people walk through them when they arrive."

There was a pause while we all digested this. Joanna had been listening intently.

"Do spiders go to heaven?" she asked.

"Well . . . I guess they do," I replied. "I mean 'all God's children' means creatures, too."

There was another pause. Then, with an enormous sigh, Jo said, "Oh, *dear*."

I REMAINED CONCERNED about the constant separations from Blake and the effect they were having on our marriage. Our phone calls were all too brief, and I was anxious about how much time he was spending with Lynne and Peter. I felt foolish and paranoid, since I knew that Blake's job required him to pay close attention to his lead actor, especially one as needy as Peter. Nevertheless, my intuition was still nagging me that something more was going on. Eventually, I became so uneasy that I flew to London for a few days, where my worries were not assuaged to the degree that I had hoped.

The problems with Peter had escalated, and he was more of a handful than ever. One time he showed up to work drunk and was abusive to crew members. An important take was ruined, and Blake had to settle for it. Looking back, I suspect that Peter had become as concerned about his marriage as I was about mine, since Lynne was ever present, often dressed in provocative attire and being seductive with Blake. I was also aware that Blake was self-medicating again.

I wrote:

Every line between Blake and me feels crossed. I want to talk with him, yet know he's distracted and busy, and I feel tongue-tied with insecurity. It's clear he's attracted to her, and he's certainly allowed to look at other ladies. Probably that's all there is to it. But I'm becoming more anxious by the day and feel as if I'm in the way here. It makes me angry that this slip of a girl is creating so much havoc in our lives.

Finally, the stress got the better of me and I found the appropriate moment to speak with my spouse. I told him I was aware that he was preoccupied with Lynne. He threw a small, exasperated fit, citing the film and his responsibilities. Then he admitted he was flattered by her attentions.

I said, "I don't want us to bullshit each other, Blake. Do you still want our marriage? We can end this right away, if that's what you'd prefer."

He thought for a moment.

"I *do* want our marriage," he finally responded. "Very much."

From then on, things were markedly better between us.

PRINCIPAL PHOTOGRAPHY FOR *Revenge of the Pink Panther* finished in April, and Blake and I headed back to Los Angeles. The girls and their new nanny had flown there a few days prior, and Emma and Clare were there to welcome us. It was a great feeling for me to take up the reins again with most of my family under one roof.

Blake began editing the film. He also began attending group therapy. After his first session, he came home awed and weary. "Don't worry," he said to me. "Our marriage *is* going to work. I needed this." He seemed much relieved, as was I.

A few weeks later, our boat broker telephoned us. "You won't believe this," he said. "Your lovely *Impulse* is for sale again, and going for a song."

Blake and I looked at each other and firmly

agreed on all the reasons why we should not repurchase her: she was that much older, she was made of wood, there were surely so many better boats out there. Then we promptly bought her on the spot, feeling foolish and thrilled at the same time. Blake's uncle Owen, and his wife Lucille, who were adept sailors, offered to bring her back to the States, where she could undergo repairs.

OUR HOUSE IN Malibu was finally beginning to feel like a real home. The children were happy there; friends often came by for dinner and a movie on Sundays; and Blake's parents and Aunt Thyrza visited regularly.

The press premiere of *Revenge of the Pink Panther* was scheduled to take place in Hawaii at the end of June. A few days prior to our planned departure for the event, Blake suddenly decided that the final scene of the film didn't work and needed to be replaced. With as much courage as inspiration, he came up with a new ending, and within two days he'd raised the necessary funds, brought most of the company back together, procured a soundstage at MGM, and had a set built.

After the premiere, I wrote:

Well, my Blackie's done it. Based only on instinct, that clever man re-shot the last scene of the film, re-edited it, and didn't see the complete result until the screening this evening.

I was so nervous for him—we all were—to be so down to the wire and to take such a gamble, but everything worked, brilliantly. The film is funny—the most surreal, the most mad of all the *Panthers*. Thinking back on the sheer pressure of it all, plus putting up with Peter's behavior, and then pulling off this last-minute coup, I can only say, "Bravo, Mate!"

Revenge of the Pink Panther was a success, and Blake quickly received word that a screenplay he had written in Gstaad a year or two prior, called *10*, had been approved for production by Orion Pictures, a new company that had been formed that year. It was about a man in midlife crisis, who, on a whim, pursues a beautiful young bride he perceives to be a "10." Filming was to begin that fall in Los Angeles, which meant that Blake had to start preproduction immediately.

We had been planning to charter a boat and tour the Greek Islands with Emma and Clare—Blake's idea, as he had long wanted to visit there, and he thought it might be nice to spoil the girls a bit.

Now he was unable to go. He suggested that I take the girls anyway.

The Greek Islands were surreal in their beauty. I felt as though we had landed on the moon, with the sun-bleached white villages and baked landscapes against the crystal-clear aquamarine sea. It was wonderful to spend concentrated time with Emma and Clare. We swam daily, and to our amazement, we were accompanied by the ship's cat, who had been found abandoned dockside and adopted by the crew. As a means of keeping her cool and free of fleas, they washed her in the sea, and to their great surprise, she had taken to the ritual. Now, every time we jumped into the water, she followed. It occurred to me that a story about a cat that lived at sea and loved to travel would make a charming children's book. I began to make notes.

Early one morning, after we put in to a small island port, the "head" in my cabin overflowed. Desperate to protect the carpet, I began to bail it out as best I could with a small garbage can, rousing Emma in the process by dashing into her bathroom to empty it. She gamely began assisting me, and we were busy squelching back and forth, trying not to alert the crew, when we heard a stranger's voice calling "Hallo-ooo?" from the main deck.

"See who it is!" I hissed at Emma, who quickly

threw on some clothes and disappeared upstairs. Moments later, she reappeared.

"Mom—it's the mayor!" she said. "He wants to introduce you to his wife, who is a big fan, and wants to be an actress."

I gasped. "Keep them occupied! I'll come up as soon as I've changed."

Emma held the fort, serving coffee and making small talk, until I appeared, having donned a pair of jeans, a floppy hat, sunglasses, and a daub of lipstick.

I swanned onto the afterdeck, putting on my best Hollywood charm, and was aware of Emma stifling giggles. The mayor was effusive. He introduced me to his wife, who was taller and considerably younger than he. Clad in the tightest of bustiers and sporting an abundance of gold jewelry, she gushed, "You look *just* like Mary Poppins!" Nothing could have been further from the truth. We did our best to graciously wrap up the visit as quickly as possible, so as to get back to the pressing matter below.

THERE FOLLOWED yet another period of back and forth between Gstaad, London, and L.A. for both Blake and me. Blake was totally consumed with preproduction for *10*. Tony Adams had served as associate producer for all the *Panther* sequels, and Blake had now promoted him to producer, since he was doing fine work and our friend Ken Wales had moved on to other projects. I was to play a role in the film, but for now, my mission was to keep the family "topped up" in our various home bases by spending as much time with each member as I could, while maintaining our Swiss residency, a task which seemed to have fallen more and more on my shoulders. Fortunately, Jen and Clare would be back in Los Angeles with Emma for another year, which was a huge help.

Toward the end of September, I flew back to L.A. with Amelia, Joanna, and the new nanny to begin preparing for my work on *10*. The day after I arrived, Jennifer announced that her marriage to Tom had ended, and asked if she and her daughter, Kayti, now two years old, could move in with us for a while, since they had nowhere else to go. We made hurried arrangements to accommodate them in our already densely populated house.

To add to the family dramas, Blake approached me with an astounding request: "Darling, would you mind terribly if I asked Patty to design the clothes for *10*?"

I was aghast. The idea of attending fittings—revealing all to my husband's ex—was unthinkable . . . not to mention everything that had transpired between us over the years. I made my feelings known.

"I know it's a lot to ask," Blake said. "But she's in desperate need of money. This way, she can get into the designers' union. It's the only thing I can think of to truly help her."

I reluctantly agreed. To my surprise, Patty's choices made me look fresh and hip. She dressed me in snug leather jeans, luxurious jackets, and great boots, and I recognized that I looked the better for her efforts. Although her personal problems were ever-present, working together did improve our relationship.

Patty also introduced me to a man who was to become one of my closest friends and professional colleagues. John Isaacs was at the height of his fame as a brilliant hairdresser and cofounder of the esteemed Michaeljohn salon in London, with a second salon in Los Angeles. John agreed to style my hair for *10*. Little could I guess the number of other films and projects that he and I would work on together in the future, and how close our families would become.

THE SEARCH FOR a gorgeous young actress to play the title role in *10* was the biggest challenge for Blake. Recommendations were made by casting agents and other industry colleagues, and he and Tony conducted dozens of screen tests. One afternoon, he phoned to say he'd found the perfect "10."

Bo Derek was the third wife of actor/director/ photographer John Derek, and she had been recommended to Blake by an industry colleague. Blake had set up a meeting with her.

"I walked into my office and came to a skidding halt," he told me. "There she was, dressed in some sort of hopsack and very little else, and I just *knew*."

"Can she act?" I asked.

"Jesus. I don't *know* . . ." he said, but it was quite obvious that he couldn't care less. Bo never did a screen test. But she did do makeup and hair tests, as we all did—and she asked Blake's permission to try the iconic cornrows she wears in the film. Blake readily agreed to the look. In those days, it was considered an inspired choice. Today, we recognize it as cultural appropriation.

GEORGE SEGAL WAS originally cast to play the lead role in the film. A week before we were to start shooting, for reasons I still don't fully understand, he withdrew. It was devastating for Blake. Orion promptly shut down production, and everything came to a grinding halt.

Dudley Moore happened to be attending the same group therapy as Blake.

"There I was," Blake said, "looking right at him. I suddenly knew that was the way I wanted to go."

This choice surprised me. Dudley was so different from George Segal, and the way the character had originally been written. I was to play Dudley's long-time girlfriend, whom he forsakes for the fantasy of his "10," but returns to in the end, a wiser and more devoted partner. I worried that Dudley looked younger than me, and I was certainly several inches taller than he was. I told Blake that I would understand if he wished to replace me with someone more compatible with Dudley on-screen. Blake said he actually wanted that contrast.

"Think of Sinatra, or André Previn," he said. "Neither man is tall, yet both are incredibly attractive and charismatic." I instantly comprehended what he was getting at.

My first day of shooting for *10* was in early November. We shot a scene on the beach, just up the road from our house. The following day, all hell broke loose with our babies' new nanny. Tensions had been escalating, as she was not happy being in Los Angeles. Amelia was sick, and I had to go to work. When I returned home that evening, the nanny was nowhere to be found. She had left Amelia and Joanna in the care of our housekeeper, packed her bags, and boarded a flight back to London.

Fortunately, I was not scheduled to work the next day. I canceled other appointments and focused on the children. The next stretch of filming was to take place in Mexico, and I had been planning to go there a week ahead of the company since the days allotted on my U.S. visa were almost up. Blake and I decided that I should take the girls with me. Five days later, Amelia, Joanna, and I departed for Las Hadas, in Manzanillo. Blake, Emma, and Clare were to join us there the following week.

Las Hadas was a pretty ocean-side resort, looking much like an iced wedding cake against the parched landscape. Amelia and Joanna settled in easily. We swam every day, Amelia eventually learning to do so independently, and both children reveled in getting undivided attention from their mum. We made cards to welcome Blackie and the older girls when they finally came down, and arranged flowers for everyone's rooms. Emma and Clare took maximum advantage of the sun, sea, and sumptuous dining.

Blake was in rare form, clearly enjoying this film, which despite its bumpy start was now proceeding smoothly. Dick Crockett was ever-present at his side, directing all the stunt sequences and second unit photography, as he did for most of Blake's films. I noticed that Blake wasn't taking any pills, which made it all the more pleasant for us to spend time together.

Watching some of the scenes being shot, it was quickly apparent that Dudley was going to be superb. There was a scene in the hotel bar with Dudley at the piano, playing his own arrangement of Henry Mancini's lovely theme song. An accomplished pianist, Dudley often played extemporaneously on the set. He was a brilliant comedian, endearingly authentic and generous, both on-screen and off. I looked forward to working with him in the New Year.

The company took a brief hiatus for the winter holidays, which we spent in Gstaad. While we were there, I learned that my mum was very ill with bronchitis. She hadn't been to the doctor because she knew that he would put her in the hospital. Auntie reported that Mum was experiencing severe depression. I felt desperate to do something to help once again, but what? She was too ill to travel. I hoped I might persuade her to come visit in the New Year, once she was well enough to do so.

Emma was having her own difficulties. Now sixteen, she was feeling her oats. She had begged to be allowed to go to Alderney for Christmas with Jen and Clare. I understood her desires, but I told her that I wanted her with me. She then arranged to join her dad in New York for the second half of the holiday. I tried to be supportive, but it made me blue.

On the day after Christmas, Blake confessed that he had been flirting with pain pills again. I had sensed it. I knew he must be feeling out of phase, having stopped working so suddenly after having been so creatively stimulated in the prior months. Peter and Lynne Sellers were in town, which made things uncomfortable, since we bumped into them here and there. Also, Blake's back had been troubling him again—always a red flag.

Although completely sober during the day, by the dinner hour he became distant or argumentative, often disappearing upstairs to our bedroom as early as possible. I found myself making excuses to the kids, saying "Dad's feeling tired tonight," in order to cover for him. Thankfully, Charley had returned to us for a spell, which brightened their spirits.

When Blake finally confessed his problem to me, he became tearful, asking me to be patient, and to try and help him. Afterward, his mood lifted considerably, as it so often did once he had unburdened himself.

I did my best to do as Blake asked. At this point in our marriage, I was aware that his issues with drugs were all about calming his anxiety and stress levels. He didn't take uppers, nor did he drink, smoke, or take recreational drugs. Prescription pain medication was always his panacea of choice, and since I knew his pain was real and chronic, I found myself between a rock and a hard place in terms of what to do. I was torn between compassion and the suspicion that he might be using his physical challenges to enable his addiction.

On New Year's Eve, I wrote:

Another difficult year. However, Blackie has now resolved yet again to try to keep away from the drugs. The difference when he does is phenomenal. He's human, and reachable. This evening he stayed up until 2 AM playing Scrabble with us all.

Happy New Year, world. I wonder what lies ahead of us next year.

When we returned to Los Angeles, Blake resumed shooting on *10*, and I started filming my scenes a few days later. I was initially aware of watching myself too carefully and felt my performance was contrived. Eventually I settled into the role and began to enjoy myself.

There was a secondary plot in the film involving a neighbor who, in contrast to Dudley's character, has a prolific sex life. Blake hired a consultant from the adult film industry to assist with the casting and staging of an orgy scene. He came home on the first day and said he couldn't remember a funnier or more bizarre experience at work, and that I must come and visit the set to see it for myself. I arrived to find naked bodies strewn around, waiting for a shot, as if it was the most natural thing in the world.

When the assistant director said, "Touch-ups, please, for the next scene!" I was astonished to see combs produced and pubic hair teased and fluffed, with no embarrassment whatsoever.

Blake conceived an adorable shot of Dudley walking naked between two tall women, his arms encircling them both. It started as a headshot of the three, then as they pass the camera and climb steps to a telescope, it revealed the rear view: three bums, with Dudley's considerably lower and smaller one in the center.

"I've never been so happy in my life!" his character says dreamily.

This was a lot to ask of Dudley. He was self-conscious about his body, having been born with a clubfoot. Blake promised he would be very discreet and shoot above the knees. He even offered to allow Dudley to wear a towel, but Dudley gamely opted to strip down and go for the comedy. Later, Blake said how impressed he was by Dudley's courage.

A week later, we received shattering news: Dick Crockett had committed suicide. We had noticed in Las Hadas that his voice, always gravelly, had become nothing but a hoarse whisper. I instinctively knew that something was very wrong and had mentioned it to Blake, who said he would encourage Crockett to see a doctor. Apparently, he had been diagnosed with throat cancer, and had been told that he would need immediate surgery. He opted for oblivion instead. He left a note for Blake, who was utterly devastated. Later, Blake dedicated *10* to Dick Crockett.

17

CROCKETT'S PASSING WAS the first in another series of family dramas. I learned that my mum had again broken two ribs, this time due to excessive coughing from her lingering bronchitis. Geoff suffered broken ribs as well, along with a fractured hand, due to a tiff with his girlfriend's brother. Jenny and Kayti, who had temporarily moved back in with Tom, returned to live with us again. Amelia and Joanna began acting up as a result of all the tension in our packed household. Jen and Clare moved into a rented mobile home just up the road from us, and Emma began spending more and more time up there. I could hardly blame her.

At breakfast one morning, Amelia, Joanna, and Kayti were bickering. I suddenly heard myself saying, "We *will* have harmony in this house!" as I whacked a pancake onto a plate.

I RECEIVED A script entitled *Little Miss Marker*, a remake of the Damon Runyon film starring Shirley

Temple as a little girl who is left as a marker for a bet. Sorrowful Jones, the bookie with whom she is left, was to be played by Walter Matthau. Tony Curtis was costarring, and the film was to be directed by its screenwriter, Walter Bernstein, at Universal Studios. The chance to work opposite Matthau appealed to me, and I accepted the offer to play the widow who becomes romantically involved with him.

The film was set in the 1930s, and I wore some beautiful costumes designed by Ruth Morley, famous for her work on *Annie Hall*, *The Miracle Worker*, and *Kramer vs. Kramer*, among others. My new friend John Isaacs was brought in to do my hair, but I was in search of a new makeup artist. Lorraine Roberson, who had been my hairdresser on *Hawaii* and *Star!*, was working at Universal at the time. She called me and said, "There's a young man I think would be perfect for your makeup. I've seen his work, and he's great. Come and meet him?"

Rick Sharp seemed absurdly young, but the makeup tests we did looked terrific. From then on, Rick became my go-to makeup man, and he remains so to this day. He and John Isaacs hit it off immediately, and working with these two gents was, and continues to be, a true pleasure. Their moods are light, and they tease me and each other affectionately, making long and arduous workdays pass more quickly and joyfully.

In early March, a few weeks before filming was to commence and before I'd had a chance to ask her myself, my mother uncharacteristically telephoned to ask if she could come for a visit. Her arrival would coincide with my work on the film, which involved time away on location, but of course I said yes. I arranged for her to have a complete checkup with Dr. Tanney, who confirmed that she was not a well lady and put her on several different medications.

Despite the fact that I was working, Mum seemed to enjoy herself. She had her hair done, visited the set, and spent time with Joanna and Amelia, now four and five, and with Emma, now in her junior year at Brentwood School. Emma had just made the Honors List, and a little later was elected senior prefect and editor of the school yearbook. I was immensely proud.

Working with Walter Matthau was delightful. He was funny, and surprisingly shy. Because he'd had heart issues, he maintained a rigid discipline in terms of his work schedule—always quitting at 6 p.m. on the dot, and never working on weekends, which suited me fine.

The film company flew to Palo Alto for two weeks' location shooting, and my mum went to San Juan, Mexico, to spend the last part of her holiday with my brother Donald, who had relocated there. He had separated from his first wife and was now remarried to a lovely woman named Alma. (Chris had also remarried, and was still living in England. He was working as a photographer, and though struggling financially, was trying to stay sober.)

After *Little Miss Marker* wrapped, Emma, Jen, and Clare headed to Alderney, where they would be spending the better part of the summer. Blake and I went to Gstaad with Amelia, Joanna, and Charley.

Instead of the summer of idyllic peace we had hoped for in Gstaad, we very quickly found ourselves in the midst of the usual Edwards chaos. Jenny and Kayti arrived a few days after we did. I had promised Aunt Joan that she could visit while we were there, and she arrived soon thereafter.

Blake then received word that the top brass at Orion Pictures, who had committed to *S.O.B.*, his screenplay about the madness of Hollywood, were now questioning budget issues and threatening to pull the plug. He began pitching the film to other studios. We had to make a quick trip to London the same week, for screenings of the latest cut of *10*, and for me to record the theme song for the film with Henry Mancini. We rather nervously left Auntie, Jenny, Charley, and the three children behind at the chalet, and wondered what problems might arise from that mixture of personalities.

Our trip happened to coincide with my mother's sixty-ninth birthday, so we arranged to take her to dinner. She was in a dark mood and made little effort. Blake and I found it exhausting to keep the evening light and festive.

When we returned to our hotel, we watched a televised program about Luciano Pavarotti. Song after song poured out of the great tenor, and the beauty of his voice made me tearful and filled us both with awe. After the program ended, Blake asked me what I felt made great singing so moving to listen to.

"I think, when singing, one exposes one's soul," I said.

"How so?"

I struggled to explain. "Dancers can look at a mirror, a writer can look at a page, and a painter can look at a canvas and see their work reflected back at them. But singers can only hear and feel what they are doing. After all the training, technique, use of breath, and placement of sound, it boils down to an emotional response to music and lyrics—and the way they touch one's heart and soul."

Blake nodded understandingly. We kissed, said good night, and turned out the light. About ten seconds passed, and in the darkness, I heard a slight clearing of the throat, and in a little voice like that of a child, Blake began to sing "Sweet Leilani."

I exploded with laughter and turned on the light.

"Don't laugh," Blake said. "I'm showing you my *soul*."

He then proceeded to sing a medley of golden oldies, from one corny love song to another, in the same little-boy voice. His eyes glinted with delight at his own antics, and I laughed until I literally wept. I had one of the best night's sleep of my life.

BLAKE MADE A few trips back and forth to Los Angeles to do some reshoots and work on the marketing for *10*, which was due to open in October. He also received word that Lorimar Pictures was now on board to produce *S.O.B.*, which was to begin shooting in the New Year.

It had never occurred to me when we made the great escape from Hollywood that residency in Switzerland would eventually lead to such long periods of time away from my husband and children. At the end of the summer, I was once again facing just three weeks left to me in the United States until the end of the year.

Despite having set up a wonderful support system—Jen and Clare in L.A. for Emma, Charley for Amelia and Joanna—I was worried stiff about what the long-term consequences might be for them without the consistency of a mum and dad in residence full-time.

My anxieties were somewhat mitigated by the knowledge that Emma was having one of the best summers of her life on Alderney. She and Clare were living with another friend in Patmos, our little cottage. They had been enjoying a form of freedom, living independently yet being quietly monitored from a short distance by Jen Gosney, and Mum and Dad Walton, who had now retired on the island, and whom they saw often. The girls had found jobs—Clare managing a small clothing boutique, and Emma working as a waitress and chambermaid at two of the island's small hotels. There was of course a lively social scene, and they were having a ball.

Near the end of August, however, I received a terrifying phone call from Jen, telling me that she and Emma had been in a car accident. Jen had accompanied Emma from Alderney back to England, and was about to put her on a plane to New York to visit her dad. En route, Jen's car blew a tire, resulting in their careening into the guardrail, and then back across the highway and down into a ditch. The car had accordioned and was smoking profusely, but miraculously, Jen and Emma emerged unscathed, except for a mild case of whiplash. It was the stuff of my worst nightmares—the very thing I worried so much about whenever any of my family were away from me. Though I longed to rush to Emma's side, I refrained, since she was on her way to see her dad.

I scheduled my return to L.A. for the end of September, a week after Emma and Clare went back to school, in the hopes of making the most out of the short time my visa allowed me in the States before having to leave the country again. Just before my departure from Gstaad, I received another call from Jen. She relayed to me that Emma and Clare were miserable in L.A. School was not the pleasure it had once been, and they were asking for a change of plan: Clare wanted to return to England, and Emma was asking to move to New York permanently. My heart sank. Although I had long expected this request from Emma, and we had occasionally discussed the possibility, I had not anticipated it happening so soon.

I asked both girls if they could finish out the school year with us, but Emma, who was now a senior, explained that this was perhaps her last chance to experience living with her father before she went to college. She requested to transfer to Trinity School in Manhattan, where Bridget was also in attendance.

Blake did not take this news well. Perhaps he saw it as an indictment of him as a stepfather, which in some ways it probably was. He'd always had a hard time expressing his affection and respect for Emma, and he was often resentful of my love for her. He tore into Emma, saying he'd be hard-pressed to forgive her for hurting me in this way. He thought he was speaking for us both, when in fact I understood what the girls felt they needed to do and why. I conveyed this to Emma, but Blake's confrontation with her was unpleasant, and it resulted in her leaving even earlier than planned.

The morning of her departure, I gave her a hug and my blessing. I wanted to tell her that she went with my love, and that she must try to listen to her instincts and not be overpowered by internal or external pressures over the next few months. Unfortunately, Blake came downstairs at the last minute. He launched into another diatribe, and it became more important to get her out of the house and away from him as quickly as possible, so she left before I could say all I wanted to. After she'd gone, I simply wept.

Clare and Jen remained in L.A. for a few more weeks, then headed back to England. It was an acutely painful time.

Because I had to leave the States again for a while, Blake and I decided to head to Gstaad for a couple of weeks, to spend some time together and attempt some real communication.

While we were in Gstaad, I wrote:

Blake and I had a huge talk last night, and I became more aware of how much he knows about himself. He admits to childishness with Emma, competition, manipulation in many areas—and much more.

My question was: "You know so much, voice so much . . . why do things that are so hurtful?"

He talked of the "madness" he'd always lived with, the habits he'd learned, and his huge swings back and forth between extreme generosity and petty anger. He claimed that he wasn't totally aware when he was being hurtful, that it's never preconceived, just something that comes out on the spur of the moment. He said he's working hard on it, but his improvement is slow. I must try to be vigilant and, in my turn, not afraid to speak out about what I see. I replied that he must be vigilant about not becoming angry and defensive if I do hit a nerve by speaking out. We talked of drugs, and how they lead to avoidance of feelings. We talked about fear. Then in typical fashion, he turned the conversation around and went on the attack, making me the one who avoided feelings. This time I realized what he was doing, and steered the subject matter back to the two of us. It was 3:15 when we turned out the light.

We had other meaningful discussions, and when I spoke to Emma on the phone, I was relieved to hear her sounding settled and happy. All too soon it was time to leave, as Blake had to return to L.A. for further promotion on *10*, which had opened to favorable reviews, and for preproduction on *S.O.B.* Just before we had departed for Gstaad, Blake and I had slipped into the back of a cinema in Westwood to observe the audience reaction to *10*. The attendees were roaring with laughter and clearly loving the movie, which had been a tonic for us both.

Rather than stay on by myself in Switzerland, I returned to California with Blake for the few last days allowed to me, to be with Amelia and Joanna. In order to stay out of the country but also be nearer home, we arranged that I would take a quick trip to Mexico on *Impulse*, which had by now been returned to us, newly refurbished. Blake, Amelia, and Joanna planned to join me for the first leg of the journey, which coincided with the girls' school break. He would then return with them to L.A. and hopefully come back aboard near the end of the trip.

The time period coincided with Blake's and my tenth wedding anniversary, and as I often did for special occasions, I wrote a poem for him as a gift:

Thoughts for a 10th Anniversary

In all my years, I've never met another one
　　like you.
You drive me mad, you make me laugh and cry
　　and set me about my ears. You do.

My mate. My dearest love. Anniversary man.
Let me capture "essence of Blake." If I can.

Black prince. Mercurial knight with a rugged
　　face.
Too proud. A broken body. Martial arts grace.

A whirling dervish. A desperado child.
"Sudden and quick in quarrel." Open-hearted,
　　wild.

Tough, yet soppy-soft. You'd like to save us all.
Generous. Extravagant. Twenty feet tall.

You "make bold," you "cut a dash." Diamonds
in your style.
Noble. Even-handed. Manipulative guile.

Calculating. Fire eater. When threatened, you
attack
And hammer at the truth until I cannot answer
back.

You tear your hair and lecture on the follies
of excess
And tell me we'd do better if we could live on less.

I agree. I really see and feel your anxious pain.
Then you blithely turn around and spend and
spend again.

You twist and turn and tie your soul. The knots
are inches thick.
Guilt and fear. Grief. Remorse. Those toxins
make you sick.

You flirt with death yet embrace life. Shake it
by the tail.

Doing first, thinking later. Making loved ones
  pale.

You steal a bit, and wheel and deal to gain the
  upper hand.
You heal, and play the doctor. Your bedside
  manner's grand.

Magic touch. Gentle touch. I melt within your
  arms.
You seem to know me inside out. I can't resist
  your charms.

So, when all is said and done, this lady's by
  your side.
For the wild fun, the fierce pain, the laughter
  in the ride.

And, dearest, when I show you this, I know
  what you will say.
"What else?" You'll grin. "What else—will you
  write of me today?"

On our first night aboard *Impulse*, we anchored
in a quiet cove. Blake and I lay in our bunk, enjoying our beautiful boat, feeling profoundly grateful

that she was ours again. When we turned out the lights, I became aware of the night sounds.

"Oh, Blake!" I said. "Listen . . . there's a bird out there somewhere. Can you hear him calling?"

"Mm-hmm."

". . . and the water slapping against the hull?"

"Mm-hmm."

"This is magical. I love you darling."

"I love you, too. G'night."

"Good night."

There was a pause of about ten seconds. Then I heard a familiar little-boy cough, and in the darkness, Blake began to sing "Red Sails in the Sunset."

I exploded with laughter, and he followed with a medley of sea shanties, until, as usual, I wept.

WE HAD HIRED a new skipper, who seemed qualified. As Blake departed for his return to L.A., he said to the skipper, "Take care of my lady, please." After Blake and the girls departed, we put to sea and began a leisurely cruise toward Cabo San Lucas, stopping at various ports and harbors along the way.

I began to suspect that our skipper was taking Blake's request a bit too seriously. I occasionally received an unbidden peck on the cheek, or pat on the back, and far too much proximity whenever

I was up on the bridge. One evening at bedtime, there was a tap on my cabin door. The skipper entered, clad in his bathrobe, his hair and beard slightly unkempt. He sat on the edge of my bed.

"Everything all right?" he asked, patting my thigh.

The other crew members were in the forward quarters, and my cabin was in the aft section. I don't recall my exact words, but I firmly dispatched him and kept my door locked from then on. I knew, however, that I needed to take stricter measures to protect myself going forward.

I attempted to alert Blake via the ship-to-shore radio, but had to speak in code since the skipper was ever present. Telling him a made-up story that was part of a word game we often played with the kids, I secretly spelled out "S-K-I-P-P-E-R-H-O-R-N-Y. H-E-L-P!" Alas, Blake had no clue what I was talking about.

Upon arrival in Cabo, I went to the nearest hotel to find a landline. When I told Blake of my plight, he became irritated by the inconvenience of it all, which wasn't exactly what I'd hoped for. But he said he would send Gerry Nutting, my former tour manager who was now a member of our production company, to join me. I was extremely grateful.

When I told the skipper we were expecting a guest, he was equally irritated. He managed to miss

Gerry's arrival at the airport, and Gerry had to find his way to the boat by himself. I spied him waving from a distance as he approached on a water taxi, and I was inordinately pleased to see him.

The following day, when Gerry and I tried to reach Blake again, we discovered the ship-to-shore was broken. We had the dinghy brought around so we could head into harbor. But as Gerry descended the ladder steps, the ties gave way and he disappeared into the water up to his chest and had to change his clothing.

We put out to sea again, this time on a long journey around the tip of the Baja Peninsula, heading for La Paz, where we planned to disembark. I can't prove it, but I'm sure the skipper must have known that a major storm was in the forecast. Within an hour we were in a full-blown gale. The sea was coming at us from all sides; *Impulse* reared up and smashed down into wave after massive wave.

About three and a half hours of hell ensued. The contents of the refrigerator exploded all over the galley floor. Glasses smashed, plants fell over, and furniture slid. At one point, a chair broke free on the aft deck, and Gerry went out to tie it down. The boat listed, and he suddenly slid out of view. Mercifully, he didn't go overboard, but he collided with a stanchion that left an egg-sized lump on his forehead.

I worried what the storm might do to our beloved *Impulse*; it felt like she could splinter apart, but her construction was so solid that she held firm.

When we finally made it to La Paz, we discovered that our trusty skipper had neglected to reserve a berth for us. We dropped anchor, piled our luggage into the dinghy, and Gerry motored us ashore. He jumped into the water, removed the luggage piece by piece, and carried it aloft until he reached the sand. I rolled up my trousers and waded in after him, soaking my travel outfit.

Sometime later, *Impulse* and her crew made it safely back to L.A., at which point the skipper left our employ.

FOR CHRISTMAS WE returned to Gstaad, where Blake put the final polish on his script for *S.O.B.*, and I attempted to begin my story about the ship's cat that I'd been planning since the trip to Greece. We also attended to a project that Blake and I had undertaken for the village.

In winters past, I had noted the rather skimpy illuminated decorations hanging over the town's main street. I said to Blake, "It's such a pity that this beautiful spot isn't lit like a fairyland for the holidays."

We conveyed to the village elders our interest in donating lights to line each chalet rooftop along the main street, plus the church steeple and the bridge. Although the tourist bureau knew we were behind the plans, I asked them to keep our involvement under wraps. When the lights were finally being installed, my heart was in my mouth, but happily, the results were gorgeous. Quickly thereafter, shop owners relit their windows to match, and the surrounding homeowners across the valley also began to line their rooftops with similar lights, which remain to this day.

BLAKE AND I became involved in another cause that year. In the spring, two young lawyers in California had organized an effort to bring much-needed relief supplies—food, water, medicine, shelter—to the Vietnamese "Boat People" (as they were called at the time). They procured the supplies and a plane to deliver the goods, but they lacked the fuel to get the plane off the ground. When Blake and I heard of their efforts, we volunteered to pay for the fuel. The delivery was successful, and Operation California (now Operation USA) was born.

The young men returned with a list of needs twice as long as the first, and further relief efforts were planned for the refugee camps along the borders of Cambodia and Laos. Tony Adams volunteered to accompany the next flight, which would be the first international relief effort to enter Cambodia since 1975. He returned with truly harrowing stories of mass killing sites, prisons, graves, orphanages, people sick and having breakdowns. The only good news was that the journey had paved the way for further flights and deliveries there.

I wanted to contribute more. Blake and I agreed to join the board of Operation California, and to host a television special as a fund-raiser early in the New Year. I also began to think about traveling with the organization myself in the not-too-distant future.

18

IT WAS THE start of a new decade—1980—and I knew it was going to be a very busy year. In addition to the fund-raising concert for Operation California, I had agreed to do another Japanese tour in February, and I had asked my mother and Zoë to accompany me. I often invited Mum to join me on such trips—location filming and so on—and most of the time she demurred. This time, to my surprise and delight and for reasons I'm not sure of, she accepted the invitation. It pleased me to know that I would be able to share Japan with her.

Blake's film *S.O.B.*, in which I would play the role of the producer's wife, had been acquired for production. Six years had passed since Blake first wrote the screenplay in Gstaad, and every studio he'd submitted it to had admired it, but passed on it, fearing the characters in the script might be based on them. In fact, no character in the film was entirely based on any one person; although almost all the events in the film were rooted in fact, the characters were amalgams of several different Hollywood people. Finally, Lorimar Pictures had been brave enough to sign on, and shooting was scheduled to begin in March.

I traveled to New York to visit Emma, whom I hadn't seen since she left California. I was so looking forward to spending time with her, and when she arrived at my hotel, I was relieved to find that she looked well and happy. She seemed very stimulated by living in New York. Her new school had a phenomenal performing arts program—Emma had joined an a cappella group, and was soon to be acting in the school play. A great piece of the puzzle about her desire to live in New York fell into place for me.

We spent three special days together, chatting, shopping, and going to the theater. We saw the original production of Stephen Sondheim's *Sweeney Todd*, starring Len Cariou and Angela Lansbury, and both agreed it was one of the best musicals we'd ever seen. Several songs had us in tears. (I always weep at Sondheim. It's the emotion in his music, the sheer brilliance of his lyrics, the essential truths he writes. He makes us see the best and worst in ourselves.) During the song "Not While I'm Around," Emma held on to my arm, and we both wept quietly. The lyric, about protecting a loved one from harm, had so many overtones for us both. Of course, we later talked of all that had occurred in Los Angeles, and became emotional again, putting everything to rest as best we could. It was wonderful to spend so much concentrated time together, yet also deeply moving. I could hardly bear to say goodbye.

I flew back to L.A., and the following morning the doorbell rang at 6:30 a.m. It was Lorimar's production crew, having arrived to begin construction on our beachfront for the set for *S.O.B.* Blake had elected to build there rather than find a house on location, because there were so many specific requirements. I wondered how I would manage the next few chaotic months.

At the end of January, I taped the benefit concert for Operation California at the Dorothy Chandler Pavilion. Tony Adams and Blake produced the evening, which was to air on television in February. *Because We Care* featured an astonishing roster of performers: Alan Alda; Glen Campbell; Natalie Cole; Billy Crystal; Jane Fonda; Robert Goulet; Michael Jackson; Walter Matthau; Dudley Moore; Mary Tyler Moore; the Muppets; Bob Newhart; Peter, Paul and Mary; Frank Sinatra; John Travolta; and Jon Voight, among many others, all of whom donated their services for the evening. Rick Sharp and John Isaacs also gave of their time, doing everyone's makeup and hair. The event raised more than $1 million for Cambodian relief, and was a marathon to pull off, but the feeling throughout the day was one of great warmth and generosity.

Two weeks later, I departed for my second Japanese tour. Mum and Zoë were with me, as was Gerry Nutting and many of the musicians from the first tour. My musical director this time around was Alan Ferguson, a colleague and friend of Jack Elliott's. Blake stayed home to work on preproduction for *S.O.B.* and to be with Amelia and Joanna.

Mum seemed so happy to be on the trip. She helped out backstage, and loved hanging out with the musicians and attending the concerts, which for the most part went smoothly. One evening, Mum got swept up by the enthusiasm of the fans waiting outside the auditorium and as we drove away she began waving to everyone like the queen. I guess you can take the girl out of show biz, but you can't take show biz out of the girl! It was adorable.

Zoë was positively bubbling throughout the trip as well. She visited the Noh and Kabuki theaters, and went shopping with Mum, who alternated between great bouts of chat and giggles, and long, contented silences. After the final concert, I took my gang to a disco. Our producer, Mr. Sakata, danced with Mum and she really cut loose, which everyone loved.

On our return to Los Angeles, Mum went off to a little apartment that I had found and set up for her. I had managed to persuade her to stay on for a few months in an attempt to see what living in L.A. might be like. As usual, the house in Malibu was overrun with people, but it was wonderful to see Blake, and Amelia and Joanna, who were in good form. As I was tucking Amelia into bed that night, she said, "Don't forget to say I love you as you go out the door . . ."

"But I always say that," I replied.

"I know," she said. "But this time I might want to say it back."

At breakfast the next morning, Jo said, "I've got a present for you!" then hugged and kissed me fiercely. Then she said, ". . . and here's another present!" five more times, and hugged and kissed me again.

FILMING FOR *S.O.B.* commenced two weeks after my return from Japan. At the first read-through, it was a delight to see William Holden, Robert Preston, Richard Mulligan, and Robert Webber going through their paces. They were all so consummate in their work, and picked up on Blake's suggestions so effortlessly. Stories were swapped, and laughter and affection abounded.

Blake seemed nervous, but I knew he would be—so much rested on this film. It was his most personal project to date, and he had waited more than six years to get it off the ground. Now it was a reality, and in our own backyard: the film crew swarmed all over our property, and trucks, trailers, port-a-potties, and generators were parked everywhere. Our dream house had been built, furnished, and was now functioning on our beachfront—yet it was merely a film set, and would be demolished as soon as we were done.

The esteemed designer Theadora Van Runkle, who had done *Bonnie and Clyde*, *Mame*, and *The Godfather: Part II*, among many others, was creating the costumes for the film. Her designs were spot-on for every character; you knew exactly what Hollywood stereotype each one represented by what they wore.

Blake had written my character of Sally Miles as a comic send-up of my own Hollywood image. Sally is a singer/actress, most famous for her Oscar-winning performance in *Peter Pan*. Her latest film, produced by her husband, Felix Farmer (played by

Richard Mulligan), is a disastrous flop, and Felix conceives the idea of reshooting it as an erotic musical in which Sally will bare her breasts.

Obviously, I was nervous about this, but I'd had six years to prepare, and the scene was character- and plot-driven, rather than gratuitous. Blake promised to shoot it on a "closed set"—no press, no visitors—and I knew he would handle it tastefully, despite the satirical nature of the film.

Since the scene is an erotic nightmare of sorts, Theadora had designed a red chiffon gown with multiple layers of fabric, to swirl around me as I moved past wind machines and mirrors. The bust was made to break away at the appropriate moment, revealing, as Theadora called it, my "*belle poitrine.*"

During the first fitting at Western Costumes, Blake came over to see how the effect would work. I was already mortified, in that a number of seamstresses and assistants were in attendance.

Blake said, "OK, show me."

I screwed up my courage and ripped open the breakaway top, which was intended to reveal just one breast.

Blake waved his hands in front of his face as if erasing chalk from a blackboard. "No, no, no!" he declared. "It won't do. It has to be both boobs."

"BLAKE!" I gasped.

"Sorry, honey, but it really doesn't work otherwise."

The dress was remodeled to reveal the entire *poitrine*. Thankfully, by the time we actually shot the scene, we had rehearsed so much that I hardly thought about it.

S.O.B. was one of the most enjoyable films to make, and I believe that everyone involved felt the same way. The film was such a send-up of the industry, and we all took wicked pleasure in the mischief-making, tilting at Hollywood instead of conforming to its standards. The cast—which also included Loretta Swit, Shelley Winters, Robert Loggia, Robert Vaughn, Marisa Berenson, and Larry Hagman, plus Blake's daughter Jennifer and Rosanna Arquette as two starstruck hitchhikers—became a repertory company of sorts. Actors who weren't scheduled to work would come down to the set just for the camaraderie and shared laughter.

When the film had finally finished shooting, we held a screening of the first rough cut for the company.

I wrote:

The film is not yet scored or dubbed, just an assemblage, but it is all there. It is so funny, and brilliantly shot. The lead-up to the "belle poitrine" is tasteful and scary and creative . . . all done with mirrors. I was so proud of Blackie, I could have burst. Good comments afterwards. My only fear is that the public won't fully appreciate the film. It is such an unusual animal.

Prior to filming *S.O.B.*, Blake had seen a small German film from the thirties by Reinhold Schünzel entitled *Viktor und Viktoria*, about a female singer who impersonates a man impersonating a woman. Blake was intrigued, and thought it could be a marvelous role for me. Although I found the idea of playing with gender daunting, when I saw the original film myself, I was able to imagine how stylish it could be in Blake's hands, and what an interesting comment it might make about true love. By the time *S.O.B.* had concluded, he had obtained the rights, had begun working on the screenplay, and had secured the go-ahead from Lorimar to begin production.

A decision had to be made as to where the film would be shot. The story was set in Paris, so we initially thought that filming there would be the obvious choice. But it quickly became clear that, as had been the case with *Darling Lili*, there were too many problems with shooting it on location—modern equipment on rooftops, variable weather, and so on. Blake suddenly remembered that Pinewood Studios in England had two large soundstages that were connected to each other. They shared a sliding door, and for big projects, such as the James Bond films, they often accommodated a single set spanning both stages. It occurred to Blake that he could shoot the entire film indoors, creating Paris in the 1930s as he needed it to be. That way, he would have total control over every aspect, and given that Pinewood also offered preproduction and editing facilities, it would be far more economical. We began to make plans to base ourselves in London once again in the following year.

IN JUNE, I traveled to New York to attend Emma's graduation from Trinity School. She had been accepted into Brown University, and I was unbelievably proud. We made plans for her to come back to L.A. for a brief visit, since my dad and Win would also be there, and I was hoping to take them all on a trip to British Columbia on *Impulse*.

When Emma arrived, Blake wasn't home, but I could tell that she was very nervous about seeing him, as this was their first reunion since she had moved to New York. I was nervous, too, but Blake made it easy for us. Emma and I were sitting in the Jacuzzi together when he got home, and he walked straight into the water with all his clothes on and gave her a big hug. Emma spent a day or two catching up with her friends from Brentwood, then she and I traveled to join Dad and Win on the boat for a few days.

It was wonderful having Emma with me, but she was quiet and a little withdrawn; probably sorting out all that had happened and the unknowns that lay ahead.

We did some salmon fishing, and enjoyed the magnificent scenery—the waterfalls, the bald eagles, and of course our beloved boat. All too soon, Emma was heading back to New York, Dad and Win were heading back to England, and I was on my way to Washington, DC, to host an episode of *The CBS Festival of Lively Arts for Young People* called "Invitation to the Dance," with Rudolf Nureyev, Ann Reinking, and other guests.

I danced a nerve-wracking waltz with Nureyev, whom I'd known in my London days through Svetlana and Zoë. He was gracious, and I managed to not trip over my feet.

While I was in DC, I heard the terrible news that Peter Sellers had died of a massive heart attack. I phoned Blake immediately, and he was very unglued. Despite their differences in recent years, their friendship had been long, and they had shared so much laughter together. His loss came as a real shock. We'd known for a long time that Peter had a weak heart, but we had come to take it for granted somehow, never imagining that he would die so soon. He was only fifty-four.

A month later, Blake's and my good friend Gower Champion passed away at the age of sixty-one. The two events hit Blake hard. He flew to New York for Gower's funeral, and returned in bad shape. I knew he was grappling with his own mortality after the loss of his two good friends, but he became severely depressed and confided in me that he had been having suicidal thoughts. This disturbed me greatly. I tried to be understanding, and prayed he would eventually work through it, since he was still in analysis.

Having been married to Blake for eleven years, I was aware that he suffered bouts of depression, and he had told me early in our relationship that his mother had been suicidal at times in his youth. The only other time I had worried that he might do himself harm was during *The Carey Treatment* and the James Aubrey debacle, when he had nearly broken the hotel room window in his despair. Thankfully, he was writing the script for *Victor/Victoria,* and having a creative project always helped. Over the ensuing weeks, his mood began to lift.

Despite the decision to control costs by shooting in the studio, the film still had a very substantial budget. The Lorimar executives began to balk. They threatened to pull out unless Blake could bring everything in at a more reasonable price. For a day or so, it seemed the whole movie was canceled. Then Blake opted to defer his salary and take a larger portion of the "back end," if the film were to be successful. This did the trick, and production was back on track.

We would need to be based in England for at least six months starting in the New Year, so we began looking for another place to live in London, plus a school for Amelia and Joanna. Fortunately, we found both in fairly short order: a large apartment on Hampstead Heath, with the American Community School just down the road.

I traveled to Rhode Island to visit Emma at Brown, where she seemed relatively happy, but admitted she was waiting for something to really inspire her there. As always it was hard to say goodbye, but we made plans to meet up in Gstaad over Christmas.

Over the next few weeks in L.A. I did looping

for *S.O.B.*, and tried to put in as much time as possible with Amelia and Joanna.

There was a second drama with the Lorimar execs when they suddenly announced that their company was having serious financial problems and they needed to withdraw from *Victor/Victoria*. They gave Blake permission to shop the film elsewhere, but said they would stay on until a new home was found, since preproduction had already begun. After a few days of frantic phone calls and meetings between Blake, Tony Adams, and various agents, producers, and lawyers, MGM—no longer led by James Aubrey—finally came on board. But its decision-makers stipulated that they wanted a two-picture deal, one of which would be a new *Pink Panther*. With Peter Sellers now gone, Blake initially resisted the idea, but eventually he accepted the terms and decided to cross that bridge when he came to it, so that work on *Victor/Victoria* could continue.

Because of my visa limitations, I had to return to Gstaad in November, and Amelia, Joanna, and Charley joined me there. Near the end of the month, I wrote:

Two lovely things happened today. Henry Mancini phoned and played three songs for me that he had written for *Victor/Victoria*. They are just great. All different, nice textures, and one super-beautiful ballad. It has no lyrics as yet, but it is the prettiest melody, another great waltz, and I know from its style and the way the melody climbs what it ought to say. Hank was funny and dear, and I sat listening with the phone to one ear and fingers in the other, since he was none too handy with the microphone on his end and there was an almighty banging coming from workmen hammering in the room above me. At one point, when the music climbed especially high, I said, "That's a bit range-y, isn't it, Hank?" He chuckled, and said, "Piece of cake for you, Jools." I hope I can prove him right.

Then Blake called at about 1 PM my time, which was 5 AM for him. He had just finished the script for *Victor/Victoria* and phoned to tell me so. He was weary and happy, having worked on the final pages for about fourteen hours straight. I said to him, "So, we have a new baby." And it is like welcoming a new life into our family. A new creative venture.

Rehearsals began at Pinewood in early January. We settled into our new apartment, and Amelia and Joanna began attending the American Community School. Unfortunately, Charley was leaving us once again, which meant the girls had to adjust to yet another new nanny. It was tough on them, as always, and I did everything I could to boost their spirits. But it was difficult, as I was also busy with fittings and rehearsals for *Victor/Victoria*.

I had expressed doubts to Blake that I would be believable as a man. Even though my character is only masquerading as one, she passes as male to her audience, and therefore I thought I needed to do the same.

Blake said, "Honey, your audience will believe that Victor is a man because the audience on-screen believes it. It's poetic license."

This helped, but I knew I had to do my homework. I started to watch every man that crossed my path, and began to find a few clues as to how to behave. I noticed that men tend to be less "fussy" in their movements. They often sit with legs apart, rather than crossed, for example, and put their hands in their pockets rather than gesturing with them. Their facial expressions can be less animated than women's. I decided that aiming for "stillness" was my best bet.

I found the layers of men's clothing somewhat claustrophobic—the starched collars, dickeys, vests, suspenders, and cravats that the period called for. Then there was the question of what to do with my hair. We decided that a vibrant red would make both Victor and Victoria stand out best. My own hair was cut and dyed with three different layers of red for Victor's "natural" hair. This required regular visits to the hairdresser every ten days to preserve the richness of the color. For Victoria, and for all of Victor's performances in drag, I wore a variety of wigs and headpieces.

Makeup tests were extensive, but thankfully my British makeup man was superb. After one exhaustive session, I wrote:

Amazing how *one* face suddenly becomes a vast terrain of lumps, bumps, cracks, crevices and hollows, to be discussed and disguised. Oh my!

There were daily rehearsals with Paddy Stone for the dance numbers, and of course, we had to prerecord the songs. I attempted to change my voice in a subtle way, pitching it lower, warmer, and huskier as Victor, so as to sound somewhat masculine and less recognizable. For the big production numbers, I suggested climbing two octaves to a high note at the end, so it would sound like I had a female impersonator "gimmick." I doubt I fooled anyone, but Blake's words about believability saw me through.

After work and on weekends, I did my best to put in quality time with Amelia and Joanna. I took them to the zoo and the ballet. I made them breakfast each day before school, and read them bedtime stories at night. It was hard to find time to study my script, and, once filming began, to learn my lines, but I was aware of the stress that Blake's and my work hours and the new nanny were creating for our girls.

In spite of my efforts, they both began to act out. Eventually, I voiced for them how hard it must be to cope with Charley's departure and my busy schedule. I reinforced how much we loved them, wanted them, and said that we would never leave or let them down. I promised that I would be home every evening, and would carve out special time to listen to stories of their day and have cuddles. I said that no matter who came and went in our lives, or how busy we sometimes were, Daddy and I would always be constant, and there for them. It seemed to help for a while, though I sensed these issues would probably come up again.

FILMING FOR *VICTOR/VICTORIA* began on March 2. Rodger Maus, our production designer, had worked wonders with our two-stage set. The Paris streets were so realistic that it was easy to forget we were actually indoors. There were real drains for snow and rain runoff, and the buildings and storefronts had myriad authentic details, like letter boxes, glass windows, lamps, and street signs. One side of the street was more "up-market," and the other more run-down. Cars could literally drive along the roads. Most of the interior sets had been built in their designated spaces behind the building façades—the hotel lobby, the restaurant, the patisserie, the seedy bar. The nightclub and hotel rooms were separate sets, and they glowed with Art Deco flair. The lamps were genuine antiques from the period, as were many of the wall hangings and other decorative items. The authenticity was staggering, and it made it so much easier for us actors to do our work.

Our cinematographer, Dick Bush, showed me postcards of Montmartre and other areas of Paris, painted by Maurice Utrillo. Dick said, "Even though the story takes place in winter, I don't want the film to look cold. So I've borrowed Utrillo's idea of throwing color onto the snow, warm reflections from the storefronts, street lamps, and so on." It

was a great lesson in the importance of the cinematographer's contribution, and how subliminally
the audience can be influenced.

"The Shady Dame from Seville" was the first
musical number we shot. It was also my first
opportunity to pull the wig off and reveal Victor
beneath. I tried to remain expressionless as I did
so. It was always difficult to know whether to focus
on being masculine, even when in a dress, or to
show hints of the woman beneath the male façade,
depending on the scene. I struggled to remember
which one was leading at any given moment. It felt
like patting my head and rubbing my stomach at
the same time.

It was a joy to work with Robert Preston once
again, though the role of Toddy was such a departure from the doctor he played in *S.O.B.* When
we finished shooting my part of "Shady Dame,"
it was Preston's turn to use the same setup for his
mock version. He was so brave, bursting out of his
costume, lipstick smeared all over his mouth, false
eyelashes askew, and tottering about in high heels.
He had the company in stitches, and Blake just let
the camera roll. Toward the end, when Preston was
dropped unceremoniously onto the floor by his
dancers, he too collapsed with laughter, and Blake
never yelled "Cut!" It's all there, on film.

When we sang the duet "You and Me," I was reminded of my days in vaudeville, watching an act called the Western Brothers from the wings of the theater. Dressed in white tie and tails, they would lean against the piano with ease . . . always suave, elegant, and stylish.

I was also delighted to be reunited with James Garner again. We had bumped into each other a few times since making *The Americanization of Emily*, and our friendship had never wavered. Blake said to me one day, "Watch Garner, Jools. He's not only a great actor, he's a great *reactor*." It was the reason Blake chose him for the role. Garner conveyed so much with the mere lift of an eyebrow, and his expression when he first sees Victoria revealing herself to be Victor is priceless. After our first on-screen kiss in *Victor/Victoria*, when his character says, "I don't care if you *are* a man," my legs buckled again, just as they had done so many years before.

An entry from my diary:

Difficult doing the love scene in front of Blake. I wanted to do it well. Garner was tactful and dear, Blake took it all in stride, and I was a basket-case!

The kiss was cinematic craziness, in that it

was supposed to be snowing, and we had to have twice the amount of fake snow in order for it to register onscreen. We were getting flakes in our noses and eyes and teeth, and a build-up on shoulders and hair that looked like dandruff. Also, Jim and I are both so far-sighted now that we couldn't see each other in the close-up, especially with snow pouring over and between us. It was ridiculously funny.

My relationship with Jim was always platonic, but the fun and mutual affection we shared was ever-present.

Learning to throw a punch was a real challenge for me. I've never even been able to throw a ball, so I had no idea where to begin. Our stunt coordinator, Joe Dunne, had worked on many of Blake's films, and it was his job to make me look authentic. I practiced for days, almost throwing out my elbow in the process. In the end, I was surprised to discover how much I enjoyed the moment, and how high on adrenaline I felt afterward.

In truth, there was hardly a day on *Victor/Victoria* when I wasn't full of doubt about my performance . . . but there was one day when I got a terrific ego boost. A group of guys—

Garner, Preston, and some of the cameramen—were standing together, chatting casually. I was dressed as Victor in a tuxedo, and I sauntered over to join them. Normally in a situation such as that, they would have made some accommodation for my presence—a physical shift, an arm placed about my shoulder, a kind of deference to my being a woman. In this case, they simply carried on without any adjustment whatsoever. I realized with delight that I had been perceived as "one of the guys."

Geoff, now twenty-one, was working in the editing department once again, and Blake gave him a small role in the film, as a chorus boy who admires Victor. Emma flew in for a visit, and Blake put her in the audience behind me during the opera scene, when Victor is weeping copiously at *Madame Butterfly*. She had made the decision not to return to Brown University for her sophomore year. Having so recently moved to New York, she missed the stimulation of that city, and the proximity to the theater scene. She opted to return there and enroll in an acting conservatory. I had mixed feelings about this, but she was persuasive in her assessment of the situation, and I always trusted her judgment.

Dad and Win came to visit the set from time

to time, as did Auntie and Mum, and of course, Amelia and Joanna, whenever possible. One Sunday, Blake and I took the girls to visit Dad and Win at their home in Ockley, and we made a trip to Leith Hill to see the bluebells, which were creating the illusion of a lavender mist as they moved in the breeze. It was a pleasure to share with my girls something I had so loved in my own childhood.

Although *S.O.B.* hadn't yet opened, reviews had begun to come in, and we were relieved to learn that they were mostly positive. *Playboy* and *Life* both raved. Vincent Canby said in the *New York Times*, "It's difficult to remember a film as mean-spirited as *S.O.B.* that also was so consistently funny." I was pleased for Blake, and proud that he had made something so creative, and wickedly hilarious, out of such adversity.

Toward the end of filming for *Victor/Victoria*, I began doing publicity interviews for *S.O.B.* I discovered that the only thing anyone seemed interested in talking about was how I felt revealing my bare chest on-screen. I did my best to turn the focus back to the film itself.

Victor/Victoria finished shooting in June. I wrote:

I feel vaguely relieved. A strange sensation. I wish I had given the role a lot more thought and care. Could I have? Yes—but at what expense? And would it have been better if I had sacrificed family, or husband? Or did I do OK under the circumstances? Not questions I can answer yet.

19

DESPITE THE MOSTLY favorable reviews, *S.O.B.* was not the box office success we'd hoped it would be. It seemed the black comedy and the Hollywood send-up were a little too "inside" for the average cinemagoer. Blake was miserable about it, particularly since it had been such a catharsis for him to write, and everyone involved in making the film had so believed in its worth.

Although Blake had more work lined up with the next *Pink Panther* film, it wasn't work that appealed to him. He fretted as to how to write a new script about Inspector Clouseau without the actor who'd created him. Eventually, he settled on the idea of making two films: one primarily comprised of outtakes from previous *Panther* films, in a story about Clouseau having mysteriously vanished, and the other about a new and equally hapless American detective (yet to be cast) who was hired to find the missing Clouseau.

Blake invited Geoffrey, now almost twenty-two,

to collaborate with him on both scripts, and in the early fall, we headed back to Gstaad, where the men began to write together. Geoff's passion for cinema had been informed by all the time he had spent on film sets in his youth observing his father at work, and, like his dad, his comedic instincts were infallible. Working with his son lifted Blake's spirits considerably; he said that their collaboration was the easiest and most fruitful writing partnership he had enjoyed to date.

Amelia and Joanna began attending the school that Emma had gone to when she lived in Gstaad, and I was happy to have at least some of my family under one roof for a spell and to be back in Switzerland again.

Once *Victor/Victoria* had been edited, it was time for me to do looping for it. Blake, Geoff, and I headed to London for a week that happened to coincide with my birthday:

I had a quiet day—and the most stupendous evening. I had said to Blake that because it was my birthday, with all its attendant emotions, I was feeling a bit blue. He replied, "I can promise you that by this evening you will be very happy." I took it to mean that the supper we'd planned at Mimmo d'Ischia with Hank

Mancini, Loretta Swit, Tony, Avril and Zoë would be pleasant, and it was.

At one point, I was chatting to Avril, and something caught my eye. I turned and did a huge double-take. Standing in the doorway, all smiles, were Jenny, Emma, and Geoff's girlfriend, Denise. Blake had flown them all in to surprise me, and they had arrived in London an hour earlier. I burst into happy tears, and hugged them all—and indeed my evening was perfect.

During the looping for *Victor/Victoria*, I saw the latest cut of the film. Henry Mancini's score was consummate, and I felt that his music even enhanced our performances. I was also delighted by how beautiful the film was to look at. I was cautiously optimistic that it might be well received.

Later that day, we received the tragic news that William Holden had died after taking a fall in his apartment. It was devastating to us all. Blake immediately boarded a plane for L.A., only to learn when he arrived that there would be no funeral, per Holden's wishes.

Perhaps in an attempt to assuage his grief, Blake once again invited a massive group of family and friends to join us for Christmas in Gstaad. We ended up being twenty-two in all, spread throughout the village.

Mum and Auntie were there, and they bickered as always. I did my best codependent dance between them, trying to appease and placate.

Mum was in bad health; she was severely overweight, wheezing, and unsteady on her feet. Her stay in L.A. had been short-lived. I had tried to set her up with everything she might need, and to make her life as easy as possible. But foolishly, it hadn't occurred to me how much she would miss her friends in Walton, and in a matter of months, she had decided to return home.

Mum had come to Gstaad a few weeks before Christmas to take a treatment at the famous La Prairie Clinic medical spa in Montreux. They gave her a battery of tests, after which she was diagnosed with a distended heart, hypertension, arthritis, kidney problems, arteriosclerosis, and emphysema. I persuaded her to come back to Los Angeles temporarily for further medical tests in the New Year. Postproduction on *Victor/Victoria* was now complete, and Blake and Geoff had finished the scripts for *Trail of the Pink Panther* and *Curse of the Pink Panther*, which were to begin filming simultaneously in California in February.

Dr. Tanney confirmed Mum's diagnoses from

the clinic and said she must stop drinking and smoking—easier said than done! He also put her on an antidepressant. There were a bizarre couple of weeks when a visit from my dad overlapped with Mum's, and they both stayed with us at the same time. Thankfully, he and Mum were easy with each other, and had pleasant chats in the evenings. It may even have helped boost Mum's spirits. But it was strange for me to have them both under the same roof at the same time.

VICTOR/VICTORIA OPENED in Los Angeles on March 16, 1982. By now, Blake had begun location filming for the next *Panther*, but I attended the premiere with Garner and Preston. Afterward, I wrote:

> Crazy world! The heavens opened up and it poured with rain. It blew away the marquee for the after-party, which was a total wash-out, but the screening was successful and a personal triumph for my Blackie. I was more aware than ever of his tremendous talent; his writing, editing, moments of pure directorial joy—of his good eye and wonderful humor. It was apparent that everyone in the audience felt the same way.

The reviews were sensational. Vincent Canby wrote in the *New York Times*: "*Victor/Victoria* is so good, so exhilarating, that the only depressing thing about it is the suspicion that Edwards is going to have a terrible time trying to top it."

I was profoundly relieved, and grateful that my anxieties about my performance hadn't been borne out. I was also thrilled for Blake, but I could tell that although he was pleased by the response to *Victor/Victoria*, he was distracted by the pressures of the new *Panther* films, and regretting having agreed to do them.

After the premiere, I was busy with press conferences, interviews, and publicity for the film—but unable to focus on much of it, due to the challenges with my mum. My worries for her consumed my every waking thought. I arranged a live-in aide and companion for her once she was back in Walton. Unfortunately, Mum became abusive to the poor lady, and eventually she left. I was heartsick, as I knew that Mum would fall back into all her old habits, and that she was now totally incapable of looking after her house or herself. But Mum was as stubborn as ever, and there was only so much I could say or do.

WHEN BLAKE FINISHED shooting his two *Panther* films, we headed for Gstaad for the better part of the summer. I tried to press ahead with my children's book about the ship's cat, while Amelia and Joanna attended summer school. As usual, Blake began to slip back into depression. He was angry with himself for having done the *Panther* films, which he felt were not what he should be focusing on at this point in his career. He was also approaching his sixtieth birthday. He had always hated his birthday, and this one made him especially miserable.

There was one evening when the situation morphed into black humor. We were in bed with the lights out, when suddenly I heard the familiar throat-clearing—and my "little boy tenor" began to serenade me once again with a medley of songs. I quickly realized that, perhaps unconsciously, he was choosing titles that were a reflection of his state of mind. He launched into "High Noon (Do Not Forsake Me, Oh My Darlin')," followed by "I Can't Begin to Tell You," "You'll Never Know," and "My Love and Devotion." Through my laughter, I found myself wanting to sing "Why Can't You Behave?" and "I Cain't Say No" from *Oklahoma!*

Knowing that we would be celebrating Blake's birthday in Gstaad, I had arranged a video of all his family, friends, and colleagues sending him well-wishes. These days, one can simply record oneself with a smartphone, but back then, it required a great deal more effort. Tony Adams and I hired three different camera crews—one in the States, one in London, and one in Gstaad—to capture all the messages, and we had the results professionally edited.

On the big day, Blake awoke in a funk, but Geoff, Amelia, Joanna, and I managed to jolly him out of his mood. By the evening he was in better spirits. He loved the video, which was truly an outpouring of affection and respect, and had turned out better than I'd dared to hope.

AT THE END of the summer, we returned to Los Angeles. Blake and Geoff had been discussing a remake of François Truffaut's *The Man Who Loved Women*, and Columbia Pictures signed on to the project. As always, the prospect of work buoyed Blake's spirits a little.

Tony Adams would be coproducing the film, as usual, but in the meantime he was committed to another trip with Operation California, this time to Thailand, Cambodia, and Vietnam. The founder of the organization, Richard Walden, invited me to join them. I was apprehensive at first, but decided it would be good for me, and would help my advocacy work if I could speak from experience. I also wanted to see Vietnam for Amelia and Joanna's sake. I felt that if they chose to visit the country themselves one day, I would be better prepared to help them do so.

I received a battery of vaccinations, and began taking malaria pills. We departed on August 30, 1982. As I hugged Blackie goodbye, I longed to tell him how insecure I felt about the trip, but I said little, since he wasn't particularly happy about my going. I climbed into the car, and Jo yelled out enthusiastically, "Have a good time in Vietnam!" which made me smile.

Our preliminary destination was Bangkok, with layovers in Tokyo and Hong Kong. Besides Tony Adams and Richard Walden, I was traveling with an American dentist named Glen Herman, who was planning to set up a dental school in Cambodia on behalf of OpCal. Also on the trip was a social worker from Thailand, who helped to process Cambodian refugees.

The experience is best described by some excerpts from the extensive diary I kept of the trip:

Driving from the airport to the hotel, I saw shanty towns of unbelievable poverty; houses tilting, falling down, open to the elements, showing single lightbulbs and families sitting on the floor.

First impressions of the city are of shuttered shops, tiny-windowed rooms above them. Tangled masses of telephone wires. The heat and humidity are intense.

* * *

Couldn't sleep last night. Dressed and went down to the lobby this morning, and it was only seconds before the perspiration started to run. We met with a colonel from the Green Berets, by the name of Mike Eiland. He is the U.S. head of refugee processing. He tried to give me a picture of all that's going on here. He wants us to visit a border camp before we leave. He said that anyone getting word back can be of great help—particularly someone who can communicate with the media.

* * *

Traveled to Saigon on the one flight that goes in and out per week. I had such mixed feelings landing at the airport. Amelia and Joanna were once on this very airfield, prior to their flight to the U.S. There must have been so much army equipment, so much U.S. machinery.

Madame Hua, head of the Saigon Pediatric Research hospital and other medical facilities and orphanages, was at the airport to meet us. She's tiny, tough, humorous, and has an aura of power.

Our hotel overlooks the Saigon River, which is full of cargo ships—Vietnamese, Russian, Indian, Chinese—all unbelievably rusty.

* * *

Must tell about the orphans who sell peanuts outside the hotel. They are heartbreaking—outcast because they are mostly mixed-race children of the war. Yet they are cheery, feisty, smiling. They all hang together and are very loving with each other. None of them wear shoes, and they beg for soap.

One of the girls took a fancy to me. I guessed her to be twelve years old. She said proudly, "I'm American, too." She didn't know where her father was, and said her mother had recently died.

* * *

Went to the street market and picked up a ton of soap for the kids, plus toothbrushes and toothpaste and some cakes, which they shared. We saw puppies, kittens, birds, monkeys, all in tiny cages, making a fearful racket. Their fate is not a good one. There was a woman on a bicycle carrying a huge load of piglets in a rope basket, and a chicken strutting on the street, plucked totally bare, except for a few tail feathers. People were asleep on the sidewalk. Others cooked over open fires.

* * *

Visited Madame Hua's hospital. She has hundreds of babies, suffering from every kind of disease; malnutrition, rickets, birth defects. Many are virtually blind. Madame cautioned us about what we would see on the other side of the compound, which is the public children's hospital, and not her domain. It is unpainted, smells of urine, and is packed with more desperately ill children. Scabies are rampant, and a lot of kids have hideous looking boils, especially around their feet and heads. Madame can "rescue" a child from here and send it to her side. When we were there, she decided on at least six kids that were so malnourished that they needed to go to her facility, but they have to wait until she has a vacant bed.

*   *   *

Saw two orphanages today. The first was state-run and immaculately clean. They were obviously prepared for our visit; the children were in their Sunday clothes and on their best behavior. The second was for handicapped children. I will remember this place to my dying day. It was run-down, bleak, and there was no stimulation whatsoever—no color, no posters, no toys. I feel that the orphans there will never get out, let alone survive.

All the children were on cots with wooden slats—no mattresses. They sleep on the hard wood and pee through to the stone floor. There were three kind-looking sisters who tried to clean, and to wipe noses and pus out of red inflamed eyes. The place was hopelessly under-staffed. Some children have encephalitis, some polio, some are blind. They all have scabies. One child could no longer take nourishment. He had festering sores and never moved, just lay staring into space.

There were children with terrible malformed

limbs, legs twisted and curled. Madame Hua said they were birth defects from exposure to a toxic chemical—perhaps Agent Orange. There were some kids with so many problems that it made others with only one problem seem like the lucky ones. There are not enough cots, so they all share. They sat on the wooden slats and just stared at us. They had nothing to do, nothing to play with, nothing to look at—just nothing.

I asked Madame Hua why, since they were so ill, they were in the worst surroundings. She said, "It is impossible to do it all. They need so much." She said staff is difficult to find, and the sisters who do help are saints. Diseases spread so quickly, they can barely catch up.

We were climbing into our car when I saw a little boy running around on all fours. A polio victim. It was as if his back had been snapped, and he will never be able to stand up. He looked at the world with his head cocked sideways, and upwards. It was simply unbearable.

I felt guilty about having to leave. As I write this tonight, it is horrible to know that those children are all still there, on their hard cots, that the stench is just as bad, and that the little boy in the orphanage is one day nearer to death.

* * *

Came down with the "tourista" today. Madame said it was probably a microbe and gave me some medicine. The Cultural Minister called this evening in a panic. Unbeknownst to me, he had arranged tickets for our group to the "Foreigners' Dance" and had promised people I would attend. They had all been expecting me and hoping I'd sing "Do Re Mi."Could I please make an effort and go? I was so ill, there was just no way. I groaned and made my apologies.

* * *

I received a letter from the lady who keeps an eye on the street kids. She asked for my help in getting her and the children out. I'll see if Mike Eiland can assist in any way.

* * *

Traveled to Phnom Penh, Cambodia. It must have once been charming, but it is now completely bombed out. During Pol Pot's invasion, almost everything was destroyed. There are seldom any windows in buildings, and there is rubble everywhere.

Our hotel is plain as plain can be, but the people running it are kind. A radio was playing as we came in. Amazing how subliminally soothing music can be. I thought of the handicapped children in the orphanage, and wondered if music could bring them any comfort.

We visited another hotel where most of the aid agencies are based. Many jeeps and vans were neatly parked there, and their names lifted my spirits: World Vision, Red Cross, UNICEF, OxFam, World Health Organization. We met with the various agencies, and my poor brain tried hard to put two and two together. I flounder a lot while trying to look as though I'm intelligent and absorbing everything. There is so much to take in.

We stopped off at the dental school where Glen will be working. Windows are nonexistent or cracked. People are sleeping in the hallways. There were many boxes and parcels from OpCal. Glen will have to start from scratch, assembling donated dental chairs, and doing a lot of other difficult work.

One of our companions at dinner tonight asked how I was doing. I got the impression she thinks I'm "Hollywood fragile," and won't last the pace. Walking home from the café reminded me of the London Blitz. Not a streetlamp was working, and only an occasional neon sign from a shop or a car headlight showed us the way. A rat scuttled out of some garbage. There are puddles everywhere. The children—always barefoot—wash their feet in the bigger puddles. There's a lot of mud and garbage, and everywhere the smells of stagnant water, excrement and cooking oil.

* * *

Cannot write adequately about what we did today. We were taken for a tour of the Pol Pot prison and torture camp, now a museum of sorts. It had once been a school. During Pol Pot's reign of terror, he had divided the rooms into small cells, barely big enough to hold a body. Prisoners there had been tortured in ways more hideous than I can describe. The grey, bleak buildings seem haunted by ghosts. I left with a sick heart, knowing that it was only three years ago that the place had been filled with such terrorized humanity.

We then drove to Orphanage No. 4. I gasped

as the car stopped and we got out. The structures look like abandoned storage buildings. Set into each outside wall, there are cubicles open to the elements. No doors, no matting, or weatherproofing—just three walls, a floor and a ceiling, and a bed. The children look dazed. Most of them work the land, such as it is. The place was crawling with ants that raced about and instantly swarmed over my shoes and up my jeans. I got in a bit of a panic and stomped about a lot.

Our host was a man named Allen, from World Vision. When we first met him, he was up to his elbows in grease and sweat, trying to mend an ancient water pump. He was there all by himself, tackling whatever needed to be done.

We met a teenage boy with one arm. The other had been shot off by a soldier, for sport. Another man had only one leg. Allen has an unflagging energy. He does not want any of the people there to think that he pities them, and he is profoundly compassionate.

They grow some food at the orphanage, and there is a cow and a couple of wells for water. But the mud, the damp, the dreariness of it, the exposure to the elements, the ants, and I'm sure rats, make it a hellhole. No sheets, pillows or covers that I could see. No music. Nothing to make the quality of life any better.

* * *

The owners of our hotel invited Richard, Tony and me to dinner. Cambodians are not allowed to fraternize with foreigners, so their invitation put them in some danger. They spoke of the things they needed to help the hotel run better, such as towels and lightbulbs. I asked what their most special wish would be. The wife answered simply, "To be more free."

* * *

We flew back to Bangkok today, via Saigon. Tony and I said a sad goodbye to Richard, who is staying in Vietnam to help Glen with the dentistry project. I delivered a package to Madame Hua from one of the aid agencies in Cambodia.

Press were waiting at our hotel. I did my best to keep my replies to their questions very simple. I need time to gain perspective, and don't wish to get into politics or offend.

I've been agonizing over the decision to either go home tomorrow, or to stay an extra day and go with Mike Eiland to the refugee camps as he requested. I finally decided to honor his request.

* * *

Woke after a bad night with the worst stomach yet. I felt incredibly weak, and thought I was crazy to consider going to the border, but didn't want to waste the opportunity, especially with Mike having gone to so much trouble. I took some medicine and ate a light breakfast.

We departed in Mike's tiny car; no room to move feet or lie down. It was pouring with rain. We stopped at his office, and I delivered the letter from the lady with the street children in Saigon. We traveled through rice paddy after rice paddy, and, thanks to the medication, despite the many bumps, bridges, and potholes along the way, I eventually began to feel slightly better.

Mike explained the differences between the border camps we would be seeing—a Vietnamese camp, a Cambodian camp, and a U.N. Refugee Camp. There are curfews from 6 PM to

6 AM, and it is after the curfew that atrocities occur. Guards take their pick of the women, and there are nightly raids by the Khmer Rouge, who steal, kidnap, and kill. Apparently the last 20 miles of a refugee's journey to any camp is the hardest, because of the mines.

As we neared our destination, we began to pass relief agency lorries parked in wired compounds, and warehouses where all the aid is stored. We drove for several more miles, lurching and bouncing on a rutted track with no signposts. How we didn't get stuck in the mud I'll never know.

We passed several checkpoints, with ridiculously young-looking men in uniform, armed to the teeth. Finally, we drove under a wooden frame with a sign, and a few yards further on, we saw some pitiful looking straw huts tilting in the mud—bamboo structures, with thin walls and floors. This was the Cambodian refugee camp that contains about 50,000 people. We drove through it and into a smaller Vietnamese camp, set inside the larger Cambodian camp.

I got out of the car and was introduced to the camp commander. Opposite his hut were row upon row of untidy-looking tents . . . dark, tattered, ragged pieces of material. As we began to walk in the thick mud, I caught a glimpse of the people packed inside each tent, with no room but for their own body space. Some were sitting, some lying listlessly, mothers nursing babies. I was told that they are not allowed to speak to or make contact with visitors. The camp was built for 700 people, and there are 2000 there at present.

We passed the camp kitchens. The refugees are given rice and fish, and very little else. There were two water taps in deep, trampled mud. People are rationed to 12 liters per day. A naked little girl was washing a tiny child, soaping its hair from one bucket of water and rinsing with the other while checking carefully for lice. Clothes were hung out to dry on anything that would hold them.

We entered a straw hut. There were three tiers of bunk beds packed with bodies—205 people. I felt ashamed to be looking in on their misery.

It was about this time that I thought I was going to faint. The pressure of so much humanity jammed into such a small space, the crushing midday heat, the humidity, my stomach troubles. I had an awful vision of slumping into the mud in front of all these sad people.

I sat on a bench and looked at the scene, trying to imprint it on my mind forever, wishing I could communicate it to someone, knowing that I was one of relatively few people in the world to have witnessed it.

We then drove back to the larger Cambodian camp and visited the hospital there. It's divided into two—one half is managed by Cambodians who prefer to practice their own medicine, the other half is staffed by relief agencies. There is no electricity, and doctors and nurses work by lantern light. Mike says these people, mostly volunteers, burn out pretty fast . . . usually after about three months. They seemed so glad that I was there. The fact that I had come all that way to see for myself was somehow meaningful for them.

I began to realize that I should not be ashamed or shy to look at anyone, to observe how they were living. A smile for them was like a gift; our presence something to remember at the end of a miserable day. Perhaps there was some small hope that we could carry a message back to the world. I began to say "Hello!" and to wave to the children. The response was so enthusiastic it was heartbreaking.

Finally, we moved on to the U.N. refugee

camp. Here there were neat little thatched huts, divided in half; eight people per side. But the people are just as destitute, and it is desperately crowded in spite of the orderliness of the huts.

Doctors and nurses from all nations work in the hospital there. There were a lot of people with limbs missing. A young man had tried to come in during the night and stepped on a mine. Part of his leg had been blown away and he had developed gas gangrene. What must he have been through during the night—in the agonizing time before he was found? What price freedom?

It was getting dark. Curfew would be upon us in half an hour, and Mike wanted us to get on our way. We had a four-hour journey back to the city. On the way home, we talked non-stop. Mike tried to help me find the correct words for all we had seen—to properly represent it to the media. He suggested I stay non-political and deal only with the human dimension. He said to blame no-one, or everyone. I asked him where the buck stopped in terms of the problems in all three countries. He said, "It doesn't ever stop. It just gets passed around and around." He said that it's foolish to believe that the global situation can be solved; the only answer is to do what you can, for whomever you can, whenever and wherever you can, piece by piece, bit by bit. Patch, and help, and do, and make people aware. Slow, painful work, with all too slow, painful results.

I am so very glad we took the extra day and went to the border. If we hadn't, we would never have seen the plight of the refugees. On the flight home, I thought a lot about my impressions and the things that I will forever remember. Not in any order:

I'll remember how impressed I was that people in South Vietnam still feel remotely friendly towards the Americans. I'll remember the dirt, the mud, the heat, the humidity. I will forever remember the children—little ones, taking responsibility for tiny babies, heartbreakingly ill ones who will never see the world as Amelia and Joanna will see it. Feisty ones whose future is bleak and empty.

I don't understand why the world as an international body isn't able to help more. The common denominator is human misery.

The most important thing I have learned is the simplest of all: people are just people—no matter their politics, their skin color, or where they live. There is no difference in our humanity; only in our circumstances.

* * *

We landed in L.A., and within minutes my Blackie was beside me. We hugged long and silently. I think I wept.

As we drove along the Pacific Coast Highway, the sea looked so beautiful, and fresh, and familiar. I had been so emotionally raw, so pried open by everything I had seen, and I suddenly had the deeply disturbing sensation of Vietnam and Cambodia slowly receding into memory. I felt ashamed, and made a promise to myself to always be vigilant, and to do all I could to help those in need.

Amelia and Joanna rushed to greet me as we arrived. Jo was hopping from foot to foot, grinning and thrusting forward to hug me. Amelia was trying to contain her excitement and her smiles, but happily, not succeeding at all. I hugged them both fiercely.

20

WITHIN A FEW days of my return from Southeast Asia, I began to do television and print interviews about my experience there. I focused on three areas of concern, as Mike Eiland had advised: the plight of the Amerasian children, many of whom were abandoned or on the streets; the Cambodian and Vietnamese refugees in the Thai border camps; and the need for aid to Vietnam and Cambodia, to help them recover from the devastating effects of the war.

The day before my birthday, I received a call from Connie Boll, a lady from the agency who had helped deliver Joanna to us. She was hoping I could reach out to the Speaker of the House, Tip O'Neill, to plead for the Amerasian Immigration Act, which was an attempt to provide a path for the thousands of Asian-born children of American servicemen to immigrate to the United States. The bill had been languishing for four years, but was potentially going before Congress the next day, just prior to their recess.

I telephoned the Speaker's office with trepidation. I had never lobbied or reached out to a government official before, and I was worried they might wonder what a British citizen was doing advocating for an American cause. But it seemed so important, after all I had seen, that I try to do *something*. The Speaker's office suggested that I call New Jersey congressman Peter Rodino at 6:30 a.m. my time the next morning. When I reached him, the congressman was very kind, and spoke at length about his passion for the bill. He then referred me to another congressman, who referred me to someone else. I thought I was being given the runaround, but plodded ahead and made my pitch each time. To my disappointment, I was eventually told that the bill would not be going to the floor that day— they had too much else to focus on—but that it might be brought forward to a lame duck session in a month or so.

However, at the end of the day, I received a wonderful surprise: a call from Congressman Rodino's assistant, who said that Mr. Rodino had asked him to tell me that the bill had in fact come to the floor, had been passed, and was now on its way to the White House for President Reagan's signature. I told Mr. Rodino's assistant that he had given me the best birthday gift I could ever have wished for.

Connie later phoned to convey her thanks, saying that my call had made the difference.

My trip to Southeast Asia changed me on a profound level. Whereas before, my creative work seemed the most significant pursuit, now a heightened awareness of the basic human right to the essential elements of life—clean water, adequate nourishment, safe shelter—had given me a new sense of purpose.

I TRAVELED TO New York to do some more press interviews, and to celebrate Emma's twentieth birthday. To my joy, she presented *me* with a belated birthday gift from *her*. She had been taking voice lessons, and had recorded herself singing an enchanting song, entitled "Mama, a Rainbow," by Larry Grossman and Hal Hackady. The lyric is about attempting to find a gift for one's mother, and in the end realizing that the most meaningful offering is to hold to a vision of Mama, forever young and beautiful, in the mind's eye.

I was a blubbering mess, knowing the courage it had taken for Emma to sing something for me. I was grateful from my soul to have a daughter able to voice such a loving thing. Perhaps it also had to do with resolving the pain that she and I had experienced when she left California.

Later, I penned the following:

In New York last week doing my interviews,
I was treated a little like some kind of monument, or legend. I certainly don't feel that way.
Blake says it's because I'm a "survivor." Emma
says it's because I have done some memorable work. All of it has been fascinating and
much of it has given me great joy, especially—
always—the music. I certainly want to attempt
more creative work, in addition to doing what
I can to support the causes I care about. I still
have the energy to bring to it all. At times, I
feel younger now than I did in my twenties.

While I don't feel like a "legend," I do feel a
little more sure of myself; a little more capable.
Another product of that trip to Southeast Asia?

Early in the New Year, we began shooting *The Man
Who Loved Women*. Both Truffaut's original film
and Blake's adaption tell the tale of a serial woman-
izer whose passions lead to his demise. In Blake's
version, the main character is a sculptor, played by
Burt Reynolds, who consults with a female analyst
(me) about his obsession and subsequently falls in
love with her. My role was challenging, in that
half of it required being seated and holding very

still in analytical sessions, while the other half was comprised of voice-over narration, since the story is told from the analyst's point of view.

I had never done narration before, and wasn't sure how to approach it. How do you engage the audience when the speaker is unseen? Should I be vocally intimate, dramatic, oratorical? I finally decided, for the first time in my life, to consult with an acting coach. I asked several people—my agents, certain friends and colleagues—who would be the best person to work with, and one name kept coming to the forefront: Nina Foch. I made an appointment to see her.

Nina's acting career spanned six decades in Hollywood, and included such films as *An American in Paris*, *Executive Suite* (directed by Robert Wise), *The Ten Commandments*, and *Spartacus*, as well as a great deal of television work. She had been teaching acting for a long time, at both the American Film Institute and USC. I wondered if I might be intimidated by her knowledge and expertise.

I was ushered into her house by an assistant, and left to wait for a couple of minutes. The main staircase descended into the living room, and I heard her voice before I saw her.

"I'm coming, I'm coming! Sorry to keep you waiting!" I watched her descend the stairs with ease and command, every bit the actress making a grand entrance, and it made me smile.

Nina turned out to be an absolute love. She was enthusiastic, perceptive, and completely frank. She began to dissect Blake's screenplay, not in criticism, but in much the same way Madame Stiles-Allen used to break down a song. Why did I never think to apply one technique to the other? For every line of dialogue, she gave me suggestions as to what my character might be thinking; her objectives, the subtext. Although we only covered a few pages of the script in that initial session, Nina gave me the foundation for my work on the role, and she quickly became a close and trusted friend.

In addition to my coaching sessions, I also began studying the Alexander Technique, a method I had been hearing about for freeing up tension in the body. This, too, I found immensely helpful.

FILMING FOR *THE MAN WHO LOVED WOMEN* spanned the next several months. Burt was delightful to work with, but he kept very much to himself. Blake had searched long and hard for a sculptor whose work might best represent Burt's character. Having recently begun sculpting himself, Blake had amassed quite a number of lovely pieces. One day, he shyly asked me whether I thought his work might be good enough to use in the film. I told him I thought it would be perfect, and he decided to take the gamble. I was so proud to see his pieces larger than life on-screen, and I feel they enhance the film considerably.

Because of the film's psychoanalytic theme, Blake had cowritten the screenplay with his own analyst, Milton Wexler, in addition to Geoffrey. Unfortunately, during production, Geoff and Blake had a falling-out due to artistic differences about the script. The two became estranged for a time, which pained Blake considerably.

Milton occasionally served as a consultant on the set. One day, we were filming an analytic session. We had been experimenting with improvisation— something Blake had done with *The Party* and was increasingly intrigued by. I wore an earpiece, through which Milton's voice guided me in my responses to Burt's musings so that they would be appropriate and correct. I had the peculiar sensation of art imitating life, and it felt more than a little bizarre.

Once my work on the film had concluded, I bounced back and forth between Europe and the States for the remainder of the year, still trying to uphold our Swiss residency while being present for my family as much as possible. These continued forced separations were tough on us all. The last two *Panther* films had not done well at the box office, and sadly, *The Man Who Loved Women* did not fare much better. Whenever I was away, I did my best to press ahead with my children's book about the ship's cat, which I had titled *Little Bo: The Story of Bonnie Boadicea.*

I happened to be in London for my mother's seventy-third birthday, and we had the rare experience of celebrating it with all my siblings under one roof. My brother John had recently remarried, a lovely lady by the name of Sharyn. Christopher was there also, with his wife, Ann, who was newly pregnant. Donald and his wife, Alma, had recently welcomed a baby son. Auntie was "starchy" as always, and as I had feared, Mum had slipped back into her old ways, but she did enjoy that evening.

Emma turned twenty-one in November, and I was able to steal a couple of precious days to fly to New York and surprise her. By now she was auditioning regularly, and performing in off-Broadway plays, television soap operas, and commercials. She was working so hard, and I was proud of her accomplishments, but I wished I could somehow help her avoid the inevitable industry challenges and setbacks that I knew lay ahead.

JUST AFTER CHRISTMAS, Blake took a meeting in Gstaad with Leslie Bricusse about adapting *Victor/ Victoria* into a stage musical for Broadway. Blake had occasionally talked about this idea, but it had always seemed to me to be a "pie in the sky" possibility, way off in the future. When he told me about the meeting with Leslie, he conveyed his hope that the Broadway version would happen sooner rather than later, and that Robert Preston and Lesley Ann Warren would join me in reprising their roles from the film.

I wrote:

Blake never asked me, "How do you feel about it?" He just assumes that I'll do it. Of course, I want to do it—I'm well aware how fortunate I'd be to have that opportunity. But I'm terrified already. It's such an enormous gamble to go back to Broadway, and it would be a huge undertaking. What of Amelia and Joanna? Our lives? What if it is a long run? Do I still have the chops, the stamina? And what happens to our marriage if I'm dedicated and busy? Would Blake keep his cool through the whole process— and with me?

Blake began to take more meetings, with various potential Broadway producers, about *Victor/Victoria*. He had also written a stylish screenplay for Clint Eastwood and Burt Reynolds. Unfortunately, the three personalities were not a good mix. Burt and Clint asked for many changes to the script, and finally wrote a version of it themselves, much to Blake's chagrin. Warner Bros. backed the actors, and eventually Blake removed himself from the project.

Fortunately, he had another project in development—a second collaboration with Dudley Moore. *Micki + Maude* was a quirky film about a confused bigamist. It was picked up by Columbia Pictures, and Blake began shooting it in Los Angeles in April, with Amy Irving and Ann Reinking rounding out the cast.

At the same time, Blake became involved in a legal battle with MGM/UA, who had sued him for overages on *Victor/Victoria* and the two subsequent *Panther* films. Blake countersued, and MGM/UA counter-countersued. It was hugely stressful—and we spent a good deal of time that year meeting with our lawyers, giving depositions, and so forth. The suits were eventually settled out of court, but the experience took its toll on Blake emotionally, as did the continued estrangement from Geoffrey.

Blake began to suffer from depression once again. He lost weight and complained of constant fatigue. Eventually, he was diagnosed with mononucleosis and Epstein-Barr.

I did my best to be supportive, and also to be as present as possible for Joanna and Amelia, now nine and ten. They were going to the same UCLA Lab School that Emma had attended years before. Amelia was showing real talent in ballet class, and Jo was passionate about horseback riding and reading. I proudly attended their respective dance recitals and horse shows.

Over the course of that year, I also gave a couple of benefit concerts, and cohosted the Tony Awards in New York City with Robert Preston. While I was there, I began looking at apartments we might rent should the stage version of *Victor/Victoria* come to pass. I also took the opportunity to spend time with Emma, who was moving into a new apartment with a fellow actress from her acting program.

I happened to be in the city the night they moved in, and after a late supper with Emma, I received a call from her saying that she had returned to her apartment to find the place on fire. It was a ground floor walk-through, and apparently a passerby had flipped a cigarette butt into the pile of empty packing cartons that she and her room-mate had left by the stairwell. The damage was extensive, and I stayed on through Thanksgiving to help the girls with the cleanup and restoration. Afterward, Blake flew in to meet me and we traveled on to Gstaad, hoping to spend a peaceful Christmas there.

Three hours after we arrived, the phone rang. It was my brother Chris's wife, Ann, who relayed that my mother was in the hospital for some tests. Apparently, Mum had been experiencing severe abdominal pain, and at first the doctors thought it might be pancreatitis. Within a day, the diagnosis was much more serious; she had an aneurism in her lower aorta. It was a ticking time bomb, and if it burst, she would most certainly die. The only hope was an operation, which in itself was dangerous, and from which recovery would be slow. Blake and I flew to London immediately.

When we arrived at the hospital, Mum was pale, fragile-looking, and in considerable pain. Blake was very dear with her; he rubbed her back, and she flirted with him a bit. It warmed me to know that her humor and life force were still intact.

The following day, my brothers joined me at the hospital. We saw X-rays and met with the surgeon, who explained Mum's problems in great detail and what he needed to do. We had family conferences, trying to determine the best course of action. I was struck by the sadness of seeing Mum so desperately ill and close to death, stoically trying to get through a hospital meal of gray roast beef and green beans.

When I returned to the hotel, I was shocked to discover Blake lying on the floor of our room in a fetal position. He claimed to be very ill—probably a gallbladder attack, he said. He was shaking and emotional. I wondered privately if his visit to the hospital had intensified his feelings of mortality; he avoided hospitals whenever possible, but had made an effort for my sake and Mum's. I asked him to phone his analyst, which he did.

The next morning, we learned that Mum was bleeding internally, and that the operation had to happen immediately. Mum said, "I just wish I'd had a little more time to prepare for this . . ." and later, "If I can just pull through tomorrow . . ." It was clear to me that she knew how serious the situation was, and my heart was breaking for her.

Later, I wrote:

I am in great distress tonight; for her fear, for her pain. I find myself praying she will be alright. She is going to have to be so strong, so brave.

The latter, she is. I hope she can muster the former. Mostly I wish her some inner peace.

I had wanted to spend that night with her at the hospital, but Blake was now in such bad shape emotionally that I ended up going back to the hotel to care for him. I was awake the whole night, trying to send Mum love and strength, and phoning the hospital every few hours to leave messages for her, while also tending to my husband. At times I found myself rocking forward and back, as if to steel myself against some impending doom.

Once the operation was over, we were told that Mum's situation had been much worse than the doctors anticipated. She had two aneurisms, one of which had ruptured on the operating table. Every artery was involved, and Mum had a graft on her main aorta from her diaphragm to her pelvis. They expected her to die within the hour, but somehow she rallied a bit and was sent to intensive care.

Blake mustered the strength to join me as we visited her in the ICU. She was on a respirator, but clearly recognized him and lifted her hand to touch his cheek. But as the days unfolded, Mum's recovery slowed, and my husband's condition worsened; he became increasingly self-absorbed and desperate. We visited a gastroenterologist, who felt his problem was more likely emotional than gallbladder-related, but who recommended a battery of tests, nonetheless. Blake regressed further, becoming almost unremittingly childlike, and at one point I caught him writing a suicide letter. I asked him to again phone his analyst, who recommended that instead of going back to Gstaad for Christmas, Blake return to L.A. for more tests and possible surgery. Within two days, Blake was on his way back to California, while I remained in London, taking things a day at a time.

Mum continued to struggle, and was given a tracheotomy to ease her breathing. The doctor advised us that she would remain in the ICU and not be awake or responsive to family visits for a while. He recommended that I leave her in his good care and return to my husband and family for the few days over Christmas. He said that he would remain in close contact with me, and since there was the possibility that Blake now needed an operation, I decided to take the gamble and join him and the children in California, and fly back to London at a moment's notice if need be.

I phoned the hospital from the airport, and was horrified to learn that Mum's condition had suddenly deteriorated. My spirits plummeted and I was in an agony of indecision—but I boarded the plane, nonetheless. I don't remember one moment of that flight. My emotions were in such turmoil: guilt, worry, confusion, *deep* sadness.

Just a few hours after I arrived home, I received a call from the doctor. He said that Mum's kidneys were failing, and that she was unlikely to survive another day. The following morning, she passed away. I will never forgive myself for not having been with her.

My first reaction was relief that she was out of pain. Then grief overwhelmed me, and I bawled. I spoke to my brothers, and Auntie, who were equally distraught. We agreed to schedule Mum's funeral in a week's time, just after Christmas. I asked Auntie if she would like to return to Los Angeles with me after the proceedings, and she seemed grateful to have something to look forward to.

ON THE DAY of the funeral, Dad, Auntie, and I formed a receiving line at the church. I was so touched by Dad's being there with us. I mentioned to him how sad it was that Mum's last years had been so unhappy.

"It is sad, Chick," he replied. "But that was your mum's destiny, not yours. Yours is to live out whatever time is given to you to the fullest extent, to relish every day and make it count."

Aunt Joan and Jen Gosney had joined forces in my absence, and had done a Herculean job organizing all the details of the service. Somehow, I got through it without breaking down completely. I managed to join in the hymns, and even sing the descant to "The Lord Is My Shepherd." I thought how Mum would have loved the music. I gave a little speech, and concluded by saying how proud I was to carry Mum's genes. It was a comfort to think of the eight grandchildren that now carried those same genes forward, including Chris's new baby daughter, Jessica.

My mother's best friend, Gladys Barker, gave a small reception at her house, which meant a great deal to me. As I left, Auntie Gladdy said, "Your mum was one of the bravest people I've ever met." I understood what she meant. Mum had had such an uphill battle most of her life—with her parents' early death, her responsibility for Auntie, her poverty, Pop's alcoholism. She had indeed been brave.

Aunt Joan accompanied me back to Los Angeles, as I had hoped. She stayed for a month, during which time we talked of the possibility of her relocating to America permanently. Her rheumatoid arthritis was by now so bad that she was severely disabled and always in chronic pain. We found a little house for her, just down the road from ours, and she lived there for several months. However, like my mother, she missed her friends and her hometown, and eventually opted to return to England.

Blake didn't end up having gallbladder surgery, since his further tests never revealed a definitive diagnosis. But he did continue to decline emotionally over the next six months. I had never seen my husband so depressed. He complained of constant fatigue, nausea, aches, and pains. There were days when he could barely function at all. He had every medical test under the sun, including exhaustive blood work and bone marrow scans, with no clear results. One doctor said it was mono; another said there was no trace of mono at all, though he may have had it at one time. One doctor said he did have a gallstone; another said he did not. He was prescribed antidepressants, but claimed to have a bad reaction and stopped taking them.

Although he was by now working on a new film—a valentine to Laurel and Hardy called *A Fine Mess*—the work didn't seem to buoy his spirits as it usually did. He seemed to be going through the motions; getting the job done each day without energy or enthusiasm, and coming home early whenever possible. It became clear that he was abusing his prescription meds again. He would wake in the night with anxiety so acute, it rendered him trembling and tearful. Many times, I found him standing by my side of the bed in the dark, in an almost catatonic state. We would go for long predawn walks on the beach, during which he would often weep uncontrollably. Sometimes he had trouble simply putting one foot in front of the other. He increased his visits to his analyst, seeing him seven days a week, and occasionally twice a day. He even sought out astrologers and psychics, and devoured books on spirituality, as well as medical journals. But he only seemed to slide further down into despair. I tried to help as best I could; I held him, listened to him, encouraged him. Nothing seemed to make a difference.

Eventually he confessed to feeling suicidal again. Several times, he told me that he had actually attempted to take his life, but didn't have the guts to go through with it, which made him feel even worse about himself. He spoke of an episode in which he had been on our bluff with a razor blade in hand. Our dog had placed a ball in his lap and begged him to play with her so insistently that he decided it wasn't the right day to end his life. When he stood up, he accidentally stepped on the razor blade and cut his foot. He relayed this to me with a degree of humor, as if it were a scene from one of his black comedies, but I found it horrifying.

I was at a loss as to what to do. I began to keep a discreet vigil, trying to make sure Blake was never alone, without his realizing it; while protecting the family from knowing the true depths of his despair. Often, after the worst days, he would apologize and ask for my continued patience and support.

I saw my own analyst frequently. I even had sessions with Blake's analyst, who, without breaking patient confidentiality, encouraged me to stay calm. Dr. Wexler suggested that Blake was at the crux of something very important in his psychoanalysis. It was utterly baffling to me. I wondered if it had something to do with our marriage, or me personally, but Wexler's words resonated, and since I cared for my troubled spouse, I hung in there.

In hindsight, it seems obvious that Blake was having some kind of nervous breakdown. Yet with all the doctors involved, it amazes me that no one diagnosed it as such. No one suggested he be admitted to a hospital or clinic, or that any other measures be taken beyond what he was already doing.

Somehow, in spite of his despair, Blake managed to complete filming *A Fine Mess*, and begin postproduction. One day, when Jennifer was visiting the house, he suddenly said to us both, "You know what I'd really like to do? I'd like to make a very personal film, about a guy confronting his mortality who puts his family through hell. I'd cast just our friends and family members, and shoot it cinema verité–style—nonunion, very low-budget, like a John Cassavetes film. We could do it here at the house. God knows, I've abided by unions all my life. I think I'm owed one independent film at this stage in my career."

I thought to myself, "I'll believe it when I see it."

Eight weeks later, an entire film crew was assembled on our property, the union was picketing outside our gates, and shooting was under way for *That's Life!*

Blake's screenplay was indeed personal. With Dr. Wexler's help, he wrote a thirteen-page outline about a successful architect named Harvey Fairchild who is facing his sixtieth birthday and is in emotional crisis. His wife, Gillian, is a singer who, unbeknownst to anyone but her doctor, has just had a biopsy on her vocal cords, and has to cope with her fears alone through the birthday weekend while waiting for the results. During this time, Harvey seeks solace through doctor's visits, medication, confession, and psychic readings, along with attempts at adultery and suicide.

The whole idea was immensely creative, yet I felt it was a dangerous thing to attempt. I hoped it meant that Blake was finally confronting his demons and, as he had done with *10* and *S.O.B.*, was attempting artistic alchemy.

Jack Lemmon played Harvey Fairchild, who was essentially Blake, and I played his wife. Jack's real-life son, Chris Lemmon, played our son, and Jennifer and Emma played our two daughters. Everyone in the film family is absorbed with their own problems—the son is almost as narcissistic as his dad; the eldest daughter is pregnant, and her husband has a wandering eye; and the youngest has just split from her boyfriend.

The other cast members were mostly close friends—Sally Kellerman, Robert Loggia, Cynthia Sikes, and Jordan Christopher among them. Jack Lemmon's wife, Felicia Farr, had a character role as a seductive psychic.

Before shooting commenced, I went to visit my ear, nose, and throat specialist to consult with him as to what my character might be dealing with; how a singer would sound after a biopsy, and what kind of operation and future she might be facing if the diagnosis was bad. Feeling oddly superstitious about playing a character facing the loss of her voice, I asked my analyst if investing emotionally in the role could put me at risk of some psychosomatic manifestation. He assured me I had nothing to worry about.

On the first day, Blake assembled all the principals at our house and explained the process by which we would be filming. Working from his outline, we would begin by improvising a scene for which he had given us the dramatic through-line. Our script supervisor would take notes on the dialogue we came up with, and Blake would "set" the scene based on what he decided to keep or discard. We would then rehearse what had been developed, and finally commit the scene to film.

The responsibility placed on us actors was enormous; any one of us could have indulged our ego and attempted to enlarge our role. To the contrary, we became a disciplined ensemble, everyone relishing the creative license we were given, and being wholly generous with one another.

Jack was marvelous in the role of Harvey. He was brilliant at improvisation, giving Blake umpteen variations on a theme. Having worked together on *Days of Wine and Roses* and *The Great Race*, the two men had a mutual ease and trust; in fact, Blake often said that Jack was one of his favorite actors to work with.

It was simply mind-boggling to watch Blake

give direction for a character based on himself. He would act things out for Jack with such openness and honesty that it took my breath away. He knew so much about himself, but he seemed better able to admit it all on-screen than in real life. It amazed me how he could just "turn on" grief and rage in a demonstration for Jack, suddenly becoming the way he had been in real life so many times over the past year—and then turn it off again as he handed the emotional baton back to his leading man. Blake confessed that his depressive behavior had often been manipulative, and I sensed that he was experiencing a kind of catharsis as he watched Jack portray him. Viewing the film today, I am struck by Blake's honesty about his own failings, and seeming compassion for what his illness cost the family. It even strikes me as an apology of sorts— but perhaps that's wishful thinking on my part.

Two days after filming commenced, we celebrated my fiftieth birthday. Blake said that he had an early gift for me, and he led me outside while shielding my eyes. When I opened them, Dad and Win were standing in front of me. I came apart with joy, and they stayed for several weeks while filming continued, which was simply wonderful.

Though the work for the most part was happy and productive, the film itself was beset by challenges, not the least of which was the union picketing noisily outside our gate and on our beachfront every day. They set off sirens, banged drums and garbage cans, and sent up a "union rat" balloon and searchlights, forcing us to move certain shots to different locations on the property and shoot at different hours of the day. The disruptions were hard on the neighbors as well as our crew, and our wonderful director of photography, Harry Stradling Jr., was forced by the union to leave the project. Thankfully, a British cinematographer by the name of Tony Richmond took over, and he turned out to be excellent.

There was also a period when the dry Santa Ana winds caused massive fires to erupt across Malibu, perilously close to our house, necessitating that we stop filming for several days. In addition, it was a challenging time for Amelia and Joanna. They weren't involved in the film, and they had to continue attending school and living life as usual, despite the fact that there were people, trucks, and trailers around at all hours.

These challenges notwithstanding, *That's Life!* was a joy to make. It was lovely to work with Emma and Jenny, and I was immensely proud of the authenticity they brought to their roles. Emma had to play the saxophone in the film, and she took lessons with Joe Lopes, who had headed up the woodwinds section on my Japanese and American tours, and who also appears in the film.

To a person, the cast and crew were warm, loyal, and tireless. One morning, after a very late night of shooting, I woke to find that our cameraman and some members of his crew had never gone home, and were setting up for the next day's work. Because we were filming in our own house, I often found myself being "Mum" to everyone, making scrambled eggs and cups of tea for predawn breakfasts or middle-of-the-night snacks. On evenings when we shot in our own bedroom, Blake and I sometimes found ourselves preparing for bed while crew members were still removing cables and lights. At any given time of day or night, there were bodies parked on sofas and chaises, or sacked out on our carpet.

One day, the company was filming on location at a church adjacent to a school. I wasn't in the scene, but I was visiting the set and apparently word got out that I was there. Children kept coming over for autographs, and most of them seemed disappointed that I didn't look more like Mary Poppins. Eventually their visits began to interfere with the filming. One boy leaned directly across me and asked Tony Adams, "Have you seen Mary Poppins?"

"She's gone," Tony fibbed.

"Damn!" the boy said, and turned away.

Later, an elderly parishioner came up to me and said, "You do nude movies, don't you?" She then proceeded to lecture me on the sins of money and fame. Bizarrely, the pastor of the church was a member of the Screen Actors Guild, and had copies of *Variety* and the *Hollywood Reporter* on his desk.

We shot *That's Life!* more or less in sequence, which meant that near the end of the filming, we finally arrived at the challenging scene where my character confronts Jack's, and tells him that unless he changes his attitude and begins to appreciate all that is under his nose—"a loving family, a wife who thinks he's the best thing since chopped liver"— she will leave him.

I wish I could say it was art imitating life, but in fact, these were not words that I had ever said to Blake, although I'd sometimes imagined doing so. I'd seen so much conflict in my childhood that my instincts as an adult were to avoid confrontation whenever possible. In addition, after most of Blake's digressions, he apologized, which always gave me fresh hope that things would improve, and that he would eventually return to being the loving and generous man that I married. Now, because the film was so autobiographical, my husband was giving me free rein to tap into all my frustrations of the past year and vent them. It was surreal, and cathartic, and the words simply poured out of me.

After just one take, Blake said, "Print it."

When I questioned him, he smiled tenderly and said, "Trust me."

ONCE THE FILM was edited, Blake hosted a screening for family and friends. Geoff came, since shortly after filming had concluded, Blake and he had happily arrived at a rapprochement. Amelia and Joanna were also in attendance, as were Nina Foch, Joe Lopes, Henry Mancini, and most of our cast and crew. I worried that the film might seem self-indulgent—nepotism run rampant—but instead, it knocked me out.

Afterward, I wrote:

I recognized tonight how much better Blake is now, in every way. He looks fit, he's not morbid, and he's made a powerful little film. Our lovely home is immortalized forever, and the work speaks for itself. It's moving, honest, sweet, funny . . . and all about love.

So, what had happened with Blake? I'm not sure to this day. He was indeed a serious hypochondriac. Had he simply exhausted the list of things that could have been wrong with him? Had making *That's Life!* rid him of his demons? Was there some dark secret he had kept from me that he'd finally worked through, or was there something about true depression that I didn't fully understand? Had the reunion with Geoff helped set him back on his feet? I only know that I was grateful for the reprieve—and despite the dramas, the transgressions, the ups and downs of our marriage, I still loved him deeply. We remained married for another twenty-five years before he passed away at the ripe age of eighty-eight.

WHEN IT PREMIERED in September of 1986, *That's Life!* received generous reviews. The *New York Times* said the film was "full of sunlight, warm feelings and wonderfully rude gags . . . Yet *That's Life!* may be this singular director's most somber comedy to date." The *Los Angeles Times* wrote: "This is one of the funniest, and perhaps the most life-embracing, movies Edwards has made . . . The currents of despair give the humor a deeper bite. [It's] a film that took considerable courage, love and craft to make."

That's Life! was the last film that I made in Hollywood for many years, and coincidentally it was Blake's and my last film together, before we headed to New York to embark upon the next big chapter of our lives—adapting and preparing *Victor/Victoria* for the stage. I would later return to Hollywood, and there were other creative ventures along the way, but for now, Broadway was beckoning once again.

EPILOGUE

THE MANY PATHS my life has taken continue to astound me. I am often asked how I feel about the success I have enjoyed. Am I proud of my work? What informed my choices? Did I know I would *be* a success?

But what is success?

Is it the pleasure in doing the work, or the way it's received afterward? The latter is ephemeral. The doing is everything.

THE TRUTH IS, I never anticipated any of it. I just took the opportunities that were in front of me and waded in. I wobbled, and I waffled, and there were certainly challenges along the way. But so many people helped—nudged, encouraged, pushed me out of my comfort zone.

Was I scared? You bet. Did I feel inadequate? All the time. Did I want to overcome those feelings and succeed? Absolutely. Thankfully, I was willing to pay my dues, and to learn. And I never took anything for granted.

When we were touring, my mum would drill into me:

"Don't you dare complain about anything . . . not the cigarette smoke in the theater, not having a cold, or waiting long hours. It won't do a thing for you, and nobody cares. Don't pull rank, or boast. There's always someone who can do what you do better than you. Get on with it, and you'll be respected so much more."

So I began to build a work ethic, which gave me a solid foundation from which to fly.

Today, when asked what advice I might give to aspiring performers, my answer is always this:

"Learn your craft. Do your homework. Opportunity will come along when you least expect it, as it did for me. You may not even recognize it at the time. Your job is to be as ready as possible when that good fortune comes your way."

THERE AREN'T MANY truths of which I am certain, but writing this book, I was reminded over and over again of one that I am rock-solid sure about:

I have been lucky.

To have been given the gift of song—and to recognize that it *was* a gift; to have been mentored by giants, who taught, influenced, and shaped me; to have gained resilience from hard work; to have loved, and been loved; and to have sometimes felt an angel on my shoulder, a reassuring presence that helped center and guide me when I needed it most . . . actually, that's more than luck.

I am profoundly blessed.

ALSO BY JULIE ANDREWS

Mandy
The Last of the Really Great Whangdoodles
Little Bo—The Story of Bonnie Boadicea
Little Bo in France—The Further Adventures of
Bonnie Boadicea
Home: A Memoir of My Early Years

BY JULIE ANDREWS AND EMMA WALTON HAMILTON

Dumpy the Dump Truck
Dumpy at School
Dumpy Saves Christmas
Dumpy and the Big Storm
Dumpy and the Firefighters
Dumpy's Happy Holiday
Dumpy and His Pals
Dumpy's Friends on the Farm
Dumpy's Apple Shop
Dumpy's Valentine
Dumpy to the Rescue!

Dumpy's Extra Busy Day
Simeon's Gift
Dragon: Hound of Honor
The Great American Mousical
Thanks to You—Wisdom from Mother and Child
The Very Fairy Princess
The Very Fairy Princess: A Fairy Merry Christmas
The Very Fairy Princess Takes the Stage
The Very Fairy Princess: Here Comes the Flower Girl!
The Very Fairy Princess Follows Her Heart
The Very Fairy Princess: Teacher's Pet
The Very Fairy Princess: Sparkles in the Snow
The Very Fairy Princess: Graduation Girl!
The Very Fairy Princess: A Spooky, Sparkly Halloween
The Very Fairy Princess: Attitude of Gratitude
The Very Fairy Princess Doodle Book
Little Bo in Italy
Little Bo in London
Julie Andrews' Collection of Poems, Songs, and Lullabies
Julie Andrews' Treasury for All Seasons:
Poems and Songs to Celebrate the Year

BY EMMA WALTON HAMILTON

Raising Bookworms:
Getting Kids Reading for Pleasure and Empowerment

ACKNOWLEDGMENTS

As with my first memoir, this book would not have been possible without the immeasurable contribution of my daughter, Emma Walton Hamilton. Throughout the many years of putting this together, Emma has been at my side both figuratively and literally. A fine writer herself, she subjugated her own life, needs, and talent to assist me. She listened, encouraged, researched, transcribed from my diaries, organized, assembled, edited—without bias or reproach, and with all the gentle wisdom that an adult daughter who has shared so much of my journey can offer. It wasn't always easy to open up and reveal certain truths. I didn't want to reawaken old wounds, or inflict new ones. But she remained steadfast, nonjudgmental, curious, compassionate, loyal, and unafraid. Thank you, my darling Emma.

Leslie Wells edited my first memoir, *Home*, and it was unthinkable to attempt this second book without her. We are so grateful that she agreed to come aboard once again. Ever astute, honest, and kind, she steered Emma and me clear of many pitfalls and cheered us on when we needed it most. I recall with pleasure the hours we spent poring over photographs spread all over my dining table and floor, and the fun of being "just gals" together, while in the face of deadlines that seemed all but impossible.

Mauro DiPreta, founder and former VP and publisher of Hachette Books, served as our senior editor and stayed the course with us even after relocating to a new publishing home. We begged him for so many deadline extensions that he must have despaired of ever seeing the finished manuscript, but he was always patient and supportive.

Brant Rumble, executive editor at Hachette, came aboard seamlessly and has been a joy to work with as well. Our most sincere thanks also to Susan Weinberg, SVP/publisher at Perseus Books, and Mary Ann Naples, VP/publisher at Hachette.

Steve Sauer, my longtime manager and friend, was steadfast in protecting us from distractions, and helping us navigate the many other obligations, professional and personal, that threatened to derail the project from time to time. Thank you, dear Bubba, and thanks also to Jane McKnight, Steve's indefatigable assistant.

Acknowledgments

Boundless gratitude to Amy Slack, my personal assistant, whose tireless efforts on Emma's and my behalf encompassed everything from organizing files, photos, and supplies, to embarking on research, all while keeping my home and life in order and ensuring always that we were well fed and supplied with bottomless cups of tea. Amy's cheerful, gentle, and loving presence kept our spirits up every day. Thanks must also go to her patient husband, Michael Cinque, who never complained about how busy Amy was or how much we asked of her.

As she did for my first memoir, Francine Taylor, another dear friend and longtime assistant, spent hundreds of hours without complaint transcribing the interviews that Emma and I recorded together, even when the audio was interrupted by dogs barking, doorbells ringing, and vacuum cleaners humming. Her occasional witty inserts into the transcripts always made us smile.

Julie Colbert, our agent at William Morris Endeavor, has been our champion throughout this project and beyond. Her constant support and gentle nudges of encouragement kept us going, and her sense of humor and clear judgment continue to refresh and inspire us.

Thanks must also go to other cherished members of my superb team, Ginny Davis and Christine

Jardine, who have been with me for decades and who supplied data from archives, pulled materials out of storage, and held the fort for me in every way.

The vast majority of the photographs in this book were taken by my close friend Zoë Dominic. When she passed away, she transferred the rights to her work to her devoted friend, assistant, and photography colleague, Catherine Ashmore. Thank you, dear Catherine, for your profound generosity in providing us with the photographs contained in this book, and for seeming to drop everything at a moment's notice to hunt for a specific image whenever we asked.

So many people helped with research for this book: Ted Chapin, president and chief creative officer of Rodgers and Hammerstein, and Kevin Kern, Brian Sibley, and Edward Ovalle at Disney Archives all provided valuable materials and information regarding *Mary Poppins* and *The Sound of Music*.

Tony Walton, my former spouse and Emma's father, generously shared his datebooks and his memories (apologies, Tone, for the diary that went missing in a taxicab!). Tony and his loving wife, Gen LeRoy Walton, have been encouraging throughout, in spite of my sharing some personal stories that must have been painful to revisit. Tony's sisters, Jen Gosney and Carol Hall, were also helpful in supplying memories and research materials. Emma and I thank you all, and love you dearly.

Needless to say, our entire family has contributed so much to this book, and their patience alone deserves our most profound thanks. Jennifer, Geoffrey, Amelia, and Joanna came to the rescue when our memories failed us, and gamely allowed us to reveal family stories, as did my brothers, John Wells and Donald Andrews, and my half sister, Celia (Shad) Day. My niece, Jessica Andrews, could not have been more supportive in giving her blessing to my revealing some painful truths about her beloved dad, my brother Chris, who sadly passed away several years ago.

An extra hug goes with gratitude to Emma's husband, Steve Hamilton. This mother-in-law deeply appreciates your patience, guidance, and tact—not to mention the many superb meals and the shared laughter. Thanks, also, to Steve and Emma's children, Sam and Hope. Sam's computer skills often saved the day, as did his good eye, which helped us see little things we might never have spotted. Despite the frequent inconvenience of having Mum and Granny working such long and focused hours, Hope made her own contribution to the book by remaining patient, respectful, and resourceful throughout, knowing how much it mattered.

Emma and I extend heartfelt thanks to all at Hachette Books who have helped produce this memoir, including Michelle Aielli, Michael Barrs, John Colucci, Sarah Falter, Anthony Goff, Amanda Kain, David Lamb, Tom Louie, Michele McGonigle, Monica Oluwek, Adam Schnitzer, Cisca Schreefel, and Rick Willett, as well as Alan Samson, Maura Wilding, and Simon Wright at Orion Publishing Group in the UK, and the wonderful Cynthia Daniels and her team at Monk Music Studios for the audiobook version.

Finally, between 1963 and 1986, the years that this book encompasses, there were so many people who touched our lives. Many of them are mentioned in the book, but to have referenced them all would have made it twice the length. That said, I would like to acknowledge a few who are not referred to by name but who nevertheless played an important role in our lives during those nearly three decades:

Richard Adams
Jack Bear
Peter Bratschi
Trish Caroselli

Acknowledgments

Junius Covington
Joe Cranzano
Nicole David
Carrie Dietrich
Hedi Donizetti
Dorothy Drake
Jackie Fabitore
Judee Fraser
Linda Friedman
Setzi Ganev
Paul Glass
Jamie Gosney
Dwight Hemion
Leoni Hürlimann
Lynni Hutton
Mike Kaplan
Chris "QP" King
Buz Kohan
Kim LeMasters
Audrey Loggia
Walter Ludi
Arlene Ludwig
Ginny Mancini
Stan Marin
Michael Oliver
D.W. Owen
Patricia Poirier

Acknowledgments

Mary Prappas
Theodor Romang
Richard Rosenberg
Sol Rosenthal
Gene Schwam
Gary Smith
Jack Stevens and Reg Allen
Syri Stoll
Rosemary Taylor
The family Von Siebenthal
Bob Wells
Ken and Mitzi Welsh
Michael Wolf
Susan Wolf

JA & EWH
Sag Harbor, 2019